Praise for Ann Douglas

"For sleep deprived Moms desperate to emerge from a bleary-eyed state of newborn or toddler exhaustion, help has arrived from parenting guru Ann Douglas."

—Stacy DeBroff, author of *The Mom Book: 4278 Tips From Moms for Moms* and the founder of MomCentral.com

"A one-stop, no-guilt answer book on sleep where *every* bleary-eyed parent can find wise, rational advice on any sleep issue from A to ZZZZZs."

—Paula Spencer, contributing editor to *Parenting* and *Baby Talk* magazines

"Solutions that fit like a glove, no matter what your lifestyle or sleep concerns."

—Julia Roslen, Senior Editor *ePregnancy* magazine

"No mother should have to lose sleep over sleep again!"

—Andi Buchanan, author *It's a Girl: Women Writers on Raising Daughters*

sleep
solutions

The Ultimate No-Worry Approach™
for Each Age and Stage

for your
baby, toddler
and preschooler

ANN DOUGLAS

Author of The Mother of All® Pregnancy Books

**WILEY**

John Wiley & Sons Canada, Ltd.

National Library of Canada Cataloguing in Publication Data

Douglas, Ann, 1963–
     Sleep solutions for babies, toddlers and preschoolers : the ultimate
no-worry approach for each age and stage / Ann Douglas.

(The mother of all solutions series)

Includes bibliographical references and index.
ISBN-13 978-0-470-83633-0
ISBN-10 0-470-83633-4

1. Infants—Sleep. 2. Toddlers—Sleep. 3. Preschool children—Sleep.
4. Child rearing. I. Title. II. Series.

RJ506.S55D69 2006   649'.122   C2005-906426-9

Production Credits:
Cover design: Sharon Foster Design
Front cover and spine images: Royalty-Free/Corbis
Back cover images: (left photo) Royalty-Free/brandx, (middle photo) Lauren Burke/The
Image Bank, (right photo) Emma Thaler/Photographer's Choice
Illustrations: Kathryn Adams
Interior text design: Pat Loi
Printer: Printcrafters

John Wiley & Sons Canada, Ltd.
6045 Freemont Blvd.
Mississauga, Ontario
L5R 4J3

Printed in Canada

1 2 3 4 5 PC 10 09 08 07 06

To the Writermamas:

For being there for me when I found myself up in the night, tending to a sleep book that wouldn't go to bed, and for sharing my passion for making a difference in the lives of other mothers.

—Ann

Acknowledgements

Back when this book was at the conception stage, I e-mailed friends asking them if they knew people who might be interested in being interviewed for a book on babies, toddlers, preschoolers, and sleep. And then *those friends* talked to *their friends*, and so on, and so on.

Activating the mom-to-mom grapevine—plus getting a wonderful e-mail boost from the National Association of Mothers' Centers, who were kind enough to tell their members that I was looking for parents to interview for this book and its sister book, *Mealtime Solutions for Your Baby, Toddler, and Preschooler: The Ultimate No-Worry Approach for Each Age and Stage*—was the secret to finding the parent stories that (I'm sure you'll agree) are the best part of this book. My in-box overflowed with replies from parents who were eager to tell me what they had learned through the Sleep School of Hard Knocks in order to help out some other sleep-deprived parent.

Because those parents' voices are the heart and soul of the books in The Mother of All Solutions™ series—along with the books' sister series, The Mother of All® Books series—it only seems fitting to give those parents star-billing. So a huge thank you goes out to the following moms and dads for sharing so much of their lives with me: Tracy Aisenstat, Johanna Armstrong, Stephanie Ashton, Pam Aziz, Erin Bailey, Tanya Balgie, Krysta Barberi, Pamela Baribeault, Kevin Barnes, Sara Beresford, Tanys Bingham, Susan Blackmer, Brandy Boissonneault, Tanya Bonham, Sonya Boyes, Erin Branchflower, Darla Brownlee, Jennifer Cabralda, Michelle Camazzola, Brandy Carrelli, Dawn Carrier, Nathalie Caso, Jennifer A. Cavanaugh, Wendy Cellik, Marcelle Cerny, Helen Chanfat, Anna Chapin, Will Chapin, Jodi Chetcuti, Crystal Chretien, Laura Korbe Clark, Anne Clarke, Clinton Clarke, Lisa Clarke, Patricia Clouse, Tabitha Connor, Maggie Cox, Christine Cristiano, Colleen Curran, Susanne Davis, Sharon DeVellis, Ann DiMenna, Jennifer Dodds, Stephanie Dolejsi, Lori Anne Dolqueist, Dani Donders, Tracy Dougal, Marcia Douglas, Elisabeth Doyle, Stephanie Drew, Sarah Egelman, Anna Epp, Caroline Erdelyi, Georgina Eva, Nicole Fenwick, Bonnie Frampton Faust, Trudy A. Kelly Forsythe, Marie Gallo, Dawn M. Garcia, Amy K. Gates, Marla Good, Sarah Gordon, Sarah Gratta, Michelle Hamer, Kimberly Hart, Rachel Hartman, Jennifer Henderson, Christine Hennebury, Christine Hibbard, Kristi Honey, Tom Honey, Brenda Hubbard, Christine Iacobucci, Arlene Ignaczewski, Nancy Irvin, Bonnie Jarvis, Jason Jarvis, Amie

Jones, Christine Jordan, Kimberly Kilduff, Suzanne King, Jenn Kreske, Claire Kusu, Samantha Lamb, Renay Langdon, Jodi Lastman, Julia Lawn, Jennifer Lawrence, Natasha Le Blanc, Marianne Lee, Heather Lind, Carolyn Loy, Michele Lurie, Wendy MacDonald, Sharon Marks, Karen Mazza, Sasha McCorrister, Scott McCorrister, Amanda McDowell, Shana McEachren, Melissa McEathron, Sharlene McKinnon, Laura McSloy, Mireille Messier, Jamie Millette, Robin Millette, Billy Mitchell, Wendy Morgan, Laura Morrison, Sabrina Mullen-Forestell, Zaheeda Nasser, Lorraine Neal, Sharon Newton, Anne-Marie Nichols, Tania Obljubek, Cathy O'Brien, Emily O'Brien, Shelley O'Brien, Tami O'Dette, Kerri Paquette, Heather Paul, Fawna Pears, Julie Pellerin, Jennifer Penick, Gillian Hutchison Perry, Julie Pettit, Maria Phillips, Stephanie Phoenix, Karyn Positano, Jennifer Power Scott, Keri Puglisi, Sarah Ramsay, Sarah Richards, Sue Robins, Samantha Robinson, Judy Roche, Sharon Rose, Jen Sammut, Tina Scherz, Christine Schofield, Michelle Sevilla, Christine Silliphant, Julie Singleton, Caroline Smialek, Erin Smith, Laurie Smith, Amanda Snyder, Leanne Steen, Marie Stone, Nikki Stoughton, Tanya Stuart, Erin Sullivan, Maureen Sweeney, Cathleen Takahashi, Eileen Tan, Patricia Tast, Laura Tedesco, Annemarie Tempelman-Kluit, Michael Thomas, Michele Thrailkill, Dianne Vroom, Amy Wadsworth, Claire Wafer, Leslie Walker, Paige Wilkins, Michelle Williamson, Sue Wilson, Marina Wolanski, Chelsea Wolfe, Jennifer Woodard, Nicholas Woodard, Lynn Worthington, Karen Wright. Thank you all.

Next, I would like to thank the book's technical reviewers for their incredibly thorough, detailed, and thoughtful comments on the book's manuscript:

- Heidi Koss-Nobel, CD, BA, CLE, Washington State Coordinator for Postpartum Support International and DONA International's 2005 Individual Doula of the Year, and a practicing Postpartum Doula in the Greater Seattle Metro Area

- Ian MacLusky, MBBS, FRCP (C) Paediatrics, FRCP (C) Respiratory Medicine, director of the Sleep Disorders Laboratory at the Hospital for Sick Children in Toronto, Ontario

- Sallie Page-Goertz, MN, CPNP, IBCLC, clinical assistant professor, KU Pediatrics, University of Kansas School of Medicine and University of Kansas Medical Center, Kansas City, Kansas

- Marla Good, editorial consultant and the proud mother of 21-month-old Josephine (a toddler who, like many of her age-mates, is still somewhat skeptical about the benefits of sleep)

I would also like to thank:

- Mary McCormick, executive director of the Canadian Foundation for the Study of Infant Deaths, for her detailed and helpful suggestions on the chapter on safe sleep

- Katherine Finn Davis, PhD, RN, CPNP, of the Emory University School of Medicine Department of Pediatrics—Division of Infectious Diseases, Epidemiology, and Immunology, for generously taking time from her busy schedule to answer a lengthy list of my sleep-related questions

- the hard-working staff of Wiley Canada: executive editor Joan Whitman; project manager/wizard Liz McCurdy; project coordinator Pam Vokey; book designer Pat Loi; freelance copy editor Valerie Ahwee; marketing and publicity gurus Terry Palmer, Erin Kelly, Christiane Cote, Erin Goodman, Sarah Trimble, Meghan Brousseau et al.; publisher Jennifer Smith; and Wiley general manager Robert Harris (who published my first book back when I was sleepless with baby number four), for teaching me so much about the world of publishing.

Finally, I would like to thank the members of my book-writing posse and support team: Sekoiaa Lake, Robin Millette, Lisa Clarke, Nicole Tetreault, and Barb Payne for their behind-the-scenes administrative help and research assistance; my agent Ed Knappman, of New England Publishing Associates, for going above and beyond the call of duty on occasions too numerous to mention, and my trademark attorney Valerie G. Edward, B.Arts.Sci., LLB, *ditto;* Cheryl Froggett and the rest of the Starbucks Peterborough gang, who cheered me on each morning when I picked up my Venti Bold and who even gave me *a free mug* to keep me going when I was heading into the home stretch; my real-world and on-line friends (who convinced me to get back to my keyboard on days when I was feeling tempted to see if Cheryl was hiring); my PWAC buddies; the members of The Good Girl Club (including our honorary non-girl member); my long-suffering friends who have had to put up with yet another one of my book-writing disappearing acts; and, last but not least, my husband, Neil, and our four kids, Julie, Scott, Erik, and Ian, who made sacrifices above and beyond the call of duty while I was living and breathing "sleep book." I think it's my turn to do the dishes.

I know I have probably forgotten to thank someone—chock it up to sleep deprivation, if you will—but please know that if you passed along a bit of sleep wisdom; encouraged me to keep plugging away on the book (or to take a break from the book, if that seemed like better advice at the time); told me you'd once read something of mine that made a difference in your life; said something nice about one of my kids; or left me a cheery note in my blog (Marla, Dani, Jen, et al.); well, all that meant more to me than you could possibly know. Thank you.

About the Author

Ann Douglas is an award-winning pregnancy and parenting author. She is the author of *The Mother of All Pregnancy Books, The Mother of All Baby Books, The Mother of All Toddler Books, The Mother of All Parenting Books,* and *The Mother of All Pregnancy Organizers* (all part of the internationally best-selling The Mother of All® Books series), as well as the two debut titles in the newly launched The Mother of All Solutions™ series: *Sleep Solutions for Your Baby, Toddler, and Preschooler: The Ultimate No-Worry Approach for Each Age and Stage* and *Mealtime Solutions for Your Baby, Toddler, and Preschooler: The Ultimate No-Worry Approach for Each Age and Stage.* She is also the co-author of other highly popular titles in the pregnancy and parenting category, including *The Unofficial Guide to Having a Baby* and *Trying Again: A Guide to Pregnancy after Miscarriage, Stillbirth, and Infant Loss* (both co-authored with John R. Sussman, MD) and *Choosing Childcare for Dummies®.*

Ann delivers keynote addresses at parenting and health conferences across North America; teaches on-line pregnancy courses through WebMD.com; is a Mom Expert with ClubMom; delivers parenting workshops through the Ella Centre for Pregnancy and Parenting and workplace-based parenting training through Lifespeak Inc; serves as a member of the National Advisory Board for Invest in Kids; and is the president of Page One Productions Inc., an award-winning marketing and communications firm that specializes in mom-to-mom communications.

Ann writes columns for *Conceive Magazine, Glow,* and CanadianLiving.com and is a regular contributor to numerous other pregnancy and parenting publications. She is frequently quoted in such publications as *Parenting, Parents, Fit Pregnancy, American Baby, Working Mother,* and *Canadian Living* and is a popular radio, TV, and on-line chat guest.

Ann and her husband Neil have four children, ages eight through 18. Her children started sleeping through the night anywhere between three-and-a-half weeks and two-and-a-half years of age. (It was her youngest child who took the longest to start sleeping through the night.)

Table of Contents

CHAPTER 6
The Real-World Guide to Solving Your Baby's Sleep Problems 159

CHAPTER 7
The Real-World Guide to Solving Your Toddler's Sleep Problems 193

CHAPTER 8
The Real-World Guide to Solving Your Preschooler's Sleep Problems 220

Introduction

WHILE SLEEP DEPRIVATION isn't the worst thing that's ever going to happen to you, it's not exactly the stuff of which a new parent's dreams are made. (Or the dreams of a parent of a toddler or a preschooler, for that matter.) It can make it tough to get through the day and the night and the following day and the following night. The days tend to blend together, after all. If you're tuning into Sleep Deprivation TV, they'd be better off asking, "It's 11:00 p.m. Do you know what day of the week it is?" Then if you did, you could call in and win big prizes, like the services of a sleep doula or something. I tell you, I'm onto something big here. But before I get too carried away with my Sleep Deprivation TV concepts, let me tell you about this book.

Another Book about Sleep?

I KNOW. IT'S not like there's exactly a shortage of books about sleep. In fact, there's actually a sleep book baby boom going on right now. Everyone from Dr. Sears to Dr. Ferber—and sleep experts representing pretty much every sleep school of thought in between—seem to have a new book on the shelves these days. You can find books that will tell you that the secret to getting your baby to sleep through the night is to let your baby cry until she falls asleep, or to not let your baby cry at all. You can find books that promise to teach your baby to sleep through the night by age three months, and books that insist that babies aren't even ready to *start* sleep training until five to six months or later. You can find books that will tell you that bed sharing is the only way to go if you want a happy and well-adjusted child, and books that make the point that bed sharing is the worst way to go if you want your child to start sleeping through the night before he's seven or eight years of age. You can find books that will make you feel guilty for making a particular sleep choice, and books that will make you feel even more guilty for *not* going that very same route. And I've only just scratched the surface when it comes to hinting at the breadth and depth of the debate when it comes to this particular issue. Is it any wonder that so many parents are losing sleep about sleep?

So why on earth did I decide to write a book on sleep? Trust me, there were times during the researching and writing of this book when I asked myself that very same question. This is easily the most complicated and controversial issue I've ever tackled, and I've tackled some pretty hot topics in my time. But after experiencing my fair share of sleep deprivation along the way, I concluded that there was a spot in the sleep book universe for the book I intended to write. Here's what makes my book stand out, as I see it:

- **The Mom factor.** This book is the first to take a mother-centered approach to the sleep issue. Just as previous generations of pregnancy books were guilty of overlooking the fact that pregnancy actually had something to do with the mom (e.g., it wasn't all about "the fetus"), sleep books have been guilty of losing sight of the mom piece of the sleep puzzle, too—of being so focused on solving the child's sleep problem that they've forgotten to consider how that problem is affecting Mom (and, of course, Dad, too). I'm just focusing on Mom here because, statistically speaking, during the early years, it's still Mom who does much of the nighttime parenting in most families. And if Mom is perpetually running on empty, she won't have the physical or emotional resources to deal with her child's sleep problems; she'll coast along on auto-pilot, doing whatever it takes to get through the night and the following day. That's why this book starts out by giving the low-down on some of the physical, emotional, and relationship fallout that may result from parental sleep deprivation, and offering moms concrete strategies to minimize those effects.

- **No one-size-fits-all solution:** This is also the first book to provide you with the tools you need to decide which of the major sleep schools of thought is most compatible with your child's age and temperament, your parenting philosophies, and your family's day-to-day realities and needs. Rather than trying to pretend that a one-size-fits-all sleep solution—or couple of variations on that same theme—will meet the needs of all parents and all children without taking into account the sometimes complex and messy variables that go into any parenting equation, this book:

  o provides you with a crash course in sleep science so that you can understand what is happening to your child developmentally and ensure that your "sleep expectations" are age appropriate and realistic

  o gives you the low-down on what specific sleep strategies have been proven to increase the odds that a particular child will end up developing healthy sleep habits

  o summarizes the latest research on children and sleep (and helps you to put the latest American Academy of Pediatrics sleep recommendations in context) so that you have access to the most current sleep information that was available as this book was going to print

  o provides you with an exhaustive list of suggested sleep resources so that you can continue to stay on top of new developments in the world of sleep

  o includes a smorgasbord of checklists, charts, and other tools, including a handy sleep log, that are designed to help you to troubleshoot your child's sleep problems in a low-stress and parent-friendly way.

- **The no-worry approach:** I can't eliminate all of the worry of being a parent, but I can ease your mind at least a little by reassuring you that other parents have experienced many of the same "normal" (but crazy-making) sleep behaviors in their kids. And because this book contains ideas, tips, strategies, and stories from the more than 200 parents who agreed to be interviewed, it won't be me talking away throughout this entire book. Not only would that be boring, you'd be getting only my point of view as opposed to the collective wisdom of more than 200 parents. (More about that in a minute.)

- **And as a bonus—no guilt:** I wish there was an "official guilt-free zone" sticker on the cover that would alert you that I'm not going to do a guilt number on you in this book. Your sleep choices are your own sleep choices. Enough said. It's my job to provide you with the most accurate, unbiased information I can and to present it in a non-bossy way. That's the approach that made The Mother of All Books series a highly trusted information source for parents, so I'm going to stick with it in The Mother of All Solutions series as well.

So What Is This New Series about Anyway?

THE MOTHER OF All Solutions is the sister series to The Mother of All Books series. Like all siblings, they've got some things in common, but there are also some key differences. While the books in The Mother of All Books series are designed to follow each age and stage—*The Mother of All Pregnancy Books, The Mother of All Baby Books, The Mother of All Toddler Books*, and *The Mother of All Parenting Books* are each devoted to a particular chapter in your life as a mom or a mom-to-be—the books in The Mother of All Solutions series zero in on a key parenting problem that you may be facing at a particular stage of motherhood. The two kickoff titles in the series—*Sleep Solutions for Your Baby, Toddler, and Preschooler* and *Mealtimes Solutions for Your Baby, Toddler, and Preschooler*—focus on two perennial challenges for parents with children under the age of four: helping your child to become a great sleeper and encouraging healthy eating habits in young children right from day one.

If you've read the books in The Mother of All Books series, you know how central "mother wisdom" was to the success of that series. We're carrying on that tradition with The Mother of All Solutions. You can expect that same "real-world" tone and feel to these books: practical tips, ideas, and solutions that can only come from another parent who has done his or her time in the sleep-deprivation trenches. Caught the "his"? We've got a growing number of dads providing input, too, because their perspective is truly invaluable. When baby has been crying for three hours straight and no one is getting any sleep or your toddler has been refusing to eat anything but macaroni and cheese for three days in a row, it's easy for moms and dads to lose sight of the fact that they are playing for the same team. This series tries to bridge that gap by having both moms and dads actively engaged in the dialogue.

Want More Experts? We've Got Experts!

OF COURSE, THIS book wasn't based on the input from parents alone, although they really were the true experts driving the *Sleep Solutions* mothership from start to finish. Not only did I conduct exhaustive research by pouring through all the leading sleep and pediatric journals and reading thousands of sleep-related articles from science, parenting, and other magazines and newspapers published over the past 15 years or so (to say nothing of dropping an obscene amount of money in the sleep books aisle of my favorite bookstore), I also interviewed sleep authorities and had the manuscript vetted by a panel of four experts who were handpicked by me, not only because of their outstanding credentials and real-world experience, but also because they each brought a unique perspective to the technical review panel. You can "meet" the fab four by flipping to the acknowledgments page of this book.

The Sleep-Deprived Parent's Quick Guide to This Book

IF YOU'RE TOTALLY exhausted and the only thing that's on your mind as you flip through this book is how to get your baby to nap starting today, you probably want to a quick overview of how this book works and where you can find the information you want—and fast. Here's a quick overview. (You can find more details in the Table of Contents and a keyword guide in the Index.)

This Section of the Book Focuses on ...	You'll Want to Read This If You Have a		
	Baby (Birth to Age One)	Toddler (Ages One and Two)	Preschooler (Ages Three and Four)
Chapter 1: Sleepless in Suburbia — The "Mom's guide" to sleep. The physical, emotional, and relationship fallout of sleep deprivation, along with practical solutions for maximizing your opportunities for sleep and lining up the support you need.	✓	✓	✓
Chapter 2: The Sleep-Deprivation Survival Guide	✓	✓	✓
Chapter 3: The Science of Sleep — The biology behind your child's sleep-wake cycles, how much sleep your child needs at each age and stage, the low-down on the key sleep-related milestones, and how your child's sleep patterns are likely to evolve over time.	✓	✓	✓
Chapter 4: Winning at Sleep Roulette — What you can do to increase your odds of ending up with a child who is a healthy sleeper, the low-down on the basic sleep-training schools of thought, and how to come up with a customized sleep solution that seems right for your family.	✓	✓	✓
Chapter 5: Bedroom Politics: Where Will Your Baby Sleep? — The scoop on choosing a sleeping location for your baby, sleep safety, the co-sleeping debate, and more.	✓	✓	✓
Chapter 6: The Real-World Guide to Solving Your Baby's Sleep Problems — The scoop about newborns and sleep, night waking, napping (and non-napping), early birds, and the most common first-year sleep problems.	✓		

Chapter	Description		
Chapter 7: The Real-World Guide to Solving Your Toddler's Sleep Problems	The truth about toddlers and sleep, bedtime-resistance tips, naptime survival strategies, and top toddler sleep problems.	✓	
Chapter 8: The Real-World Guide to Solving Your Preschooler's Sleep Problems	Preschooler bedtime fears, morning sleepyheads, and other sleep problems during the preschool years.		✓
Chapter 9: Sleep Disorders: What Every Parent Needs to Know	Information about nightmares, night terrors, bedwetting, and some less common sleep disorders.	✓	✓
Sleep Tools	In this section, you'll find a six-step method for troubleshooting your child's sleep problems; a comparison of the major sleep-training methods for babies, toddlers, and preschoolers; a bedtime resistance checklist; a summary of the major reasons why babies, toddlers, and preschoolers wake in the night; and a sleep log. Note: The sleep log is designed to allow you to track your child's sleep patterns in a concise and easy-to-analyze format. (If you like sleep logs, use it. If they make you crazy, forget I ever included this page.)	✓	✓
Appendices	The directory of organizations, list of on-line resources, and book list may be helpful to you if you want to do further research or keep yourself up to date on further developments in the sleep field.	✓	✓

Same Old, Same Old ...

IF YOU'VE READ the other books in this series, the look and feel of the book will be familiar. You'll even recognize a few of the ever-popular icons that alert you to noteworthy facts, figures, or the much-loved Mom quotes.

 MOM'S THE WORD: Insights and advice from other parents.

 MOTHER WISDOM: Bright ideas, practical tips, pop culture tidbits, and more.

 PILLOW TALK: Facts and figures related to the always fascinating world of sleep.

 CRIB NOTES: Leads on sleep-related resources that are definitely worth checking out.

So, as you can see, *Sleep Solutions for Your Baby, Toddler and Preschooler* is quite unlike any other sleep book you may have read. It's comprehensive, thoroughly researched, fun to read, and based on real-world advice from other moms and dads who've done their time in the sleep-deprivation trenches, and who want to pass their best baby bedtime, toddler naptime, or preschooler nightmare-soothing tips along to you. Here's wishing you the stuff of which dreams are made (or at least *parental* dreams are made): a good night's sleep.

Ann Douglas

P.S.

When you reach the final page of the last chapter of this book (go ahead, take a peak—it's okay), you'll see that I am big on the idea of parents helping other parents. I hope you'll pass along some of the sleep solutions that were helpful to you to some other sleep-deprived parent. I also hope that you'll write to me to pass along other sleep solutions that have worked well in your family so that I can ensure that future editions of this book are as helpful as possible to other parents. You can write to me care of my publisher—you can find their coordinates on the copyright page of this or any of my titles or contact me via my website at www.having-a-baby.com. I always love to hear my readers' suggestions, tips, ideas, and comments, so—please—keep them coming!

CHAPTER 1:

Sleepless in Suburbia

I was obsessed with sleep. It was all I could talk about.
My "sleep log" was never out of reach. ... I would pore over my
sleep log for hours, searching for the key, the missing clue.
—LAURIE, 38, MOTHER OF ONE

S LEEP IS A lot like sex. If you're not getting it as much as you'd like, it can become a bit of an obsession. Suddenly, all you can think about is when you last had it, how great it felt when you had it, and what you can do to get some again. And if you end up sounding as desperate as a 20-something single guy on the wrong side of lucky—well, that's to be expected. At this stage in your life, sleep is in every bit as short supply as sex is in his. "When you're chronically sleep deprived, it's hard to think rationally about sleep," insists Kara, a 33-year-old mother of a toddler and a young baby. "You become desperate. My friends and I compared our sleep obsession to an addiction. *How much did you get? How did you get it? Where did you get it? Was it any good?*"

As the days and nights blend together into one continuous, unending day, you may find yourself developing an elaborate fantasy life that revolves around sleep. You find yourself daydreaming about sleep and you may be shocked to find that your steamy R-rated dreams have been replaced by decidedly G-rated fantasies. If a Hollywood leading man happens to saunter into one of your dreams these days, he's no longer flashing his bedroom eyes at you and beckoning you to come hither. He's gently cradling a sleeping baby in his arms and whispering the words that every sleep-deprived mother wants to hear: "It's okay, honey. I've got him. You just roll over and go back to sleep."

In this chapter, moms talk frankly about how sleep deprivation really feels—why sleep is such a huge issue for so many parents and how sleep deprivation can take its toll on your life in some powerful and often unexpected ways. Then, in Chapter 2, we switch into solutions mode, zeroing in on mom-proven strategies for maximizing opportunities for sleep, boosting your energy, combating stress, and taking the best possible care of yourself.

Why the Sleep Deprivation of Early Parenthood Comes as Such a Shock

GIVEN THAT PRACTICALLY every parent on the planet either attends prenatal classes, visits a pregnancy website, reads a pregnancy book, or watches a pregnancy reality TV show before giving birth, why aren't new parents better prepared for life in the sleep-deprivation trenches?

Society Doesn't Do a Particularly Good Job of Preparing New Parents

People may be willing to talk about the sleep deprivation of new parenthood before your new baby arrives, but not in a way that's genuinely helpful, insist many new parents.

"As a society, we do a terrible job of giving parents practical tools for dealing with the loneliness and desperation that strikes in the night," says Julie, a 29-year-old mother of one. "All society does is joke about it when you're expecting, instead of having an honest dialogue about the realities of sleep deprivation."

"The only thing people—even other new parents—told me about sleep was 'You won't be getting any,'" adds Samantha, 31, who gave birth to her first child eight months ago.

"I think I believed the sleep deprivation was going to be like finals week in college, says Chelsea, a 31-year-old first-time mother. "But the reality was much more difficult."

Learning about Sleep Might Not Have Seemed That Important While You Were Pregnant

Something else that conspires against new parents finding out the facts about babies and sleep before they find themselves in the sleep-deprivation trenches is the fact they have a hard time focusing on anything beyond childbirth until they get past that particular hurdle. In her book, *Talking with Mothers*, Dana Breen talks about how expectant mothers tend to apply "the hurdle model" to preparing for childbirth. They focus so much energy on trying to prepare for what they perceive to be the marathon of mother-hood—giving birth—that they tend to momentarily overlook the fact that they're actually going to need to know what to do with the baby after the birth.

"All of the books I read before I gave birth were about pregnancy," says Michelle, 31, who gave birth to her first child nine months ago. "In retrospect, I should have been reading about sleep habits and other aspects of baby care before he was born."

And even those parents who *do* manage to hit the baby books prior to giving birth tend to gravitate toward subjects other than sleep. "We never had a game plan for encouraging healthy sleep patterns for our baby, even though we were conscientious about everything else, like safety and nutrition—even the toys she played with and the books we read to her," recalls Sarah, the 32-year-old mother of 13-month-old Lilith. "I guess we thought sleep was something that would happen naturally."

Falling on Deaf Ears

Even if you were lucky enough to have a group of mom-friends who were determined to give you the lowdown on life in the sleep-deprivation trenches or a childbirth class instructor who covered infant sleep patterns as part of her prenatal class curriculum, you may not necessarily have been able to understand everything they were trying to tell you until you made your own journey to Motherland.

"Because our society doesn't provide much in the way of real-time exposure to child rearing in any of its forms, most of the reality of

MOM'S THE WORD

"When I was pregnant, I had one or two friends who talked honestly about what it can be like when you've been up all night and the baby has been crying for three hours and you're desperately tired. I found that information to be tremendously valuable when I was in the throes of it—just knowing that this was normal, that I wasn't alone, and that there was a possibility that we might all live through the night. I don't think you can truly prepare parents for what it's going to be like for them, but if you hear experienced parents talk about the realities of nighttime parenting honestly before your first baby is born, at least when it happens to you, you feel less alone."

—*Julie, 29, mom of one*

---

actual baby care is a shock," explains Erin, a 34-year-old mother of three. "A friend who recently gave birth to a beautiful baby girl called me in tears after a few weeks, wondering why no one had ever told her how hard it was going to be to take care of this child. And the thing is that we *did* tell her. But until she actually did it, had the baby, and the sore breasts, sleep deprivation, and the shattering love-anxiety-depression cocktail kicked in, she couldn't really understand what we were trying to tell her. I mean, what childless person looks at a sweet, small baby and can actually see how totally enslaved young parents can become to the whims and needs of this creature? And then there is the whole 'sleeping like a baby' cliché—which, it seems, is simply a cruel, cruel joke because babies don't really sleep all that well."

Unexplainable Degrees of Exhaustion

Even if you were lucky enough to have a friend who took you aside and told you the Sleep Facts of Life in painstakingly graphic detail before your baby arrived on the scene, you still may have found yourself in for a rude awakening during those early weeks of parenthood. After all, it's one thing to sublet someone's life for a couple of days; it's quite a different experience to purchase that lifestyle for yourself.

"You can't tell a parent-to-be about babies and sleep," says Marla, a 36-year-old mother of one. "It's like telling someone about a roller coaster ride. You can tell them, but it doesn't take the place of that feeling when your stomach starts flipping. You can say 'sleep deprivation' and they don't know what it means just like I don't know what it means to be a surgeon or a jockey. They don't know it's not just about being tired: It's about layers and layers of tired, and having to function through them, and then having the one thing that your nerves can't take even on a good day happen over and over again."

Jennifer agrees. "Most parents don't have a realistic idea about infant sleep patterns, but it's not because of a lack of education," the 28-year-old first-time mother insists. "We heard about the sleep deprivation from the doctor, the nurse, other parents, and so on. It's because you don't actually live it until the baby is here. I knew I'd be up with Rose at night, but I didn't know what it was going to be like dragging myself to her for the fourth time and feeling like I just wanted to lay down and cry because I was so exhausted."

The Mother of All Sleep Debts

Sleep researchers like to use the term "sleep debt" to describe a person's level of sleep deprivation. It is used to describe the gap between the amount of sleep you need to function at your best and the actual amount of sleep you are getting on a day-to-day (or night-to-night) basis. Just as you can quickly run into trouble with your credit cards if you consistently add more to your credit card balance than you pay off each month, you can run up a sizable sleep debt if you end up shortchanging yourself on the sleep front night after night.

Pregnancy Sleep Debt

Perhaps because Mother Nature is a big believer in on-the-job training, pregnancy tends to be one of those times in a woman's life when she's likely to find it pretty difficult to stay on top of her sleep debt. The first and third trimesters tend to wreak the most havoc on a mom-to-be's ability to catch some zzzz's. The hormonal changes of early pregnancy can result in fatigue, nausea, tender breasts, middle-of-the-night trips to the bathroom, and generally disrupted sleep patterns, while the sheer discomfort of sharing your uterus with a growing and increasingly active baby (to say nothing of leg cramps, backaches, and those never-ending trips to the bathroom) can make it difficult to get a decent night's sleep as Labor Day approaches. A study by sleep psychologist Jodi Mindell, PhD, concluded that 97 percent of pregnant women are no longer sleeping through the night by late pregnancy; and 92 percent are sleeping restlessly. Of course, that's not to imply that most moms-to-be are treated to blissfully uninterrupted sleep during mid-pregnancy: fetal movements and heartburn can lead to sleep disruptions during the second trimester as well. But if there's one trimester of pregnancy when you actually have at least a fighting chance of getting a decent night's sleep, that is it.

And, needless to say, the sleep deprivation associated with having a baby doesn't end with the first labor contraction. (As if!) If you end up with a long, drawn-out labor that stretches out over a period of days and that causes you to miss out on many hours of sleep, you may be completely exhausted by the time your baby arrives on the scene. Of course, you may be so pumped with birth-related adrenaline that your body refuses to give into sleep when you try to settle down for that first post-birth slumber, so you may end up addressing all your birth announcements instead.

New Mom Sleep Debt

But then reality comes rolling in and suddenly sleep is in both high demand and short supply. Not surprising, some moms get a little obsessive about tracking sleep—theirs and their babies' in particular. In her 2003 "momoir" (a.k.a. motherhood memoir) *Dispatches from a Not-So-Perfect Life or How I Learned to Love the House, the Man, the Child,* Faulkner Fox mentions a tired parent she knew who inquired about the sleep habits of everyone she met. "A friend of mine started referring to herself as 'the sleep accountant' soon after her son was born. She took to asking friends, colleagues at work, and veritable strangers how much sleep they'd gotten the night before. 'What were you hoping,' I'd asked, 'that no one would have gotten less sleep than you, or that someone would be down in the bottom percentile keeping you company?' 'I was just so jealous of people who were sleeping,' she'd replied. 'I just wanted to know who they were so I could hate them.'"

So what kind of sleep-debt numbers can you expect to rack up during the first year of your child's life? According to Tracy W. Gaudet, MD, author of *Consciously Female: How to Listen to Your Body and Your Soul for a Lifetime of Healthier Living*, most women need eight hours of sleep per night. Moms with young children typically get a total of six-and-a-half hours of sleep in each 24-hour period—something that results in a sleep deficit of one-and-a-half hours per day. If you continue to lose sleep at that rate during baby's first year, you will have racked up a sleep debt of 550 hours of lost sleep—the equivalent of *68 sleepless nights or two months of lost sleep!*—by the time your baby blows out the candles on his first birthday cake.

If you'd prefer to look at lost sleep for both moms and dads (as opposed to moms alone), the figure is about 400 hours of lost sleep per parent by the end of baby's first year, according to Paul Martin, author of *Counting Sheep: The Science and Pleasures of Sleep and Dreams*. Most new parents lose about two hours of sleep per night for the first four or five months (when babies are eating and sleeping around the clock) and about an hour of sleep each night for the remainder of baby's first year (when sleep becomes more consolidated, meaning that babies sleep for longer periods at one time, and your baby's sleep/wake patterns become more predictable. This makes it easier for you to grab a few hours of sleep in a row without feeling like you could be awakened by your baby at any moment—something that for many new moms is the most stressful aspect of parenting a newborn. (And since getting at least three hours of uninterrupted sleep at a time dramatically improves the quality of your sleep, you're likely to feel a lot better, too.) Of course, these numbers are just averages, which means that while some new parents are enjoying considerably more sleep because their offspring has decidedly Rip Van Winkle-like tendencies, some other moms and dads are getting by with so little sleep that they should offer themselves up as subjects for some study on the long-term effects of sleep deprivation—assuming they could keep their eyes open long enough to dial the number for the sleep lab.

More Sleep Debt: Toddler and Preschool Years

Most new parents have what it takes to psych themselves up for the short-term sprint of sleep deprivation associated with caring for a young baby ("One hundred days of hell, our friends called it," says Jennifer, 33, a first-time mother). But if that sprint ends up being more like some kind of crazy race with no finish line in sight and you're *still* getting by with less sleep than you need, you may very well be tempted to drop out of the running. You see, there's a certain expectation that your child will be sleeping well at night by the time you've made it through the baby stage, explains Jennifer, a 37-year-old mother of three. "Parents who have suffered through babies not sleeping are really looking forward to the next phase, and are horribly dejected when that phase is delayed or never comes." Based on what Jennifer says, there are an awful lot of bummed-out parents stumbling around, waiting for the Sleep Fairy Godmother to visit their homes and take them out of their misery. According to the National Sleep Foundation's 2004 *Sleep in America Poll*, a significant number of parents can expect to remain sleep deprived well into their children's toddler and preschool years. The study found that 25 percent of parents of toddlers and 24 percent of parents of preschoolers get by on less than seven hours of sleep per night—only a marginal decrease from the 31 percent of parents of infants who survive on this little sleep. That kind of chronic sleep deprivation starts to take its toll over time. "After pregnancy and infant care, my resources are low," says Sharon, the 41-year-old mother of a toddler. "That's what makes toddler sleep problems so challenging. It's getting harder and harder to recharge my batteries." The fact that there's a widespread belief that "all babies" are sleeping through the night by age six months only adds to the frustration of parents of night-waking toddlers and preschoolers. "I find it trickier to be tired now that my child is a toddler because people just assume you are well rested as opposed to the baby years when they understand that you never get enough sleep," explains Anne, a 29-year-old mother of one.

Why Sleep Is Such a Huge Issue for So Many Parents

IS SLEEP DEPRIVATION worthy of an SOS? It can certainly feel that way, particularly if you've been without a decent night's sleep for many days and nights. Here's why.

You Never Know When Your Sleep Is Going to Be Disrupted Next

Sleep deprivation is bad enough. Falling asleep and not knowing when your sleep is going to be disrupted again is even worse, according to Stanford University biology professor Robert Sapolsky, who is quoted in Katherine Ellison's book *The Mommy Brain: How Motherhood Makes Us Smarter*. Many mothers find that it's hard to relax and enjoy a restful sleep knowing that they could be roused from sleep again at a moment's notice. That's the downside to having a powerful "mother radar" that allows you to be highly responsive to your baby's needs around the clock. It's the randomness and unpredictability of sleep disruption that really starts to wear you down over time. "When our reluctant napper does finally go down for a nap, I never know how long I will have: 10 minutes or two hours," says Jennifer, 30, the mother of 12-month-old Amanda. "Falling asleep and having to get up five minutes later is much worse than not napping at all."

So just how often can you expect your sleep to be interrupted at night during the baby, toddler, and preschool years? According to the National Sleep Foundation's 2004 *Sleep in America Poll*, 80 percent of parents of infants, 70 percent of parents of toddlers, and 64 percent of parents of preschoolers are awakened in the night at least once a week by their child.

According to the sleep experts, you'd lose even more sleep if it weren't for the filtering work that your brain does while you're slumbering away. The frontal lobe of your brain processes sound information and then activates your body's "emergency-response system," letting you know whether the sound that you just heard warrants a four-alarm hop-out-of-bed response on your part or whether you can merrily happily doze on: "I still don't wake up from thunderstorms, or our cats running and playing, like other people tend to do," says Sabrina, 27, mother of one. "But I hear any peep that my child makes." *Note:* If your built-in "baby surveillance system" forces you to be on hyper-alert 24 hours a day, you could be suffering from postpartum anxiety or one of the other postpartum mood disorders. Talk to your doctor or another trusted person about how difficult it is for you to relax and unwind.

You Get Conflicting Advice from the Experts

The experts have always liked to duke it out over child-rearing issues, but rarely have their views been as polarized as they are right now. As Susan Cheever notes in her motherhood memoir *As Good as I Could Be*: "In every generation, the pendulum swings wildly back and forth between child-raising experts who advocate discipline and structure, and the experts who tell us to listen to our instincts. Currently both methods of raising children ... are being aggressively promoted."

Ah, the experts. A worried mother's best friend and worst enemy all at once. "First-time mothers—particularly of my own 30s generation—have such a strong tendency to search for the one true answer to motherhood in books and periodicals that we tend to trip all over ourselves on the way to the local bookstore. We are so education-driven, we have such a strong need to be 'in control' at all times, and we have not been taught as women to trust ourselves and our intuition, that the inherent instability and craziness of infant rearing feels unnatural and wrong to us," says Nathalie, a 34-year-old mother of two. "It frightens many. And, unfortunately, the books out there tend to do one of two things: They either give us conflicting information on any imaginable topic (one says schedule, the other tells us to be totally child-driven) or they are written so matter-of-factly that they make the millions of choices one needs to make seem as if they should be as easy as opening a can."

"There were extremes in approaches that I found unhealthy and disturbing," adds Kristi, a 27-year-old mother of one. "In the end, I decided to listen to my newfound motherly instincts and to go with what felt right for me and my daughter."

See Chapter 4 and Sleep Tool 2 for more about the various sleep schools of thought and for some practical advice on coming up with sleep solutions that feel right for your family.

And a Lot of Unsolicited Advice, Period

As you've no doubt noticed by now, the fact that you're a mother with a young child makes you an advice magnet. Even random strangers on the street feel compelled to pass along child-rearing tips and—naturally—to ask you how well your child is sleeping.

"The first question everyone asked during the first six months was how my daughter was sleeping," adds Kimberly, 31, mother of 12-month-old Nora.

You may not mind answering that question when things are going well on the sleep front, but it's not quite so fun to deal with people's reactions when your baby's getting up a lot in the night. Maggie, a 30-year-old mother of one, explains: "At eight weeks old, Ewan started sleeping eight hours straight and I was getting sleep, and it was wonderful. But what was even more wonderful was when people would ask me how he was sleeping and I could say, 'Great, he sleeps through the night.' People would give me these wonderful looks of approval. Then when he started sleeping horribly at five months and he was getting up every hour to two hours and people asked how he was sleeping, the looks quickly changed. I thought for sure I would get looks of pity, but I got the 'Oh, you're a terrible parent' look. The 'What are you doing wrong' look."

Of course, parents sometimes get competitive about how much sleep they're not getting, adds Elisabeth, 38, who is currently pregnant with her second child:

"I think there's some sense for some parents that being sleep deprived is expected, necessary, and almost a badge of honor."

Aside from the pressure to have a baby who sleeps, the sleep advice can be laced with scary predictions about what will happen if you don't get on top of your child's sleep problems pronto.

"What I really hated were the dire warnings people would give," recalls Jennifer, the 28-year-old mother of one. "Like, 'If you don't have the baby sleeping through the night by six months of age, the baby will never sleep through the night.'"

And as for the advice that comes your way from family members, however well meaning, that can prove to be a source of frustration, too.

"You would think our own mothers would be able to offer some guidance, considering their experience, but they can't," says Patricia, a 31-year-old mother of one. "Mothering was so much different back then."

Marla, a 36-year-old mother of one, agrees: "If you ask my mother and my aunts and their friends, all of whom are in their sixties, 'sleeping through the night' means the baby goes in the crib at 7:30 and you leave her there until 8 the next morning, no matter what. Their memories are frustratingly revisionist."

Perhaps the most maddening thing of all about the sleep-related advice that tends to come your way is the fact that it tends to be heavy on the criticism, but sorely lacking in practical solutions.

"I felt like everyone was dishing out advice on how much Mikaela should be sleeping, but no one was giving us the formula to get it done," says Michele, a 30-year-old mother of two.

Leanne, a 35-year-old mother of two, agrees: "Everyone seems to know exactly what we're doing 'wrong,' but no one can tell us how to fix the problem."

Your Child's Sleep Problems Can Take a Toll on Your Parenting Self-Esteem

In her book *Mothering from the Heart: Lessons on Listening to Our Children and Ourselves*, Bonnie Ohye notes that society continues to value independence in even very young children: "In spite of revisionist ideas and research, the image of the independent child as the child esteemed above all others remains a cornerstone of our understanding of children and of ourselves as mothers. It is the gold standard, the litmus test of whether a child is a good and admirable child, and whether a mother is a good mother." It's hardly surprising then that mothers of older babies and toddlers who still aren't sleeping through the night can feel like they've somehow failed as mothers. Krysta, a 28-year-old mother of one, remembers feeling this way while her daughter Gianna was repeatedly waking in the night: "I often felt that I just be doing something wrong as a mother if I couldn't get my daughter to sleep through. I'd think, 'I have a master's degree, but I can't get a one-year-old to stay asleep for more than four hours at a stretch.'"

Lorraine, a 37-year-old mother of one, thinks that the standards that society sets for mothers—and that mothers set for themselves—are often impossibly high: "Our society places so much stress on mothers. It's kind of like the beauty myth—that ideal body type presented by the media that genetically occurs in maybe 1 percent of the general population. All these girls and women striving to meet the impossible ideal are left feeling inadequate, depressed, unworthy. I think the same applies to parenting today."

Naomi Stadlen, author of *What Mothers Do: Especially When It Looks Like Nothing*, thinks it's time that we turned the stereotype of the sleep-deprived-mother-as-failure on its head: "If a mother says she is short of sleep, this could be a sign not of her failure, but of how well she may be mothering."

How Sleep Deprivation Makes Parenting Harder

IT'S DIFFICULT TO overstate the effects of sleep deprivation.

"I can remember telling Nick, in a moment of intense frustration, that waking someone up as soon as they fell asleep was a form of torture," recalls Jennifer, a 28-year-old first-time mom.

Here's what you need to know about the more noteworthy effects of sleep deprivation—specifically how they can make parenting feel like you're running uphill.

Your Brain Starts to Feel Foggy and Sluggish

Are you constantly misplacing your car keys? Do you forget about doctor's appointments or meetings at work—or show up on the wrong day? While you may feel like you have been kidnapped and whisked off to Planet of the Mommy Zombies, you're simply experiencing one of the more noticeable side effects of sleep deprivation. Research has shown that losing just one night of sleep causes a 30 percent decline in cognitive performance. Lose two nights and you're down 60 percent. Or, to look at it another way, by the time you've been awake for 17 to 19 hours, your reaction times have slowed to the point where you're functioning about as well as a drunk driver. And you don't have to lose an entire night's sleep before the brain fog starts rolling in. Losing as little as 1.5 hours of sleep in a single night reduces your daytime alertness by about one-third. And if you're less alert, you'll have a more difficult time remembering things (like where you put those car keys or whether or not that doctor's appointment is today or a week from now) and making even the simplest decisions.

And, not surprisingly, now that your brain has geared down, your productivity is nose-diving, too. It's not just because you may have a baby in your arms, a toddler clinging to your leg, or a preschooler who's constantly asking you questions (although these are certainly factors). It's because you're so unbelievably tired. And as for holding on to your long-held title as the Maven of Multitasking? You can forget about that for now, too. One of the first cognitive abilities to disappear when we become seriously overtired is our ability to handle more than one task at a time. So if you pop some toast in the toaster, put on the kettle to make some tea, and zip off to check your e-mail while your baby is enjoying his morning nap, you could end up with a kitchen flambé rather than a morning snack.

PILLOW TALK

The National Sleep Foundation's 2004 *Sleep in America Poll* reported that 48 percent of parents had driven while drowsy, 10 percent had fallen asleep behind the wheel, and 1 percent had been involved in an automobile accident as a result of daytime sleepiness.

Your Communication Skills Plummet

You're talking to a friend on the phone and you suddenly realize that you no longer sound like yourself. You sound a bit drunk and kind of thick-headed. You keep using the same words and expressions over and over again, and your voice is nowhere near as lively and expressive as it usually is. You can't find the right words to express exactly what it is you want to say. Suddenly it dawns on you why the expression "stupid tired" was coined. Or you don't bother telling your partner what's he's doing that's driving you crazy because you don't want to get into a long—and potentially energy-draining—conversation. Instead, you decide to say nothing for now in the hope that things will get better on their own. And then one day when you're feeling particularly tired or particularly frustrated, you launch into a heated tirade that—from your partner's standpoint at least—appears to be coming out of nowhere. He had no idea what was bubbling under the surface until the mom volcano finally blew.

Your Problem-Solving Skills and Your Creativity Begin to Nosedive

It's the sleep world's equivalent of a classic catch-22: being sleep-deprived short-circuits your creativity, making it difficult for you to come up with a list of possible solutions for dealing with your child's sleep problems. You lose your ability to think flexibly, preferring instead to stick with your current game plan, even if it's not working for you.

MOM'S THE WORD

"When you're sleep deprived, it's easy to get stuck in a parenting rut," says Amanda, a 23-year-old mother of one. "When I was lacking the energy to go out for a walk even, I found my days all melding together in what felt like a scene from the movie *Groundhog Day*."

You May Feel Impatient and Edgy

Most parents find that their patience is one of the first things to go when they start missing out on sleep. If you don't get at least one three-hour stretch of uninterrupted sleep in a 24 hour period, you'll find it difficult to think rationally because you'll be missing out on slow-wave (or delta) sleep—the deepest and most replenishing stage of sleep.

You Feel Zapped of Your Usual Energy and Drive

Raising young children demands huge amounts of physical and emotional energy, so it's not surprising that so many parents of babies, toddlers, and preschoolers report feeling tired. And being deprived of sleep on a regular basis will only add to your fatigue. (The National Sleep Foundation's 2004 *Sleep in America Poll* found that 50 percent of parents of infants, 66 percent of parents of toddlers, and 63 percent of parents of preschoolers reported having much less or somewhat less energy for parenting as a result of their child's sleep problems.)

You May Experience Insomnia

Missing out on sleep in the night because your child needs you may be frustrating, but it's a whole lot less frustrating than not being able to get to sleep or stay asleep during those hours of the night when you might otherwise be catching up on some much-needed shut-eye. According to the National Sleep Foundation, insomnia is a common problem for parents of young children: 29 percent of parents experience insomnia at least a few nights a week, with 12 percent experiencing insomnia every night or almost every

MOM'S THE WORD

"The few times my toddler has slept straight through, I have woken up at each interval when he would normally awaken and lain there waiting. I would try to get back to sleep, but would find it hard to turn off and relax, thinking 'He'll be up at any minute anyway.' I bet I get less sleep when he sleeps through the night than on the nights he actually gets me up."

—Leanne, 35, mother of two

---

night. It's quite common for parents to have difficulty getting back to sleep after they've been up with their child in the night. This tends to be a particular problem for parents who have a child who gets up frequently in the night. They may be so focused on how little sleep that they are likely to get before they are awakened from sleep again that they find it hard to relax enough to get the sleep that they so desperately crave: "I often lie in bed thinking if I fall asleep right now, I might get two hours of sleep before he wakes again," says Michele, 30, the mother of two young children, including 11-month-old Xander. *Note:* Insomnia can be associated with a number of different postpartum mood disorders, so be sure to mention any sleep problems to your doctor.

Insomnia can also become a problem for parents when they finally start getting some sleep: "I noticed that when Benjamin finally slept through the night, I would still wake up once or twice per night and that it would take me about 45 minutes to fall back to sleep," recalls Helen, 32, the mother of one-year-old Benjamin. "It took almost two weeks for that to wear off."

"Once Kaylei started sleeping through the night, it took several weeks for me to learn how to wind down and drift off to sleep, and to fall into a deep sleep," adds Michelle, 36, the mother of 18-month-old Kaylei. "I find—even now—that if we have a long stretch where our nights are constantly interrupted, I don't sleep well until we've had several good nights. I'm on alert for 'the cry.'"

That powerful "mother radar" can be hard to deactivate, even temporarily when someone else is on "sleep patrol" and you're supposed to be taking a break from the frontlines of motherhood

PILLOW TALK

Find yourself experiencing disturbing dreams every time you drift off to dreamland? It's a side effect of sleep deprivation. If you've been running up a hefty sleep debt, you're likely to experience what sleep researchers refer to as "rebound REM" when you're sleeping—extra-long rapid-eye movement (REM) cycles, which can lead to extremely vivid dreams or even nightmares.

---

so that you can catch up on your sleep. Judy, 32, the mother of eight-month-old Cadell, recalls how hard it was for her to relax and sleep, even when she knew her baby was in excellent hands: "I wanted to be the Martha Stewart of moms—that mythical woman who could handle anything, sleep or no sleep! But as much as I hated asking for help, I finally gave in and asked my mom to come over and take my son for a walk or play with him in the basement rec room, far away from our bedroom. I closed the curtains, turned on some music, slipped into comfy PJs, parked myself under the duvet—and lay there with my eyes wide open. *What if Cadell needed me, but Mom didn't want to disturb me? No one knew Cadell better than me. What if he needed something desperately and the one person who knew what it was had selfishly locked herself away for a few hours of sleep? How could I be so selfish?*"

Pam, 37, the mother of five-month-old Justin, has had similar difficulty relaxing enough to sleep-in on weekend mornings when her husband is available to give her a break: "I find it hard to nap when given the chance. My husband often takes the baby on weekend mornings, giving me a chance to sleep–in. The problem is I can never sleep when I feel the pressure to sleep."

If you're finding that insomnia is becoming a problem for you, you'll find some practical tips on managing this common problem in Chapter 2.

You May Start to Experience Some of the Physical Symptoms Associated with Sleep Deprivation

If you've just had a couple of particularly rough nights with your little one, you may feel like you've just been through some sort of endurance marathon (which, in a sense, you have—a sleep-deprivation endurance marathon).

Depending on how long you've been without a decent night's sleep and how quickly and how powerfully you react to sleep deprivation (we're all unique in this respect), you may find that you begin to experience one or more of the more common physical symptoms of sleep deprivation:

- itching or burning eyes
- blurred vision
- feeling cold
- increased hunger (especially craving high-carbohydrate or high-fat foods; see Chapter 2 for more on managing the nutritional challenges of sleep deprivation)
- gastrointestinal discomfort and related symptoms, like nausea, stomach cramps, and diarrhea (the production of the digestive protein that protects your stomach lining against minor irritants—e.g., spicy foods—can be disrupted if your circadian rhythms are disrupted)
- an increased susceptibility to illness (the immune system takes a bit of a beating when we lose sleep; however, the body fights back by making us extra tired when we get sick)

You May Experience Some of the Emotional Symptoms Associated with Sleep Deprivation

Sleep deprivation can make you moody. *Very moody.* (Moodier than the moodiest day of your entire pregnancy kind of moody.) In fact, getting six hours of sleep as opposed to eight hours of sleep in each 24 hour period—pretty standard for many moms with young children—can leave you feeling miserable because you simply aren't able to clock enough of the short-wave or delta sleep that you require in order to maintain your emotional equilibrium. If you're not benefiting from that kind of replenishing sleep, you lose your feeling of calmness, your sense of balance, and your ability to go with the flow. Instead, you feel more stressed, depressed, anxious, nervous, and less able to cope with the day-to-day challenges of

motherhood. (Once again, be on the lookout for the possib̄
of a postpartum mood disorder.) And as for your sense of hu.
well, let's just say it has a tendency to go AWOL when you're la͟ ͟ng
in sleep. It's hard to find much to smile or laugh about when you're
completely exhausted, unless, of course, very dark and bitter
humor counts. In that case, you might argue that your sense of
humor is alive and well, *thank you very much*.

You Are at Increased Risk of Developing Postpartum Depression

There's also a growing body of research linking sleep deprivation
and postpartum depression (PPD)—information that every
mother needs to know about. A 1992 study by researchers at the
University of Edinburgh found that having difficulty sleeping late
in pregnancy and then going through labor at night increased a
woman's risk of developing postpartum depression. And in two
separate studies conducted in 2000 and 2003, sleep researcher
Amy R. Wolfson, PhD, identified two sleep-related "red flags" that
may indicate that a particular mother faces a greater-than-average
risk of developing postpartum depression:

- an excessive need for sleep in late pregnancy (more total sleep
  time, getting up later in the morning, and spending more time
  napping), something that could either be an indication that the
  mom-to-be is experiencing poor-quality sleep at night, that
  she is struggling with prenatal depression, or both

- severe sleep disruption during pregnancy and immediately
  after childbirth

If you think you could be suffering from postpartum depression,
talk to your health care provider about how you're feeling. The
sooner you have that conversation, the sooner you can start feeling
better. (Note: See the appendices at the back of this book for information about organizations, websites, and books that may be useful
to you if you are struggling with postpartum depression. And be
sure to check out the many self-care strategies in Chapter 2, which
may be helpful to you as you start to feel better.)

Desperate Parents

SO MUCH FOR the made-for-TV version of life after baby: a camera zooms in and two completely blissed-out parents gaze into one another's eyes and then glance over at their equally blissed-out newborn, who is either wide-eyed and content or peacefully slumbering away. But while this kind of Mom, Dad, and baby camera shot may make for a picture-perfect ending for any one of the pregnancy and birth "reality TV shows" that have become hugely popular in recent years, they don't exactly capture the *true* reality of what happens during the weeks and months after partners morph into parents. (The camera crews are gone by then.)

"I swear that every couple with a new baby has the same fight when the baby's about six weeks old—the 'whose life sucks more' fight," insists Tracy, a 35-year-old mother of three. And the relationship fallout isn't necessarily a one-time deal, adds Dani, a 35-year-old mother of both a preschooler and a toddler: "I remember awful fights with my husband, hysterical tears on more than one occasion, and a lot of hours I wish I could go back and revisit, all caused by baby number two's relentless nighttime wakings."

While relationship road bumps tend to be the norm for most new parents (studies have shown that couples tend to argue eight times as often after they have children as they did before), having a child who doesn't sleep particularly well can make a difficult situation even worse. The National Sleep Foundation's 2004 *Sleep in America Poll* found that children's sleep problems cause moderate to significant stress to a couple's relationship, particularly during the infant and toddler years, with 10 percent of parents of babies and 7 percent of parents of toddlers reporting that their children's sleep habits were affecting their relationship with their partner. And when a child requires Mom or Dad to be present in the bedroom every night or almost every night in order to fall asleep at night, things tend to go from bad to worse, with 50 percent of couples reporting that they and their partner were experiencing a moderate to significant amount of stress in their relationship as a result of their child's sleep difficulties.

PILLOW TALK

Don't assume that because your partner is sleeping for more consecutive hours at night that he's necessarily feeling more rested than you are. A study conducted by researchers at the University of California found that while moms ended up having their sleep disturbed more times at night during the first month postpartum, fathers obtained fewer total hours of sleep in a 24-hour period than moms. The net result? Both moms and dads reported similar levels of fatigue.

The Sleep Deprivation Gender Gap

BEING DEPRIVED OF sleep while your partner slumbers on can lead to feelings of resentment if the sleep arrangement that the two of you have worked out starts feeling like an unfair deal to the partner who is repeatedly doing night duty—typically Mom. (The National Sleep Foundation 2004 *Sleep in America Poll* found that mothers get up 89 percent of the time with infants, 85 percent of the time with toddlers, and 71 percent of the time with preschoolers.)

"Sleep—how much and of what quality—is the main source of conflict for us," says Samantha, the 31-year-old mother of eight-month-old Sadie. "My husband gets way more sleep—and by that I mean uninterrupted sleep. I can't even remember what that is, and I get very bitter about the inequality of our situation."

"I was so resentful of the fact that he was lying there sleeping while I was getting up for the third time that night to breast-feed," recalls one mother of two. "When I'd come back to bed, I'd get in bed as noisily as possible in the hope that I'd manage to wake him up. I practically used the bed as a trampoline as I bounded back into it at 4:00 a.m. If he didn't wake up, I'd lie in bed feeling incredibly angry at him for not waking up, and that resentment would build in me until I felt like I was going to explode. And all the while, he would be having a good night's sleep without a care in the world."

"We agreed before the baby was born that while I was off work, I would get up with the baby and hubby would sleep because he had to go to work the next day," recalls Amanda, the 23-year-old mother of 11-month-old Jace. "But agreement or not, there were nights that I hated my husband when I had to get up and he could stay in bed, drooling and snoring into his pillow. Now that I'm back at work, too, we take turns getting up in the night. That's a much better idea."

If you and your partner find yourself exchanging angry words in the night or icy glares over the breakfast table, maybe it's time to clear the air about nighttime parenting issues. Here are some tips from other parents who have successfully negotiated the 3 a.m. treaty (or whatever treaty it is that needs to be negotiated to restore peace on the parental front).

Play to One Another's Strengths

ONE OF THE secrets to surviving sleep deprivation is to start functioning as a parenting team. That means considering the unique strengths and abilities that you and your partner each bring to the nighttime parenting arena and using them to your mutual advantage. "My husband and I have worked out quite a routine," adds Stephanie, 37, the mother of two boys, ages three and six-and-a-half. "Billy is the kind of guy who can wake up, triage the situation, and fall asleep again, just about anywhere. He is also a good napper. I, on the other hand, cannot nap, and once awake, rarely fall back to sleep. He takes the night wakings so that I can sleep. I take over in the morning so that he can sleep in. I am also able to go on four hours of sleep for up to four nights before becoming catatonic, so I will deal with the boys when they are sick

---

PILLOW TALK

Wonder how the Battle of the Sexes plays out in the sleep-deprivation trenches? Researchers have discovered that women are generally better at coping with the effects of sleep deprivation than men. They do better on tasks requiring a lot of accuracy because they automatically reduce their work speed in order to maintain their accuracy rate. (Men, on the other hand, tend to forge ahead at their regular speed, and their accuracy rate goes out the window.)

or upset in the night. (While Billy is good at triage, he's not good at ongoing care in the night—he kind of loses it if forced to do more than change a diaper or get a cup of water.)"

Ask for What You Need

"I used to make a bit of a production of how tired I was—I should have been nominated for an Oscar—in an effort to get my husband to come in and volunteer to take over, especially in the middle of the night," says Dani, 36, the mother of two boys, ages three and one. "It was quite silly now that I think about it. I don't know why I didn't just ask for help."

It seems like such an obvious solution in retrospect, but when you're tired and cranky (or not sure exactly what type of support your partner can provide at that given second if your baby is literally "hooked on Mom"!), it can be difficult to ask for (and get) the support you so desperately crave from your partner. "I think this was our biggest source of friction," recalls Jen, 30, the mother of 12-month-old Amanda. "My husband couldn't understand why I was resentful that he still continued all his regular activities—he is a busy guy and is out most evenings. He would come home from work and spend 30 minutes to an hour at home, eat dinner, then go out again, leaving me to bathe the baby and put her to bed every night. I love looking after her, but I need a break too! It's like I was the primary caregiver, so it was just assumed that I would be looking after her unless I asked him to. And this extended to the nighttime relationship. I always felt like when the baby cried, he didn't even hear her—it was just assumed I would get up. To be fair, I wasn't working, so it made sense that I would be the first person to get up in the middle of the night. But some nights, after being up for hours, night after night, I just really needed someone else to do it for me and give me a bit of a break. More than anything, I think that was the biggest result of our (read: *my*) sleep deprivation—irritation at my partner for not being able to read me better, and knowing when I needed to be spelled off so that I could get a bit more sleep." Rachel, the 33-year-old mother of two-year-old Byron, found that she was reluctant to ask for help, even when it was obvious to herself and her partner that she was long overdue for a break. "I think we mothers sometimes try to tough it out longer than we should," she says. "I don't know if there's something cultural making us feel like failures if we can't handle it, or what, but I do know that when I've had problems, nine times out of 10 it's been my husband who has had to set me down and say, 'Hey! Take care of yourself!' And then I do, but I think it's sad that it has to get to that point before I'll even ask for help!"

Accept That Moms Tend to Be More Tuned into Their Babies' Cries in the Night

"I used to sleep through car alarms, smoke detectors, and alarm clocks. Now the slightest whimper from my daughter and I'm wide awake," says Amanda, the 33-year-old mother of three-year-old Zoe.

"I am capable of responding to a cry instantaneously. It must be maternal wiring," adds Sarah, the 41-year-old mother of two children, ages six months and three years.

It is maternal wiring. The female brain is more sensitive to sound even before a woman becomes a parent. And the parent who provides the most care to an infant—typically the mother—gets more practice in learning what that particular infant's various cries mean. So if your partner sleeps through your baby's cries in the night, he's not doing his best to shirk his fatherly duties or win the Insensitive Clod of the Year Award: There's a very good chance he's simply not hearing the baby. Of course, that doesn't mean that dads should use biology as an excuse for not helping out in the night (assuming, of course, that the two of you have decided that it makes the most sense to have Dad pitching in on night patrol). If your partner isn't aroused by the initial sounds of your baby's rousing, he's certain to be roused by a gentle prod from you.

Accept the Fact That Sometimes Only Mom Will Do

What could be more frustrating to a dad who is doing his best to give his sleep-deprived partner a break than to end up coming up against a baby or toddler who is smack-dab in the middle of "the mommy stage" and who will accept no mommy substitutes?

"My partner feels terrible and frustrated when he tries to walk the baby, shush the baby, soothe the baby, and all the baby wants is Mom," says Sharon, a 41-year-old mother of one. "He's at his wits' end and I'm exhausted."

Dads need to know that even though a baby may want to hang out with Mom—particularly if Mom represents "the milk buffet" to a hungry baby!—dads can develop some powerful tot-soothing rituals of their own that can make them indispensable to babies (and to their baby's moms)! This is certainly how things played out for Sharlene, her partner Chris, and their baby Makenna: "To help me with the nighttime burden, Chris took the baby at 9:00 p.m. and had her until she fell asleep, they fell asleep together, or until I was ready to take the baby again. The direct result of this was the emergence of a bedtime ritual—daddy/baby time—and also Chris's amazing ability to calm the baby. After this, Chris became known as the Master Baby Calmer (MBC)." Just as that feeling of having to work at being included in the "Mom-baby" duo can be frustrating to dads, that all-encompassing sense of needed by her baby 24/7 can be overwhelming to a new mother. "I think the hardest thing for me to grasp—something that hadn't really occurred to me before—was that I didn't have a choice about getting up to feed the baby," recalls Jennifer, 30, whose infant daughter, Amanda, was breast-fed exclusively during the early months. "It was probably the first time in my life that the choice was completely out of my hands. In other situations, you might feel an obligation to do something, but you can get out of it if you really want to. This was different: a little person was depending on me to feed her, and if I didn't come, her tiny tummy would stay empty. There were many nights early on when I thought, 'I can't get up one more time,' only to have this closely followed by the realization that I simply had to. That was a hard lesson to learn, but very symbolic of everything that parenting is about, I think." Marla, a 36-year-old mother of one agrees that the intensity of the mother-child relationship changes everything overnight: "I used to think parenting was my new job. I didn't realize it was my new life."

Realize That Fair Doesn't Have to Mean 50/50

Just as those magazine articles that suggest that you and your partner divide housework chores right down the middle might not make any sense at all for your family, you and your partner may decide that having one parent up in the night (rather than having two parents up at the same feeding) is the best use of parental resources. Or you may decide that having alternate parents sharing some of the nighttime parenting duties works best because it allows each parent to get an extended stretch of sleep in the night. Or you may decide that the situation with your child has become so challenging that a "two-parents-on-deck" approach is required at every night waking. The situation is simply too difficult for one parent to handle on his or her own. You don't have to divide your nighttime parenting duties exactly down the middle in order for your "deal" to feel fair. (In fact, a 50/50 split might feel decidedly unfair to one of you, given your current circumstances.) What you want to do is to figure out a way of ensuring that you're both getting adequate rest, supporting one another, and—most important of all—functioning like members of the same parenting team. (If you're starting to feel like your partner is the enemy, that's a hint that the two of you need to renegotiate your deal. And that brings up another issue: No nighttime parenting deal should ever be final—well, at least not until Junior heads off for college with some solid sleep skills under his belt.) You'll probably find that if you start to function as a nighttime parenting team, you'll have a greater tendency to take the other partner's needs into consideration rather than wanting to look out for number one. "My husband is very supportive and he helps me tremendously," says Christine, 34, the mother of nine-month-old Emma. "So I was always sensitive to his situation, too. I knew he needed to get up to go to work the next day, so I would get to Emma before she cried when it was time to feed her and then put her back down again without disturbing him too much." "My husband has to get up at 4:30 a.m. and drive almost two hours to get to work," says Erin, 31, who is currently pregnant with her second child. "I'm more likely to tell him to go back to sleep if I know he's got to get up in an hour to go to work, even if it is his turn to get up with our toddler. Just knowing that he's gotten up before makes me more willing to help him out."

Strangers in the Night

FINDING TIME FOR one another can be a huge challenge for parents, particularly if your baby is still quite young or your child's sleep problems are either extreme or long-standing. Many moms find that it's difficult to stay connected as a couple when they're busy juggling the around-the-clock demands of parenting—to say nothing of everything else on their to-do lists. "We are like ships passing in the night," says Sharon, 35, the mother of a night-waking three-and-a-half-year-old. "I love my husband and appreciate his support, but that's about all we have for one another right now. "It's true what they say: Your heart does grow when there is someone else to love, but, sadly, the number of hours in a day does not increase in tandem," adds Laura, a 29-year-old mother of one.

"What has suffered the most for us is quality time," says Kara, a 33-year-old mother of two. "We always manage to slip in sex, but if we try to watch a movie together, I'm out cold after half an hour. We get by, but the lack of sleep has made it hard to resolve personal problems that come up between the two of us."

"We don't get much time alone," adds Stephanie, a 37-year-old mother of two. "My husband has a terrible habit of falling asleep while reading to our kids, which means he never comes to bed. And I am often too tired to hunt him down to chat. This means we struggle to find some quiet time to talk. If we need to speak about something important, we often do it with a quick e-mail or phone call when one of us is out. We also try to get away from home once in a while when we feel like we're losing our connection."

"We went to marriage counseling after the birth of baby number two because we were concerned about the overall impact of parenting two young children on our relationship," notes Erin, 34, mother of three. "We learned to set aside time for one another each week, even if it's just meeting for lunch or watching a movie together on the sofa. We find good babysitters and we use them. And we make sex a priority."

Sleep Is the New Sex

FEMINIST COMIC Beth Lapides claims that she read in *Vogue* magazine a few years back that "Sleep is the new sex." That should be great news to you if you and your partner are sleep-deprived parents who happen to like to stay on trend. The next time you're trying to muster up the energy to get some hot bedroom action happening between the sheets, you can remind yourself that the real movers and shakers are opting for sleep, not sex.

Most parents find that the sexual tide ebbs and flows depend on what's going on in their parenting lives and how much sleep they're getting at any given time.

"The adrenaline high of early motherhood made me feel sexier than usual—something I wasn't expecting so soon after giving birth," says one new mom. "But by the time my six-week checkup rolled around and I was given the okay for sex, the adrenaline had definitely worn off (for both of us, I think). Although we still felt very close, sex didn't happen for a few months and is still very sporadic. We are both just so tired. It's hard to get interested. And even now that the baby is sleeping better, it's still hard to get 'back in the saddle.' I'm exhausted from looking after her all day, he is having a busy time at work, and once you've fallen out of the habit of having sex, it's hard to get back into it. We're working on it, but we have a long way to go." "After going through pregnancy, giving birth, and living as a stay-at-home Mom for over a year, it's really hard to transition back into naughty hot sex kitten mode even just for half an hour or 10 minutes. Whatever," insists Marla, 36, mom of one. "I'm just saying, that it's like I'm a physically different person—and he's not. But given a choice to sleep or spend hours making wild, passionate love, he'd choose a quickie and some sleep too, so I don't feel like it's all on my shoulders." When there's mutual understanding, as there is between Marla and her partner, the situation tends to be a lot less stressful. Both partners simply

PILLOW TALK

Your baby isn't the only kid who arrived on the planet with a powerful ability to detect—and prevent!—parents' sexual activity. In fact, the phenomenon is reported so often by parents that researchers have been floating around a couple of theories to explain why babies seem to wake up every time things start getting hot and heavy between Mom and Dad. The top three explanations? (1) Baby may be able to smell Mom's breast milk letting down during sexual arousal; (2) there's some powerful psychic connection between Mom and baby that tips baby off to the fact that some bedroom action may be looming—and hence the threat of conception is near; and (3) Mom and Dad aren't being quite as hush-hush as they think they are, and it's good old-fashioned noise that's to blame.

---

accept the fact that there's less sex on the menu for the time being, even if neither of them are particularly thrilled to find themselves experiencing the sexual drought that they swore would never happen to them. "We were tired, and that was a fact of life," explains Amanda, a 33-year-old mother of one. "Sort of, 'If I wasn't so tired I'd jump you' and 'If I wasn't so tired, I'd like it.' And co-sleeping didn't provide the ideal atmosphere for spontaneous, before-sleep sex. Once Zoe got into a regular sleeping schedule, we started to set aside an hour or so in the evenings to spend with one another. And we rediscovered the joy of sex outside the bedroom."

When one partner is exhausted and the other partner is craving affection that the other simply doesn't have to give, that's when things can get a little tense between partners. "I feel as though I give everything to the kids during the day," explains one mother of an infant and a toddler. "I need time to myself at night, which means that my husband doesn't get the attention or affection he wants." Another mom with four young children puts it even more pointedly: "Intimacy ultimately becomes another chore that needs to be checked off on the 'to-do' list at the end of the day." Sometimes it's the simple geography of sex that's at the root of the problem. "It's very difficult to get into the mood when you can hear your baby breathing right next to you," says one co-sleeping mother of two. The solution to that, insists one veteran co-sleeping mom, is to move sex out of the bedroom. "Bedrooms aren't the only place to be intimate," says Keri, a mother of seven and foster mom of two. "Couches can be comfortable or in front of the woodstove with a nice candle glowing. There are always those 'quickies' in the shower with the baby monitor sitting on the counter—or even just before or just after the shower. Many people also have nicely finished basements that may have an appropriate place to be intimate. We actually found being 'forced' out of our own bed to be 'fun'! Also the futon on the floor beside the bed can work too!" Of course, taking the romance out of the bedroom is no guarantee that your baby won't pick up on the fact that you're actually trying to have sex: "On the odd occasion when we do connect, we are invariably interrupted by our son," laments Sharon, 41, mother of one. "It's like he has some sort of built-in radar system that keeps us from creating a new little competitor for his toys. *Weird*."

Solutions Central—The Last Word

THIS CHAPTER FOCUSED on the physical, emotional, and relationship fallout of sleep deprivation—how missing out on sleep during the early months and years of your child's life (a very normal parenting rite of passage, but an exhausting one nonetheless) is likely to affect virtually every aspect of your life.

In the next chapter, we're going to zero in on some parent-proven strategies for maximizing both the quantity and quality of the sleep that you're getting and for otherwise taking the best possible care of yourself during this crazy-busy time in your life. (Note: You'll want to share many of these strategies with your partner so that the two of you end of being better rested sooner, something that will reap huge dividends in the quality of your relationship with one another and your ability to tackle your child's sleep difficulties together.)

CHAPTER 2

The Sleep-Deprivation Survival Guide

My best advice came from my doctor, which was to pace myself for the long haul. It's not just about trying to get more sleep; it's restructuring your days so they're not as stressful.
—MARLA, 36, MOTHER OF ONE

I F EVERY BABY CAME with an operating manual that included a detailed schematic outlining infant, toddler, and preschooler sleep patterns (and a programming guide for getting those sleep patterns back on track if your child were to experience any "sleep system malfunctions" during that time), you would have a clear sense of how much sleep you could expect to get during the early years of parenting. Sure, you'd be a little sleep deprived from time to time, but at least you could prepare for the rough patches in advance. And during the most sleep-deprived nights of parent-hood, you could slide your finger across the sleep schematic and count the number of days left until Junior finally started sleeping through the night once and for all. Of course, nothing about parenting is that predictable. That's why savvy parents know that managing your resources as a parent means so much more than taking care of yourself in the here and now. You have to stockpile a bit of extra emotional and physical energy in case (unbeknownst to you) you're ramping up to a particularly grueling stretch of night-waking, a period when neither you nor your baby is likely to get any sleep. That is what this chapter is all about—maximizing your opportunities for sleep and taking the best possible care of yourself so that you will have the physical and emotional reserves necessary to handle whatever parenting curveballs may be headed your way.

Eyes Wide Shut: Maximizing Your Opportunities for Sleep

IF YOUR SLEEP debt is growing by the day and you feel physically and emotionally drained, you're no longer dealing with a sleep challenge—you're dealing with a sleep emergency. And in an emergency, you have to take a fairly drastic approach to managing your limited resources until the emergency passes. That may mean making getting sleep and caring for yourself and your child your sole priorities until you feel more rested and better able to cope. The challenge, of course, is to come up with strategies for maximizing sleep when you're feeling totally exhausted. In Chapter 1, we talked about how problem solving and creativity are two of the first casualties of sleep deprivation. Fortunately, there are ways to start getting the sleep you so desperately crave, starting today (or tonight). You're unlikely to get huge blocks of sleep at any given time (unless, of course, your child decides to give you an unexpected sleep gift!), but if you start incorporating as many of the following strategies for maximizing sleep into your life as possible, you will start getting more sleep and be in a better position to brainstorm possible solutions to your child's sleep problems.

"Sleep When the Baby Sleeps"

"'SLEEP WHEN THE baby sleeps.' I hate to say it because when people said it to me, it made me want to scream," says Cathleen, 32, the mother of seven-month-old Miyoko. "When my baby was asleep, I wanted to sleep, but I also felt like I needed to do laundry, make dinner, pay bills, and do all the other things that needed doing, not to mention relaxing or fun things like reading or calling a friend. But, really, if you are sleep deprived, there's really no other choice but to sleep when the baby sleeps."

Julie, the 29-year-old mother of 11-month-old Jacob, also hated hearing that much-repeated piece of sleep advice, so began to modify it in a way that worked for her: "I hated the advice that you should sleep when the baby sleeps. It seemed that I was never tired when he'd finally sleep, so my advice would be relax when your baby sleeps. If you're not able to sleep, then just sit on the couch and read a good book. Lie on your bed and daydream. Indulge in a few TV shows you'd not otherwise watch. But really and truly: *Let the housework go.* Don't worry about cooking decent meals. Don't worry about returning phone calls or e-mails. Really take care of yourself at all costs."

Some mothers use a combination of strategies to get through the day, including, admittedly, caffeine. For Leanne, 35, the mother of a 14-month-old and a four-year-old, that means minimizing energy expenditure throughout the day and coordinating her children's naptimes in the afternoon so that she can fit in a nap, too: "On days when I haven't had a lot of sleep, I just do whatever I need to do to cope, which usually means morning cartoons for my oldest, naps for everyone in the afternoon (me included), and copious amounts of caffeine in the form of Dr. Pepper in the afternoon, and then pure relief when my husband gets home and helps out after work. If a task can wait—laundry, cleaning, paying bills—it won't get done on those days."

Call for Backup

Leanne isn't the only mom who admits to feeling "pure relief" when the sleep reinforcement forces—in this case, her husband—arrive on the scene to provide a much-needed break. Having other people to turn to can mean the difference between treading water successfully and going under when you're a sleep-deprived parent. And, contrary to popular belief, there are plenty of things that other people can do to help out, even if your baby is still very young and you're breast-feeding. See the box "How Other People Can Help You to Be a Better-Rested Mom" for some practical suggestions.

Not everyone has a partner who is willing or available to provide hands-on help on the sleep front. And, of course, there are many

HOW OTHER PEOPLE CAN HELP YOU TO BE A BETTER-RESTED MOM

- Take care of your baby right after a feeding so that you can nap until it's time for baby to nurse again.

- Take care of your other children so that you can take your baby to bed, nurse in a side-lying position and hope that you and baby will end up taking a shared nap. (See Chapter 5 for tips on co-sleeping.)

- Offer a bottle of expressed breast milk to your baby so that you can sleep through a late evening feeding and get a solid block of sleep from right after dinner until your baby's middle-of-the-night feeding. (Note: Most breast-feeding experts recommend that you wait until breast-feeding is well established before you introduce a bottle to a breast-fed baby, ideally three to six weeks.)

- Care for your older children during the day so that you can sleep while the baby sleeps.

- Assist with laundry and other household chores, cook meals, or run errands for you so that you won't be tempted to tackle these tasks during times when you might otherwise be sleeping or resting.

parents raising children without partners. If your partner is not available or you are parenting without a partner and you feel like you could use some additional parenting support, you may want to consider one or more of the following possible sources of assistance. (Note: When you're trying to decide who to turn to for help, ask yourself who would be in the best position to provide you with the type of help you need right now and, if you have to pay for this help, at a price you can afford. Don't forget that you could ask for some postpartum help as a baby gift or barter for the help.)

Family members: While the days of having generation upon generation of family members just around the block are a thing of the past for most of us, it's still possible to tap into the support of far-flung relatives provided, of course, that they are willing to offer some of that support. Here are a few suggestions:

- See if a relative that you are particularly close to would be willing to stay with you to assist with baby care and general household tasks so that you can catch up on your sleep.

- If there aren't any relatives available to come to you, see if there are any relatives who'd be willing to provide such support in their own homes. Would your parents, in-laws, or any of your aunts, sisters, or cousins be willing to play host to you and your baby (with the aim of the visit being to allow you to catch up on your sleep)?

Friends: If you've got friends who are willing to pitch in and help, accept their offers, says Wendy, 30, the mother of one-year-old Thomas. "Instead of saying 'No, I've got everything under control' when someone asks if there is anything they can do, we need to say 'yes' and put them to work." Friends who are experienced in caring for young children can cuddle your baby while you take a nap or entertain your toddler or preschooler while you and baby take a nap together. Friends whose idea of torture is being left alone with little kids can help you out in other ways—by preparing meals, helping to run loads of laundry through the washer and dryer, cleaning the mystery leftovers out of the refrigerator, or vacuuming.

A postpartum doula: A postpartum doula (a professional support person who assists mothers and their families during the postpartum period) can provide breast-feeding and baby care advice as well as hands-on help with household tasks when you and your partner may be feeling exhausted and overloaded. Her job is to take care of the new parents—to "mother the mother" and the father, too. See Appendix A for information about and referrals to postpartum doulas.

A mother's helper: A preteen who is too young to babysit on his or her own (either legally or in your opinion) can still be an excellent source of hands-on help under your supervision. You can have the preteen play with your baby and fold laundry while you're making dinner or paying bills on-line. And, as an added bonus, when your baby is a little older and the preteen a little older, you could very well have a custom-trained babysitter who is the perfect age for taking care of your little one.

A high school student: If you have both a baby and a toddler or preschooler to care for, hire a high school student to play with your toddler three afternoons a week for an hour after school so that you and baby can take a late-afternoon nap on those days for an hour before it's time to start making dinner.

A college or university student: If there is a college or university in your community that offers courses in early childhood education, nursing, teaching, or other programs that focus on children, place an advertisement with the campus recruitment office offering part-time work to one of their students. Look for someone who is available to come to your house for a couple of hours during the daytime or evening on weekdays or weekends (whatever will work best with the student's schedule) so that you can work more sleep into your schedule.

Someone from your faith community: If you belong to a church or other religious association, you may find that the people you know through your faith community are only too happy to pitch in and help if you let them know that you could use a little extra support. Just be sure to be specific about your needs and what other people can do to help.

Another mother who is interested in doing a child-care swap: Odds are you're not the only tired mother in your circle of friends, so why not pool resources and offer to swap child-care services for "nap credits, " potentially the most valuable currency on the planet? You could take care of your friend's baby or toddler one morning while she zips home to flake out for the morning on the closest horizontal surface (likely the couch just inside her front door). Then she would return the favor so that you could do the same thing the next day. Obviously, you'd want to do a child-care swap only with someone you know well, trust thoroughly, and who has a compatible parenting style. Otherwise, you would spend your morning off worrying about your child rather than getting any shut-eye, which would defeat the entire purpose of the child-care swap!

Make Some Strategic Sleep Moves

Here's the lowdown on some sleep strategies that have worked well for other parents and that you'll definitely want to know about.

Experiment with a variety of different sleeping arrangements until you find the one that results in maximum sleep for everyone: Sometimes you have to experiment a little to find your way to sleep nirvana. Don't be afraid to scrap the plan you wrote before your baby was born. Just go with whatever works, provided, of course, that it's safe.

Become the diva of the daytime nap whether you work at home or outside of the home: Necessity is the mother of invention, and what could be more necessary to you at this time than clocking some extra minutes of sleep? While no nap will be a "miracle cure" and replace the eight hours of consecutive sleep that you wish you were getting at night, studies have shown that a 20–30 minute daytime nap can help to reduce the effects of sleep deprivation, so here's the lowdown on some powerful napping strategies that have worked for other moms.

If you work at home during the day:

- Safeguard your daytime sleep. Treat naptime as sacred, especially if you're not getting much sleep at night. Turn off the ringer on the phone and place a note on the door asking friends, neighbors, and anyone else who happens to show up on your doorstep to refrain from ringing the doorbell. If you're expecting an important delivery, be sure to leave a note letting the courier company know what you'd like them to do with the parcel— attempt delivery another time, leave the parcel on the porch, or leave the parcel with a neighbor.

- Treat your child's naptime as the midday oasis that it is. View it as an opportunity to top up your sleep stores and to prepare yourself for whatever nighttime parenting challenges may await you tonight. A couple of quick tips:

○ If your baby typically nurses to sleep, use the side-lying nursing position (go to www.sleepsolutionsbook.com for tips on how to make this position work for you) so that you can maximize the number of minutes that you get to lie down. Then either take your nap with baby or move baby to the bassinet or the crib (wherever baby typically takes naps).

○ If your preschooler has given up a daytime nap, but *you* still need a daytime nap because you're doing a lot of nighttime parenting with your preschooler or other children or because you're pregnant again, encourage your preschooler to enjoy "quiet time" in the bedroom, even if your child doesn't plan to take an actual nap. Your preschooler can look at books, listen to music, do a puzzle, or do other quiet activities until the kitchen timer goes off to signal that "quiet time" is over.

• If you have a baby and a toddler to care for and you desperately need to get some rest *before* naptime rolls around (some days naptime can seem impossibly far away), childproof an entire room and put a baby gate on each door. Set out a couple of activities that are likely to keep your toddler entertained for at least 30 minutes and that don't require a lot of hands-on help from you. You may even want to put on one of your toddler's favorite DVDs just to hedge your bets. Then flop out on a mat on the floor with your baby and nurse in the side-lying position. With any luck, you'll be able to close your eyes and rest (and possibly even grab a quick powernap) during the 30 minutes that the DVD is playing. *Hint:* If your toddler is toilet-trained, you may want to encourage your toddler to use the bathroom before the baby gates go up so that you don't have to hop up mid-nap to remove a baby gate because she suddenly has the urge to go.

• Toddler-proof your bedroom so that you'll know your toddler is safe in it if you happen to doze off and your child happens to slide down off your bed. Then encourage your toddler to come and cuddle with you while the two of you listen to soothing music. With any luck, the two of you will doze off and enjoy a wonderfully cuddly catnap together. (Obviously extremely high-energy toddlers won't want anything to do with this particular sleep strategy except, perhaps, jumping up and down on the bed.)

If you work outside the home during the day:

- Look for ways to fit a catnap into your working day.

  ○ If you take the bus, train, or subway to or from work each day, you may be able to squeeze in a quick catnap, provided you can get a seat. (If you're worried that you might sleep through your stop, figure out how long it typically takes you to get to your destination and set the alarm on your watch or a cellphone to go off a few minutes before you reach your stop.)

  ○ Take a catnap during your lunch hour. If you have your own office, lock your office door and nap on the floor or put your head on your desk. (You may want to keep a travel-sized pillow in your desk for this purpose.) If you don't have your own office, you might consider napping in any private corner you can find when you're out and about on your lunch hour—perhaps a table in a nearby food court that is reasonably secluded and that faces a wall. (You could prop your head on one arm and pretend to be reading a book, but with your eyes shut!) And remember to set the alarm on your watch or cellphone so that your catnap doesn't turn into a three-hour afternoon nap. Your boss might not be too impressed.

Know when to call it a day (or a night): Make it a rule that whatever housework didn't get done by 9 p.m. (or whatever time you start winding down before you go to bed) has to wait until the next day. Every minute of sleep is precious when you're working both the day shift and the night shift, which you are at this point in your life.

Take advantage of your baby's longest stretch of nighttime sleep: Once your baby moves through the immediate newborn stage, she will begin to differentiate between night and day and your baby's sleep will begin to consolidate into one longer stretch of at least five hours in the evening. If your baby's longest period of nighttime sleep isn't neatly meshing with your own schedule (your child sleeps from 8:00 p.m. to 1:00 a.m., but you don't head off to bed until 10:00 p.m.), maybe you can do some strategic time shifting for the next little while and head off to bed at the same time as baby. That way, you'll have a decent block of sleep under your belt before your baby launches into the "up every two hours" wee-hours-of-the-morning night-waking routine. If you have school-aged children, too, your partner could assume responsibility for tucking them in and then hit the hay, too. You'd then handle all the baby shifts in the night while he got to sleep until dawn (or whenever the alarm clock goes off at your house).

Give your baby a late-evening feeding before you head off to bed yourself: Another strategy that can help you to get a decent number of hours of uninterrupted sleep (and eliminate the need to either head off to bed early in the evening, a strategy that doesn't necessarily appeal to every mom) is to offer your baby a "dream feed" (a.k.a. a "focal feed") when you head off to bed yourself (e.g., at 11:00 p.m.). Basically, you wake your baby up and feed her when you're ready to go to bed so that she's unlikely to wake up hungry for at least the next few hours. Many parents find that this helps them to get at least a few hours of uninterrupted sleep during the first part of the night—something that makes it easier to get out of bed when baby eventually does wake up looking for a feeding. "I started waking my son up to nurse when I wanted to go to sleep," recalls Marcelle, 33, the mother of two children, ages two years and six months. "It often bought me a couple of hours of uninterrupted slumber."

Streamline and simplify nighttime parenting: Ask any experienced players and they'll tell you that the object of the night-time parenting game is simple—minimize the amount of time you spend with your eyes open and your feet on the floor. Here are some strategies that have allowed other parents to minimize the disruption to their own sleep while they are attending to their child's needs in the middle of the night:

- learning to breast-feed in a side-lying position (visit www. sleepsolutionsbook.com for step-by-step instructions)

- sharing their room or their bed with their child (see Chapter 5 for a detailed discussion of co-sleeping)

- having all the necessary changing and, if you're formula-feeding, feeding supplies close by.

MOTHER WISDOM

A focal feeding of pumped breast milk delivered by bottle can help a breast-feeding mom enjoy a five- to six-hour stretch of uninterrupted sleep. Assuming your breast-fed baby is willing to accept an alternative to your breasts and is at an age where you feel comfortable introducing a bottle, you might decide to rely on this solution on nights when you feel like you need to catch up on your sleep or as a regular part of your sleeping and feeding routine. If you don't feel comfortable offering your baby a bottle (or your baby is one of those breast-fed babies who refuses to accept any method of administering breast milk other than Mom), you might also consider another variation on the same theme: Your partner could bring the baby to you to nurse after you've gone to bed for the night and then take care of settling the baby before hitting the hay, too.

Tip: It can be tough to pump enough milk in the evening for an entire late-night bottle, so you may want to get in the habit of pumping throughout the day—or as often as practical—until you have enough milk accumulated over a 24 hour period to equal a full feeding.

Know when it's time to experiment with new sleep solutions for yourself and your baby: The sleep solution that proved to be a total lifesaver when your baby was a newborn may not work quite so well a little later on. Similarly, the arrangement that worked perfectly with baby number one may not work at all with baby number two or baby number three, so keep an open mind and be willing to go back to the sleep drawing board whenever the situation demands it (as opposed to allowing yourself to get stuck in a sleep rut). Just as there's no one-size-fits-all-sleep solution that works for every child, there's no one-size-fits-all sleep solution that fits every child from the newborn stage through the teen years. (They outgrow their sleepers and their pajamas. I guess it only makes sense that they outgrow certain bedtime routines and nighttime sleep behaviors as well.) You'll find all kinds of age-appropriate sleep strategies and solutions in the remaining chapters of this book.

Set the Stage for Sleep

Is your bedroom an oasis for sleep or the stuff of which nightmares are made? The ideal sleep environment is quiet, dark, comfortable, cool, and restful. This checklist will help you to decide whether your sleeping environment is helping or hindering your ability to get the sleep you so desperately crave.

Is your room too bright? Blackout liners and blackout shades can help to make your room darker if streetlights or the neighbors' security lights are lighting up your bedroom at night. If your room still isn't dark enough for you, you could try wearing a sleep mask to bed.

Is your bedroom too noisy? It's hard to fall asleep—and to stay asleep—if the aging rockers down the street insist on beginning their backyard tribute to AC/DC whenever you're ready to call it a night. (*Highway to Hell,* indeed.) And even if you do manage to drift off to sleep with all the accompanying partying going on, you're unlikely to get a particularly good night's sleep. Noise doesn't actually have to wake you up in order to disturb your sleep. It can cause you to switch from a more restorative stage of sleep to a less replenishing one. Fortunately, there's a simple and highly effective solution to the neighbors-from-you-know-where problem: white noise. Contrary to what you may have heard, white noise isn't just for babies. It can also be incredibly soothing for parents. You may find that running your ceiling fan, setting your clock radio between stations so that it plays static (but soothing static, not crackling static), or purchasing a white noise machine will allow you to get a better night's sleep. Other alternatives for dealing with an overly

---

MOM'S THE WORD

"When parents are taking turns listening for the little one at night, the off-duty parent should wear earplugs! My husband and I did it for about a month, and it really helped take the pressure off the one who was supposed to get the uninterrupted sleep." (Unfortunately, it can't turn off the "mommy instinct" for you.)

—*Cathy, 37, mother of 22-month-old Josie*

noisy sleeping environment include using earplugs (experiment with different types and styles until you find a set of earplugs that is comfortable and effective so that you'll have a pair on hand to use for those times when you're not the parent on duty) and using quiet background music to drown out the more annoying background noise. (Just be aware that you may eventually find it difficult to sleep without the background music. Sleep associations can be hard to break. And some people find it impossible to sleep with music playing in the background, so you and your partner would have to agree on this plan of attack, or one of you would have to use headphones and a personal stereo.)

Is your room the right temperature? If you want to maximize your chances of getting a good night's sleep (and, frankly, who doesn't?), you'll want to ensure that your bedroom temperature is 68°F (20°C) or cooler. If you and your partner have a hard time agreeing on what temperature constitutes a comfortable sleeping temperature, try making your bed with two separate top sheets and blankets so that you can each customize your own sleeping temperature without getting into a tug-of-war over blankets. And, of course, if you're sharing your bed with a baby, you'll need to ditch the blankets and dress in your warmest pajamas instead. (See Chapter 6 for more on reducing the risk of bed sharing.)

Is your room well ventilated? It's hard to get a good night's sleep if your room is stuffy and the smell reminds you of your high school gym bag in June. A ceiling fan can keep the air circulating and provide a soothing blanket of white noise and—because it's out of the reach of little ones—you don't have to worry about your toddler getting injured by jamming a finger or a toy inside the fan while the blade is moving, or electrocuted by playing with the electrical cord.

Is your mattress comfortable? Ideally you want a mattress that is firm, but not too firm. (If it feels rock-hard, you won't be able to get a comfortable night's sleep.) And when you're shopping for a pillow, look for a pillow that is supportive rather than overly soft so that it will provide adequate head support. If both your mattress and your pillow have seen better days and your post-baby finances are a little bit stretched, why not ask for gift certificates that could be applied toward the price of a new mattress for your next birthday? Don't forget to splurge on a new pillow, while you're at it.

Are you sleeping in an uncomfortable position? Sleeping on your stomach can lead to a stiff neck and a sore back—something that can make sleep uncomfortable or downright painful.

Has your bedroom become just another room? The sleep experts recommend that the bedroom be reserved for two activities and two activities *only*—sleep and sex.

Is the baby monitor making you totally paranoid? If your baby is sleeping down the hall and you're relying on a baby monitor to hear your baby, keep the baby monitor turned down to a reasonable volume so that you don't overreact to every peep and sigh your baby makes in the night. While you'll want to respond quickly to your newborn's cries, you may want to give a slightly older baby a moment or two to settle down if he or she stirs in the night.

Is your alarm clock keeping you awake? If you have to rely on an alarm clock in order to get up in the morning, either buy a clock that doesn't glow in the dark or turn the clock away from you so that you're not constantly tempted to check on the time. And if your alarm clock makes a loud ticking sound—well, obviously, it's time to give that alarm clock away.

PILLOW TALK

If you need to leave some lights on so that your children can find their way to the bathroom in the middle of the night, use a low-light night-light in the bathroom and a motion-activated nightlight in the hall. If that's still distracting to you, use an eye mask, either an unscented fabric eye mask, an aromatherapy eye mask that's has been scented with a few drops of a soothing essential oil (e.g., lavender oil, which is known to help promote sleep), or a soothing gel-filled aromatherapy mask (very soothing if you're very tired and your eyes feel like they are on fire). Bright lights in the night aren't a good idea because they can mess with your circadian rhythms by making your body think that morning has arrived a few hours earlier than it actually has, so try as much as possible to stick to the "dark at night" rule at your house. (See Chapter 3 for more about how the use of light can support the body's circadian rhythms.)

PILLOW TALK

Wearing socks to bed can help you to get a good night's sleep (even though some people think that wearing socks to bed is uncomfortable, weird, or just plain *wrong*). Having warm feet encourages good blood circulation, which, in turn, cues your brain that it's time to relax and go to sleep. Sleep vs. nerdy-looking feet. The choice is yours.

Are you watching TV (or using the computer) instead of sleeping? It's no wonder that the sleep experts give TVs and computers in the bedroom a universal thumbs down. Watching TV or surfing the Internet before you go to sleep is not conducive to a good night's sleep. Not only is there the temptation to stay up too late because you're interested in what you're doing, if you're in the habit of watching TV or surfing the Internet before you go to sleep, you may be too wide awake to fall asleep once the TV goes off. And if you *do* happen to fall asleep in front of the TV, the quality of your sleep will be affected by the noise and light from the TV. It's a lose-lose proposition.

Is Fido or Fluffy interfering with your sleep? It's been scientifically proven that pets deprive their owners of sleep, either by jumping on the bed in the middle of the night or by making such a racket with their snoring that you'd have to be wearing airport-grade protective ear-wear in order to get any sleep.

Is your partner a snorer? Research has shown that sleeping next to a person who snores can cause his or her partner to miss out on an hour of sleep per night—a hefty price to pay if you're already missing out sleep while you care for your night-waking child. If your partner's snoring is loud enough to keep you awake or to wake you from a deep sleep, his snoring is loud enough to be heard across the house, or he seems to stop breathing in his sleep, it's possible that he's suffering from a sleep disorder. Other possible signs of a sleep disorder include the following: your partner wakes up with a headache, is not refreshed even after eight hours of sleep, has difficulty concentrating, is sleepy while driving, and is tired most of the time. If you suspect that your partner is suffering from a sleep disorder, encourage him to make an appointment to see a doctor to find out what is at the root of his—and your—nighttime woes.

Practise Good "Sleep Hygiene"

The term "sleep hygiene" has about as much sex appeal as the term "dental hygiene," but it can make a huge difference in the quality and quantity of the sleep you're getting. If you're finding it difficult to settle down and enjoy a peaceful night's sleep long after your baby has decided to call it a night—or to get *back* to sleep after your toddler's middle-of-the-night "mommy" call—this checklist will help you to troubleshoot the root causes of some of your sleep-hygiene-related woes (or your bad sleep habits) and to identify some possible solutions.

Are your bedtime and morning wakeup time roughly consistent? If you can stick to roughly the same bedtime and morning wake-up time each day (or at least as much as your child will let you), you'll find it much easier to function. If you vary these times by more than an hour each day, you're basically asking your body to switch time zones on an ongoing basis and living with perpetual jetlag! If you're overtired and eager to catch up on your sleep, it's less disruptive to your body rhythms if you go to bed early than if you sleep in late. Sleeping in late can leave you feeling sluggish and out of whack.

Are you using daylight to your advantage? Making sure your body gets exposed to at least 20–30 minutes of bright light first thing in the morning (daylight works best) will make it easier for you to fall asleep when bedtime rolls around at night, while clocking at least 20–30 minutes of daylight in the late afternoon or early evening will help you to sleep better at night time. Daylight plays a powerful role in regulating your circadian rhythm—your built-in sleep-wake "clock."

Do you tend to eat your meals at roughly the same time of day? Eating plays a key in helping to regulate our circadian rhythms as well, so varying your mealtimes from day to day—or skipping meals entirely—can make it difficult for you to get a good night's sleep.

Is something you ate (or something you should have eaten) keeping you from getting a good night's sleep? Don't let what you eat interfere with your ability to get a good night's sleep. Understanding the sleep-food connection can play a key role in helping you to get a good night's sleep.

- Eat dinner at least three hours before you plan to go to bed. Eating too big a meal too close to bedtime can make it difficult for you to get a decent night's sleep because the biological clock that regulates your sleep/wake cycles relies on your eating patterns to regulate your sleeping patterns, too.

- If you find that heavy meals cause you heartburn or discomfort at bedtime, eat lighter meals at dinner and go easy on the types of foods that are known to cause upset stomachs and/or heartburn at bedtime: greasy foods, spicy foods, foods that leave you feeling very gassy, and very sugary foods.

- Forget about having wine and cheese at bedtime or—if you were so inclined—chocolate fondue. Ditto for any of the breakfast meats: bacon, ham, and sausage. All of these foods are rich in tyramine, an amino acid that triggers the release of the brain stimulant norepinephrine, which can make it difficult for you to get a good night's sleep.

- Being too hungry at bedtime can also interfere with sleep, so if you find that your stomach's grumbling when you're ready to turn in for the night, you may want to eat a light snack like a few crackers before going to bed. The carbohydrates in the crackers will help make you sleepy.

- If you wake up hungry in the night, you may need something slightly heftier. (Just don't go with an ultra-hefty snack or your body will mistake that "snack" for an entire meal.) A bedtime snack that includes both carbohydrates and protein will help you to carry through until breakfast, regardless of how many times you're up in the night with your baby. Protein triggers the release of glucagon (the counter-regulatory hormone to insulin), thereby helping to keep your blood sugar stable.

- Not getting enough sleep over a prolonged period can cause you to eat more. Sleeping four to five hours a night triggers hormonal changes that lead to an increase in hunger. You become glucose tolerant and you don't metabolize what you eat as well and you face an increased risk of developing diabetes.

• Go light with the liquids. Limiting the number of beverages you consume right before you go to bed will reduce the number of middle-of-the-night treks you make to the bathroom. (Unless, of course, you're pregnant again, in which case hormones and the pressure of your baby on your bladder will probably cause you to hit the bathroom anyway.)

Could you be overdoing things on the caffeine front? Yes, I know caffeine is a highly rated form of "mother fuel," but (as much as I hate to admit it) when it comes to caffeine, you can have too

---

SLEEPING FOR TWO: COPING WITH THE ADDED SLEEP DEPRIVATION OF BEING PREGNANT AGAIN

It's challenging enough to deal with the sleep deprivation of pregnancy without having to contend with the added challenge of dealing with a night-waking toddler or preschooler. Here are some tips on dealing with the sleep deprivation double whammy.

• Find the most comfortable possible sleeping position so that you can maximize the amount of sleep each night. If you're heading into the final weeks of pregnancy, you may find that sleeping on your left side with a pillow between your knees and another pillow behind your back or lying on a pregnancy body pillow is the closest thing to comfortable.

• Try to sneak in a daytime nap of 20–30 minutes (unless, of course, you're bothered by insomnia, in which case this strategy may backfire). If you find it difficult to nap during the week try to catch up on your sleep on weekends.

• Exercise will improve the quality of nighttime sleep and help you to avoid painful leg cramps that can wake you up in the night, so try it unless your doctor or midwife has specifically recommended against it.

• If you suffer from heartburn, steer clear of spicy, acidic, and fried foods so that you'll be less likely to experience middle-of-the-night discomfort as a result of something you ate.

much of a good thing. Consuming 400 milligrams of caffeine in a day (the equivalent of three of the smallest servings of coffee you can buy at your gourmet coffee establishment of choice—go to www.sleepsolutionsbook.com for more information on the caffeine content of common foods) can make it more difficult for you to get to sleep, reduce your total sleep time, change the ratio of light sleep to deep sleep, and increase the number of times you wake up in the night. It's also important to note that babies vary in their sensitivity to caffeine: some babies don't object at all if their moms become lifetime members of Club Espresso. Others seem to object if their moms so much as inhale the scent of java. ...

Are you using alcohol to wind down at the end of the day? While those pre-bedtime drinks will make you extra sleepy, alcohol affects the quality of your sleep, so you won't be nearly as well rested when you wake up in the morning. Not only does alcohol cause you to spend less time in the most restful phase of sleep (REM or rapid-eye movement sleep, the phase in which most of your dreaming occurs), it tends to wake you up four to six hours after you finish drinking, and can make it difficult for you to get back to sleep again. While you don't have to pass on that glass of wine entirely (if you're breastfeeding, you should be limiting yourself to no more than 2 4 oz. servings of wine, 2 12 oz servings of beer or 2 1 oz servings of liquor anyway), if you want to get a good night's sleep, it's best to consume alcohol early in the evening and to drink in moderation. And remember, if you're drinking to the point of inebriation, you shouldn't be sharing your bed with your baby: the

---

PILLOW TALK

While you've probably read about the sleep-enhancing effects of turkey, in order for the essential amino acid L-tryptophan in turkey to trigger the production of serotonin (the neurotransmitter that calms you and makes you sleepy), turkey has to be eaten on an empty stomach without any other foods. (You feel sleepy after eating a turkey dinner because you ate that turkey with carbohydrates (such as stuffing, potatoes, and cranberry sauce) and likely overate to boot, both of which can leave you feeling more inclined to snooze than to socialize with your nearest and dearest.)

risk of a parent rolling on top of a baby and accidentally suffocating the baby increases dramatically when a parent is intoxicated. See Chapter 5 for more on safe sleep.)

Are you taking a medication that could have you wide-eyed at 3 a.m.? If you recently started taking a new medication (either prescription or over-the-counter), check with your doctor or pharmacist to see if the medication could be contributing to your nighttime woes. (Note: Never stop taking a medication on your own without consulting with your doctor first.)

Could that late-night cigarette be costing you sleep? The solution in this case is obvious: Quit smoking or cut back on the number of cigarettes you smoke in a day. Smoking interferes with the quality of your sleep. It is also a key risk factor for sudden infant death syndrome and increases the likelihood of your child developing a number of other serious illnesses, which is reason enough to butt out.

Is exercise part of your daily routine? It may be hard to motivate yourself to move your weary bones, but being physically active will help you to fall asleep more quickly. Exercising for 30–40 minutes four times a week will help you to fall asleep more quickly (15 minutes vs. 30 minutes for people who don't exercise regularly, according to one Stanford Sleep Center study) and sleep longer. Just one important tip: Don't plan your workout for within one to two hours of bedtime or you may be too pumped to fall asleep. Working out right before you go to bed causes a rise in body temperature and an increase in your metabolic rate that can make it difficult for you to fall asleep.

Do you lie in bed tossing and turning—or head out of the bedroom if you're unable to sleep? The experts suggest that you get out of bed and head somewhere else if you're still wide awake 15–20 minutes after your head hits the pillow. (If you continue to lie in bed tossing and turning, you can quickly start to associate your bed with *not sleeping* rather than *sleeping*.) Don't make the mistake of getting up and trying to tackle some productive activity like cooking or cleaning, since you're not sleeping anyway. The idea is to engage in

PILLOW TALK

Understand the stress-insomnia connection. If you minimize stress throughout the day, you'll find it easier to get a good night's sleep. Here's why. It's normal for our body's cortisol levels to rise in the morning—Mother Nature's way of helping us to jumpstart our day—but if you're exceptionally stressed, your cortisol may kick in a few hours early (at around 3 a.m. or 4 a.m.), which can contribute to middle-of-the-night wakefulness.

---

a relaxing activity that will allow you to head off to Dreamland sooner rather than later, so read something monotonous in an effort to bore yourself to sleep.

Is that daytime nap working for or against you? If your child is a newborn and you're hardly getting any sleep at all, that daytime nap is a total no-brainer: You've got to grab sleep when you can. But if your child is older and following a more regular nighttime sleep schedule, you may want to keep daytime naps to a minimum or eliminate them entirely. The reason? Daytime naps can interfere with the quality of your nighttime sleep. If you are going to take a nap, here are two important points to keep in mind:

- Make sure you take your nap at least four hours before you intend to go to bed so that your nap doesn't interfere with your ability to fall asleep at night.

- Pay attention to the length of your nap: a 20–30-minute power nap or a 90–100-minute longer nap works best. A nap in the 40–60 minute range is likely to leave you feeling groggy and spaced out. If you take the wrong length of nap, you risk waking up during a non-REM sleep cycle, in which case you'll feel like you've landed on Planet of the Mommy Zombies, and the only thing that will snap you back into a state of even semi-alertness is a mixer-bowl-sized cup of coffee.

Are you losing sleep over sleep? It's a vicious circle: The more you obsess about the sleep you're not getting and how tired and miserable you're going to feel in the morning, the less likely it is you'll be able to drift off to sleep anytime soon. The next section of this chapter will provide you with some tools that will help you to relax when you're lying in bed wide-eyed, exhausted, and frustrated beyond belief, and increase the odds that you'll get some shut-eye soon.

Develop a Relaxing Pre-bedtime Routine

Children aren't the only ones who benefit from a soothing pre-bedtime routine. Stressed-out or overtired moms and dads who are frazzled and finding it hard to get to sleep may also find it helpful to establish a series of wind-down rituals that help to signal to their bodies and their brains that it's time for lights out. Here are a few tips:

Have a warm bath an hour or two before bedtime. Your core body temperature starts to drop after you get out of the tub, eventually triggering those welcome waves of sleepiness.

Dump your brain before you go to bed. That way, any sheep that you count as you make your way to Dreamland won't be tattooed with your top 10 worry or to-do list items. Instead, dump all your worries into a journal or notebook and jot down a to-do list for tomorrow so that you won't lie in bed trying to remember them instead of allowing yourself to succumb to sleep.

Master some relaxation techniques so that you'll have some tools to draw upon if you have trouble getting to sleep or getting back to sleep. There's nothing more frustrating than battling insomnia when you're already very sleep deprived.

PILLOW TALK

Whatever gets you through the night may have been a good bedtime mantra for John Lennon and Elton John, but it doesn't quite work for breast-feeding moms and bed-sharing parents. Sleeping medications (both over-the-counter and prescription) and most herbal sleep remedies are not recommended for breast-feeding mothers because they can be transmitted to the baby through breast milk. The same thing applies to bed sharing. It's dangerous to use any type of product—whether it is a medication or herbal sleep remedy—that can make you extra drowsy while you're sharing your bed with a baby because of the increased risk of rolling on top of the baby. Check with your doctor before using any such product if you are breast-feeding or sharing your bed with your baby.

Boosting Your Energy through Nutrition and Fitness

YOU MAY NOT be getting as much sleep as you want or need, but that doesn't mean that you have to feel like you're running on empty. By paying careful attention to nutrition and fitness, you can give yourself a much-needed energy boost.

Eat for Energy

When you're tired, you may be tempted to cut corners on the nutritional front, but that's the last thing you want to do right now. When you're missing out on sleep, it's more important than ever to make healthy eating a priority. Here are a few quick tips.

Eat breakfast. You need the energy burst, but don't rely on sugar for a quick fix. That sugar high will be followed by a sugar low. Stick to foods you can count on for the long term—complex carbohydrates and proteins that will give you the energy you need to get through until your next opportunity for sleep.

Don't skip meals. Your blood sugar will dip, something that can send your moods on a corresponding roller-coaster ride.

Plan healthy snacks. If you're breast-feeding, set up a "mother fuel" station near your favorite breast-feeding chair. Keep a water bottle and a healthy snack like fruit, vegetables, or whole-grain crackers within easy reach so that you can have a healthy snack while you're nursing your baby.

Do a nutrient check. Stress—including the stress associated with sleep deprivation—causes our bodies to produce increased quantities of adrenaline, the ready-for-anything hormone. While adrenaline can be very useful in readying the body for action, it can quickly drain our body of important nutrients, including vitamin C (which can leave your immune system vulnerable to bacteria and viruses) and vitamin A, folic acid, and zinc (which play key roles in the regulation of the nervous system). Some stress experts also recommend that you add 3000 mg per day of Omega 3 fatty acids to your diet in order to maximize brain function and your ability to cope with life's ups and downs.

MOTHER WISDOM

Keep a water bottle handy so you can keep yourself well hydrated throughout the day. Add slices of lemon, lime, orange, and/or cucumber to bottled water to give it a bit of zip. If you're starting to get bored of water, try herbal teas and watered down juices and sports drinks. They're delicious and refreshing, too.

Ensure that you're consuming adequate protein. Your body's protein needs jump by 60 percent when you're under stress, so include a protein source at every meal. Not only will protein give you a long-lasting energy source: it will help to keep your blood sugar (and your mood) relatively stable.

Pay attention to your fluid intake. Dehydration will only add to your fatigue. When you're dehydrated, your blood becomes thicker and your heart has to work harder to pump blood and oxygen to your organs and muscles, and to transport nutrients to your cells. It also makes it more difficult for your body to flush toxins out of the body. Rather than obsessing about how many ounces of fluid you're consuming, pay attention to the color of your urine. If it's clear or light yellow, you are drinking enough. If it's dark yellow, you should plan to increase your fluid intake. Just don't go overboard with the fluids if you're a breastfeeding mom: too many liquids can actually decrease milk production in some women.

Make sure that you're consuming a variety of iron-rich foods. It's not unusual for new moms to be iron deficient. In fact, 50 percent of pregnant women become iron deficient during pregnancy, and the blood loss associated with childbirth can reduce their iron stores further. If you are quite anemic, your health

---

PILLOW TALK

Even if you're eager to lose any extra weight you gained during pregnancy, this is no time to go on a crash diet. Trying to lose the baby weight in a hurry will only add to your exhaustion. The experts suggest that you wait at least four weeks before you start thinking about losing weight. Then don't eat less than 1,800–2,000 calories/day and be sure to eat a balanced diet so that you'll have the energy you need to enjoy motherhood.

care provider may recommend an iron supplement to boost your iron stores, but don't rely on that alone. It's also a good idea to get iron from food sources (e.g., dark green leafy vegetables, beans, and red meat). If you find that iron pills are either severely constipating or make you queasy, ask your health care provider to recommend a liquid iron supplement. Many women find that liquid iron supplements tend to be easier to stomach. And to boost the amount of iron that you absorb from food, eat iron-rich foods at the same time as foods that are rich in vitamin C, and avoid eating iron-rich foods at the same time that you consume dairy products, calcium, vitamin E, or zinc. Use the Food and Nutrition Information Center's online tools (www.nal.usda.gov/fnic/) for help in zeroing in on foods with these key nutrients.

Exercise for Energy

In addition to giving you a much-needed energy boost, exercise also triggers the release of endorphins, those feel-good, mood-boosting, aren't-you-glad-you-took-that-walk-around-the-block biochemicals, something that will help you to sleep better and that will make parenting easier. Here are some important tips to bear in mind when you're planning your workout:

- **If you haven't been active since before your baby was born, go easy at first.** Start out with a gentle stretching or moderate-paced walking program, and don't forget the warm-up and the cool-down.

- **Find an exercise buddy.** Depending on the age of your child and your fitness level and interest, you and your buddy and your junior workout companions could go jogging with your strollers, cycling with back-of-the-bike baby seats or a tow-able toddler trailer, or hiking with baby backpacks.

- **Stay close to home base if you're out and about with little ones.** Keep your walks fairly close to home so that you can zip back home if a nap, bathroom break, or diaper change is in order. And try to time your arrival home so that everyone will be ready for lunch and then naptime or quiet time after your walk, so that you can enjoy a bit of an afternoon break, even if that involves nursing the baby to sleep in the side-lying position and then enjoying a brief afternoon siesta yourself.

• **Fresh air and fitness can be terrific mood and energy boosters.** Team them up and you've got a winning combination. While getting out and about with more than one child may feel like an exercise in impossibility some days, with practice, that morning workout could become a much-anticipated morning ritual. Depending on the number and ages of your children, you may find that a stroller (double or single), a wagon, a tricycle for your preschooler, a bicycle with a baby carrier (only for older babies), a front carrier or sling, and/or a baby backpack allow you to get active while you're enjoying the great outdoors with your kids.

The Secrets of Sleep-Savvy Moms: Ways to Make Sleep Deprivation Less Crazy-Making

EVER WONDER HOW other parents have managed to make it through the seemingly endless nights of interrupted sleep without becoming completely unglued? Here are their top tips on surviving this exhausting time in your life.

1. **Balance the need to stay home so your child can nap against your need to avoid cabin fever.** You can quickly develop a case of cabin fever if you feel like you're trapped in the sleep-deprivation zone 24/7.

2. **Seek out other moms who will allow you to speak honestly about the challenges of being chronically sleep deprived.** Researchers at the University of California at Los Angeles have discovered that women are hardwired to nurture their young and seek out the support of other women during times of stress (the so-called "tend and befriend" stress response triggered by the surge of oxytocin, which is released when women are under stress).

3. **Make a conscious effort to de-stress.** Even very young babies can pick up on their parents' stress levels, so one of the keys to keeping your child from becoming totally stressed out (something

that will only make it more difficult for your baby to wind down and fall asleep) is to reduce your own stress level.

4. **Balance the need to sleep when the baby sleeps with your need to have some "me-time."** "I know that there's logic behind the advice to 'sleep when your baby sleeps,'" says Cathleen, mother of an eight-month-old. "It makes a lot of sense! But that doesn't leave time for R&R activities, whatever they might be for each person. Reading a novel, taking a bubble bath, painting your toenails—these are luxuries for moms! I gladly forfeit sleep to grab some me-time. It saves my sanity in a way that sleep cannot. Tomorrow I'll just cross my fingers and hope that Miyoko decides that she wants a nice long nap, and I'll lie down and catch a snooze with her then."

5. **Don't waste energy by fighting your child's sleep problems in nonproductive ways.** "If I can get five to six hours of sleep a night now, I'm pretty much good to go and I've certainly learned to go with the flow," says Jennifer, 28, mother of 20-month-old Rose. "That's not to say that I am not sometimes very frustrated when Rose has relapses, but I would say that I am much, much, much better at handling it all now. If I want to enjoy my baby, I have to enjoy all of her, including the night waking, so I just look at it as a normal part of my life. But it took me a long time to get this point. I guess what I've learned is that it's all a matter of perspective. If you look at it as a problem or something bad, then that's where your mindset is at. If you look at it as normal or as part of having a baby, the night waking is much easier to deal with."

Solutions Central—The Last Word

THIS CHAPTER HAS focused on strategies to maximize your opportunities for sleep, advice on creating a sleeping environment that is sleep enhancing, and tips on troubleshooting any bad habits that may cause you grief on the sleep front, as well as pointers on developing the kind of pre-bedtime routine that should guarantee you an express trip to Dreamland, provided Junior doesn't call off the trip. In the next chapter, we're going to hit the sleep science lab to get the lowdown on babies, toddlers, preschoolers, and sleep.

CHAPTER 3

The Science of Sleep

"People who say they sleep like a baby usually don't have one."
—LEO J. BURKE

YOUR BABY ISN'T "sleeping like a baby"—whatever *that* means—and you're convinced that your toddler or preschooler is shooting for the world record for most consecutive night wakings. While it can be exhausting and frustrating to have your sleep interrupted in the night, those middle-of-the-night SOS-es are a fact of life for most parents of young children. Sure, there's the odd mom or dad who ends up with a baby who sleeps through the night virtually from day one, but those babies are the exception rather than the rule. After all, babies come hardwired to ensure that their biological needs get met around the clock, even at 3 a.m. when their parents are desperately craving sleep. Understanding the basics of sleep science—why the sleep of young children is so different from the sleep of adults—can help to make nighttime parenting a little less frustrating. If you know what types of sleep-related issues you're likely to deal with as your child moves through each age and stage and how individual traits like temperament are likely to affect your child's sleep patterns, you'll be a little less frustrated when you find yourself up in the night dealing with a newborn who has not yet developed the self-soothing skills required to get back to sleep or an extra-sensitive preschooler who is frightened by the scary noise the furnace makes when it fires up in the night.

While reading this chapter and the chapter that follows won't necessarily make you any less tired, they may help to reduce the stress of nighttime parenting by relieving some of the pressure to do something about a sleep "problem" that may not, in fact, even be a problem at all. Instead of finding yourself engaged in middle-of-the-night debates with yourself about what you *should* be doing about your child's sleep problems—or, worse, forcing yourself to follow an off-the-shelf sleep training program that seems totally out of synch with your family's needs—you may decide that it makes more sense to take a wait-and-see approach or at least a wait-until-morning approach. Everything seems so much more urgent and hopeless in the middle of the night, after all.

What Sleeping Like a Baby Really Means

SOMEONE WHO HAS never done any time in the newborn trenches might mistakenly assume that parents with new babies are the best-rested people on the planet. After all, as the keepers of newborn sleep stats are only too happy to point out, a typical newborn sleeps between 10 and 18 hours per day, with a "typical" newborn clocking 13 hours of shut-eye during the early weeks (see Table 3.1). Of course, if you're actually wide awake enough to finish scrutinizing the sleep stats, it takes you only a couple of seconds to zero in on why new parents have that permanently glazed look, and why they take turns making emergency runs to Starbucks: Newborns like to grab sleep in bite-sized snacks of just a few hours at time rather than holding out for meal-sized sleeps of, say, seven or eight hours at a time (the kind of sleep that moms and dads tend to prefer). This makes total sense from a biological perspective, of course: Newborns have tiny tummies, so they need to eat frequently because they are growing at a rapid rate, and for nearly all babies, that includes middle-of-the-night feedings during the early weeks.

This means that it's normal for babies to wake in the night. In fact, it's normal for *everybody* to wake in the night. We all do it—babies, children, teenagers, and grownups alike. Night wakings in babies are an issue only because most young babies haven't acquired the self-soothing skills to get themselves back to sleep. Until they master those skills, babies need help to get back to sleep each time

PILLOW TALK

When asked what they would change if they could change something about their child's sleep, parents of infants were most likely to want to change the length of time their child slept, parents of toddlers were most likely to want to change the time their child went to bed and the time their child wakes up, and parents of preschoolers were most likely to want to change the time their child went to bed.

Source: National Sleep Foundation, Sleep in America Poll (2004).

---

they wake in the night, and given that those night wakings happen on average two to six times per night, that can mean a lot of night-time parenting for moms and dads. Once you realize that this is normal and that there's nothing "wrong" with your baby and that you're not doing anything "wrong" as a parent, you'll probably feel much more relaxed about getting up in the night with your little one. It's when you think that your baby is the only one waking up countless times in the night (even two or three night wakings can feel like "countless" when you're a sleep-deprived mom or dad) or you worry that you're setting up your newborn or young baby for a lifetime of poor sleeping habits by responding to his needs in the night (you're not) that you can start losing sleep about sleep. (Note: We'll be talking a lot about what you can do to encourage your baby to develop self-soothing skills in Chapter 4.)

Sleep-Related Milestones

ONE OF THE biggest problems with the expression "sleeping like a baby" is that it might lead some people to conclude that all babies have identical sleeping patterns when, in fact, there can be huge variations from baby to baby (even between multiples who were "womb mates" until quite recently). Some newborns sleep for five hours at a time from birth onwards. Others prefer to indulge in one-hour sleep "snacks," a sleep diet that can be rather be rather exhausting for their parents. Scientists still can't explain why some babies are natural-born Rip Van Winkles while other babies seem to view falling asleep *at all* as a sign of weakness. But whether your baby is sleeping as much as 18 hours a day or as little as 10 hours per day, you can rest easy knowing that your baby's sleep patterns still fall within the range of "normal." It's also important to remind yourself that while the term "baby" is used to describe a minutes-old newborn and a baby who is about to celebrate his or her first birthday, the sleeping patterns of those two babies have little in common. That's why I thought we should spend a little time talking about how a baby's sleep patterns evolve, and what sleep-related milestones you can expect your baby to achieve over time. Every baby achieves sleep-related milestones (like other types of milestones) on a slightly different timetable. But rest assured that your baby will master these skills when he is developmentally ready, even if it isn't during the exact week or month that the sleep experts predict. (Fortunately, as you'll learn in Chapter 4, there are plenty of things you can do to encourage your baby to develop healthy sleep habits.)

Note: If your baby was born a few weeks or months early, you should adjust the estimated time line for these sleep milestones to reflect your baby's due date rather than birth date—in other words, her developmental age or corrected age. Your premature baby has come "programmed" to demand a little extra nighttime parenting to ensure that her needs for food and round-the-clock nurturing are met.

So now that I've issued the necessary disclaimer—the fact that there's no "one-size-fits-all" set of sleep milestones that applies to all babies—here's the lowdown on the types of sleep-related milestones that babies tend to achieve and when. I've also described how your child's sleep patterns tend to evolve throughout the first year of life and during the toddler and preschool years so that you can get a sense of what types of sleep changes you can expect in the very near future.

MOTHER WISDOM

"When I discovered that the term 'sleeping through the night' is actually defined as 'sleeping for five hours straight', I realized that Zac had been 'sleeping through the night' for a while, as he would often fall asleep at 7:30 p.m. and sleep through until 12:30 a.m. or 1:00 a.m. for a feeding. So I realized that the problem was not that Zac was not sleeping through the night. It was that this was not my definition of sleeping through the night. My definition of sleeping through the night is really *me* sleeping through the night."

—*Tanys, 36, mother of two*

Your Newborn

Newborns sleep approximately 16–18 hours each day, a fact that may totally astound you if you've been stumbling around in a sleep-deprived state since Junior arrived on the scene. Because newborns aren't born with mature circadian rhythms (the circadian rhythm is the built-in body clock that regulates how wide awake and how sleepy we feel at various points in the day, and that requires resetting each day so our internal schedules will mesh with the 24-hour schedule that the world operates on), a newborn's sleep patterns are very different from those of an adult. Your newborn is a lighter sleeper than you are, has shorter sleep cycles, and experiences more transitions between sleep stages. Here are some other key things you need to know about newborns and sleep.

Newborns sleep in "chunks" of time that are fairly evenly distributed around the clock. Unlike adults, who tend to do most or all of their sleeping at night, a newborn's sleep is broken into six or seven separate periods of sleep, which are fairly evenly distributed around the clock.

Newborns spend more time sleeping at night than during the day. If you analyze a newborn's sleep patterns in great detail, you will discover that a typical newborn does spend a fraction more time sleeping at night than during the day—but just barely! Scientists don't know why this happens, but theorize that maternal hormones released during pregnancy, or the mother's sleep-wake during pregnancy may help to "program" a baby to naturally prefer to be awake during the day.

Generally, the younger the child, the later the bedtime. Babies two months of age and younger typically go to bed just before 10:00 p.m. Babies, toddlers, and preschoolers between the ages of six months and four years old typically go to bed between 8:30 p.m. and 9:00 p.m.

Babies need more sleep than adults because they are growing at such a rapid rate. A typical baby will double his weight by age six months and triple it by his first birthday. And those numbers don't even begin to account for the learning development that occurs during that time period.

The sleep patterns of babies are so different from the sleep patterns of adults that even the types of sleep have been given their own names.

- *Active sleep:* What we refer to as REM sleep (or rapid-eye movement sleep) in adults is more often referred to as active sleep in babies because the muscular paralysis that occurs in adults during REM sleep has not yet fully set in. You may be surprised how active your baby is during REM sleep (also called dream sleep since the majority of dreams seem to occur during REM sleep). (See Table 3.1.) Some parents are concerned that their babies aren't getting good quality sleep because they seem so restless during this stage of sleep, but you can feel confident that this is a perfectly normal sleep pattern for babies. Even if your baby is keeping you awake with wriggling and strange breathing, he is sleeping perfectly normally for a baby.

- *Quiet sleep:* What we refer to as non-REM sleep in adults is often called quiet sleep in babies because babies are much more restful during this stage of sleep.

Newborns spend more than half of their time in active sleep: eight to nine hours a day. This is because a lot of critical brain maturation happens after birth for humans. Researchers have discovered that this stage of sleep plays a critical role in brain development and, more specifically, the processing of all the learning that occurs over the course of a day. As sleep researcher Avi Sadeh notes in his book *Sleeping Like a Baby*, "The phenomenon can be compared to a librarian who during library hours has to assist patrons in finding, borrowing, and returning books; only after the library closes does the librarian have an opportunity to catalog, sort, and reshelve the books." So if your baby spends her waking hours staring at her hands, figuring how to make these marvelous "tools" do what she wants them to do, or learning how to make all kinds of amazing baby gurgles, at night time, her brain is busy filing away these accumulated bits of baby world learning, so she doesn't have to re-learn the same material the next day.

Table 3.1:

How Babies *Really* Sleep: Active Sleep and Quiet Sleep Explained

Active Sleep (Rapid-Eye Movement Sleep or REM Sleep)	
What you may notice your baby doing during this stage of sleep	• Your baby's eyes may dart back and forth underneath his closed eyelids (rapid-eye movements).
	• Your baby may smile or frown. He's practising using the facial muscles that will eventually turn him into Mr. Personality when he's awake.
	• Your baby may wriggle his fingers and his toes. He may even move his arms and legs around, twitch his body, or "startle" himself into wakefulness.
	• Your baby's breathing may be rapid, irregular, and noisy.
	• Your baby's heartbeat may be irregular.
	• Your baby may cry, groan, or whimper, even though he is still asleep.
Why this stage of sleep is important	Scientists believe that active sleep plays an important role in the development of the central nervous system, the brain, and other body systems. Your baby doesn't come "hardwired" with everything he needs for a lifetime when he arrives on the planet. He needs to keep adding new "circuitry" as he gets older. Scientists believe that a lot of this important "rewiring" occurs during REM sleep.
	Babies are more easily aroused from active sleep than from the deeper and more restful quiet sleep stage. This makes

sense from a survival perspective: If babies are hungry, uncomfortable, ill, or otherwise in need of attention, they can rouse themselves from sleep and let someone know that something's not right in their world. Some of the research about sudden infant death syndrome (SIDS) has, in fact, focused on whether otherwise healthy babies who succumb to SIDS might have experienced some sort of sleep arousal disorder that prevented them from awakening when they needed help. Sleep anthropologist James J. McKenna of the University of Notre Dame has argued that babies should never sleep alone: they are safer when they are constantly being prevented from falling into an overly deep sleep by the presence of another person—ideally "an actively breast feeding mother" who is sleeping in the same room or the same bed. (See Chapter 5 for more on co-sleeping.)

Quiet Sleep (Non-Rapid-Eye Movement Sleep or NREM Sleep)	
What you may notice your baby doing during this stage of sleep	• Your baby will be much more peaceful during this stage of sleep. If you watch her while she's sleeping, you will notice that she is very quiet and very still. However, you'll notice that her muscles are just a little tense.
	• Your baby's breathing is deep and regular. You may find it difficult to tell if your baby is breathing without touching her.
	• Your baby may experience an occasional startle reflex during this stage of sleep.
Why this stage of sleep is important	Quiet sleep is highly restorative. Scientists believe that the body does its basic maintenance and repair work during this type of sleep. The body releases the hormones needed for growth and development, repairs and regenerates tissue, builds bone and muscle, and strengthens its immune system while the body is at rest.

Newborns spend a lot of time sleeping, but they are light sleepers, so they tend to wake up easily and often. "During her first four months, especially if she was overtired, Edie would experience the startle reflex as she tried to fall asleep," recalls Laurie, 38, the mother of 19-week-old Edie. "It would wake her up again and again and again. It was upsetting for her and for me!" Other factors that contribute to newborn awakenings include the shorter sleep cycle for newborns and the fact that newborns experience more frequent sleep arousals (awakenings). Newborn sleep cycles can range from 50–80 minutes in length. These cycles are much shorter than the sleep cycles of adults, and your baby will experience many more sleep cycles in a day than you do. They also experience more frequent sleep arousals as they move from one sleep stage to another. This increases their opportunities for awakening (and hence *your* opportunities for awakening, too). Some parents find that swaddling their newborns and providing background sound helps to prevent babies from startling themselves into wakefulness. (See Chapters 4 and 6 for more sleep strategies.)

Most newborns and young babies are ready to go back to bed about two hours after they wake up. Some newborns have a pattern in which they take short daytime naps of 30–45 minutes. Others tend to take a couple of longer naps.

Table 3.2:

How Your Baby's Sleep Patterns Will Evolve over Time

Age	Percentage of Active Sleep	Average Length of Your Baby's Sleep-Wake Cycle
Before birth (at term)	60–80%	20 minutes
Newborn	50–60%	50–80 minutes
Six months	30%	60 minutes
Toddlers and older	30%	90 minutes

A sleep-wake cycle consists of both types of sleep—active sleep and quiet sleep—and is measured from the start of a period of active sleep cycle in one sleep cycle to the start of a period of active sleep cycle in the next sleep cycle.

Initially, your baby's sleep cycle is strongly rooted to his feeding schedule. Newborns sleep most of the time, wake up when they're hungry, eat, and then fall back asleep after they've eaten and had a chance to hang out with you for a while.

Your baby's sleep patterns gradually evolve as your baby starts consuming more calories at each feeding and starts spending more time being awake during the day. Naps become more regular and nighttime sleep becomes more consolidated (meaning that sleep gets grouped into fewer chunks of longer periods of time). But don't get too excited: You won't see any dramatic changes for a few months yet, and for good reason. Mother Nature intended for newborns to wake in the night. They have tiny tummies and they're growing at a rapid rate, so they need to dine after dark.

Breast-fed and formula-fed babies may have different nighttime feeding and sleeping patterns, but their moms end up getting roughly the same amount of sleep in a 24-hour period. Breast-fed newborns may need to be fed a little more often than formula-fed newborns (every two to three hours as opposed to every three to five hours) because breast milk is digested more quickly than infant formula. While breast-feeding your baby may mean that you're roused from sleep a little more often, research has shown that breast-feeding and bottle-feeding moms end up receiving roughly the same amount of sleep in a 24-hour period. The secret is to learn how to breast-feed lying down so that you don't have to be wide awake when you're feeding your baby in the night.

Breast-feeding delivers some major dividends on the sleep front—just not the exact payoff that most parents would prefer. Researchers have found that breast-fed babies spend a greater percentage of their sleep time in the more restorative deep sleep than their formula-fed counterparts. Even their pulse rates are lower. As Paul Martin, author of *Counting Sheep*, notes: "Breast is best, even when it comes to sleep."

Don't forget to factor in the health benefits of breast-feeding when you're considering your nighttime feeding options. "I found that mothers who were not breast-feeding were more likely to have babies who slept through the night," says Wendy, 29, the mother of 16-month-old Raiden. "But I wasn't willing to give up breast-feeding to get a solid night's sleep." For a comprehensive list of the health benefits of breastfeeding for both mother and baby, see www.4woman.gov/breastfeeding/.

Your One-Month-Old

By age one month, your baby's nighttime sleep periods will be longer than his daytime sleep periods. Around this time (age four to six weeks), your baby's sleep begins to organize itself into fewer blocks of longer periods of time. The light-dark and daytime-nighttime activity cycle, the feeding cycle, and a number of hormonal-biological processes help your baby's body to organize and consolidate sleep. (Note: You don't have to start obsessing about sleep at this stage of the game. You're still in "sleep survival mode"! But it's a good idea to start teaching your baby the difference between daytime and nighttime by exposing your baby to daylight first thing in the morning and by emphasizing the difference between your household's daytime and nighttime routines, e.g., daytime is for playing, nighttime is for sleeping. We'll be talking more in Chapter 4 about what you can do to encourage healthy sleep habits during the months ahead.) Once your baby hits the six-week mark, your sleep fairy godmother will grant you one of your most heartfelt wishes: You'll finally be able to count on your baby sleeping for at least two to three hours at a stretch. And that's not all! His longest single stretch of sleep is likely to occur during the evening hours and it may last for three to five hours.

Parents of high-need and/or "spirited" babies, there will be a slight delay before the sleep fairy godmother arrives at your house. Her ETA? When your baby is roughly three to four months old. Because

---

MOTHER WISDOM

If your baby has been sleeping through the night on a regular basis, try soothing her in non-food ways if she wakes in the night. She may be waking for a reason other than hunger. You may find this easier to do if your partner goes in to soothe your baby when she calls out in the night. After all, if you're breast-feeding, she's probably come to associate a visit from Mom in the night with food. You can always offer the breast if it becomes obvious that she needs to be fed, but you don't want to offer food to a baby who is cold, lonely, in need of a diaper change, or simply looking for a little middle-of-the-night reassurance. Otherwise, you may re-establish an after-hours "snack" habit that can be hard to eliminate down the road.

your little one is extra fussy, demanding, spirited, colicky, whatever you want to call it, it will take him a little longer to master some of these sleep milestones, but he will eventually, which means you will get the sleep you so desperately crave, too.

Your Two- to Six-Month-Old

By age three months, most babies are awake in the late afternoon and early evening. Their sleep habits are becoming more predictable. They tend to take two or three longer daytime naps, as opposed to countless catnaps of random length. Even their night wakings are becoming a little more predictable. Your baby's bedtime is shifting to early evening. By age three to four months, your baby will be going to bed a lot earlier at night—she'll be sleepy between 7:30 p.m. and 8:30 p.m. most nights. By age three to four months, your baby develops a predictable body temperature rhythm that helps to regulate her sleep cycles. Her temperature rises during the day and drops at night. This is when your baby's daytime sleep patterns start to become more firmly established and when you can start focusing on bedtime routines and thinking about sleep associations (what your baby begins to associate with falling asleep, e.g., being rocked, being nursed, being held, etc.). Up until now, you've probably been in sleep survival mode, doing whatever it takes to get through the night and the day. That's perfectly normal and perfectly okay. As Marc Weissbluth, MD, notes in *Healthy Sleep Habits, Healthy Child:* "For infants under three or four months of age, you should try to flow with the child's need for sleep. Don't expect predictable sleep schedules, and don't try to enforce them rigidly." Once your baby moves beyond the four-month mark and her sleep patterns start to mature, you may want to start thinking long term and encouraging healthy sleep habits in your child.

Your Six- to Nine-Month-Old

By the time your baby reaches this age, he is likely starting to develop a more predictable sleep pattern. He's likely worked both a morning and afternoon nap into his daily routine, and he's now doing most of his sleeping at night. While some babies this age—between 50 percent and 75 percent—are now sleeping through the night on a fairly regular basis, a fair number of babies—25–50 percent—aren't doing so quite yet, and, even if they are, most babies experience occasional night waking. (Just a reminder: In the pediatric sleep world "sleeping through the night" means sleeping for five consecutive hours in the evening or at night, which was probably not exactly your pre-baby definition.) Some babies who were sleeping through the night when they were much younger may start waking in the night again around this time. These night wakings can be triggered by physical (teething) or cognitive developments (e.g., you find your baby practising his new sitting or standing skills in the middle of the night). Sometimes six- to nine-month-old babies start waking in the night because they need an earlier bedtime. If you are putting your baby to bed between 8:00 p.m. and 9:00 p.m. and she's experiencing middle-of-the-night waking problems, try putting her to bed a half-hour to an hour earlier to see if that helps to solve the problem. Sometimes that's all it takes to encourage your baby to start sleeping through the night again. Separation anxiety is also responsible for a lot of the sleep disturbances that occur around this time. It is frequently related to a significant event in baby's life—a change in day care providers or your return to work, for example—and it is characterized by increased crying and irritability, clinginess, sleep disruptions, and a loss of appetite. It's a perfectly normal baby rite-of-passage—your baby's way of telling you that her world quite literally revolves around you: when she wakes up in the middle of the night, she needs the reassurance of knowing that all is right with the world—that you're still there.

By age six months, your baby is sleeping like an adult. (Well, almost.) By this age, babies are experiencing all the stages of non-REM and REM sleep that adults experience. However, the percentage of time that they experience in each stage of sleep doesn't quite correspond with that of a typical adult. (By age three or four, however, your child's sleep patterns will be very similar to those of an adult.)

MOM'S THE WORD

"I had a sense that six months was around the time when I would feel human again because, when I started to say to a doctor friend that I was prepared for a rough three months, he turned to me and said, 'It's six months, not three months.' I was grateful that he had given me that information otherwise I might have been pretty bitter after the three-month mark came and went."

—*Jodi, 34, mother of one*

Six-month-old babies drift into deep sleep (stage four sleep) much more quickly than adults do. This explains why you can carry a sleepy baby in from the car, take him out of his coat, and tuck him into bed without him ever waking up.

By age six months, most babies are physiologically capable of sleeping through the night and are no longer nutritionally dependent on nighttime feedings. That doesn't necessarily mean that all babies choose to forgo the late-night dining experience. Some babies will still wake up hungry in the night for quite some time. (As with anything else in Babyland, you can't apply an across-the-board rule to all babies.)

Approximately one-third to one-half of babies this age continue to wake up in the night. This should help to reassure you that you're not the only parent on the planet on night patrol if you happen to be the mom or dad of a six- to nine-month-old who is still up in the night every night.

Your Nine- to 12-Month Old

According to the National Sleep Foundation, 70–80 percent of babies are sleeping through the night most of the time by age nine months. (Of course, this means that 20–30 percent of babies this age *aren't* sleeping through the night.) And even if you swear that there's little, if any, progress occurring on the sleep front, odds are there's something very significant happening right before your very eyes. Your baby's most wakeful time of day has been shifting by about 10 minutes each day since he was born. Around the 40th week of life—around age 10 months—your baby will start waking up and going to sleep at approximately the same time each day. He may not necessarily be sleeping through the night each and every night, but at least his schedule will be a bit more predictable most of the time. But anytime he achieves a major developmental breakthrough, like learning how to stand on his own or "cruise" around the coffee table, you can expect some sleep disruptions. (Don't think of sleep as a one-way street, with your child making steady progress in a forward direction. Expect a few detours and the odd u-turn.) By the time your baby celebrates his first birthday, he is likely to be sleeping approximately eight to nine hours at night and taking two daytime naps as well (see Table 3.3). (As a point of comparison, when your baby was six months old, he was taking three or four daytime naps of between 30 minutes and two hours each in duration.)

Table 3.3

Snooze Clues: The Age at Which Naps Typically Disappear

Age	3 (or 3+) Naps Per Day	2 Naps Per Day	1 Nap Per Day	No Naps
0–2 months	76%	16%	4%	4%
3–5 months	55%	34%	9%	2%
6–8 months	29%	61%	10%	
9–11 months	11%	75%	11%	3%
12–17 months		40%	60%	
18–23 months	3%	8%	87%	2%
2-year-olds		1%	80%	19%
3-year-olds			57%	43%
4-year-olds			26%	74%

Source: Data drawn from *Sleep in America Poll*, National Sleep Foundation (2004). I have shaded the category into which the majority of children in any particular age group falls in order to highlight how naptime patterns typically evolve over time. This allows you to see approximately when the majority of children drop each successive daytime nap.

Your Toddler (Ages One and Two Years)

Most toddlers head to bed between 7:00 p.m. and 9:00 p.m. and start their day between 6:30 a.m. and 8:00 a.m. And even if no one at the neighborhood play group is prepared to admit it, between 15 percent and 20 percent of toddlers are still waking their parents at least once in the night. Most toddlers make the transition from two naps to one nap by age 18 months. The period in when a nap is being phased out can be tough on children and their parents. Sometimes two naps are too many and one nap is not enough! Going to an every-other-day nap schedule or putting your child to bed earlier in the evening are two excellent ways of easing the transition for your tired-out tot. You'll also want to make sure that your toddler is getting the amount of sleep recommended to function at his best—12–14 hours per day (see Table 3.4). That works out to 11 or 12 hours of sleep at night and a total of one to three hours of sleep during the day. In Chapter 4, we'll discuss some of the sleep cues that can indicate your toddler needs sleep. And in Chapter 7, we'll talk about why toddlers need sleep— especially when they think they don't need it!—and the price they pay physically, mentally, socially, and emotionally when they are short-changed on those all-important zzz's.

Your Preschooler (Ages Three and Four Years)

Most preschoolers go to bed between 7:00 p.m. and 9:00 p.m. and start their days between 6:30 a.m. and 8:00 a.m. Many still need an afternoon nap, something to bear in mind if your child is involved in a preschool or early kindergarten program that runs in the afternoon. Once your preschooler drops this nap, you'll need to make a concerted effort to ensure that she gets to bed on time, otherwise, she may end up missing out on the 11 to 13 hours of sleep per day that the National Sleep Foundation recommends for children this age (see Table 3.4). Because the preschool years are when a child's imagination really takes flight, this also tends to be the age at which bedtime fears (like the monster in the closet) and nightmares can become a real issue. If your child is extremely

Table 3.4

Tired Tots: How Much Sleep Your Baby, Toddler, or Preschooler Is Getting and How Much Sleep Your Child Actually Needs

	How Much Sleep Children Are Getting National Sleep Foundation's 2004 Sleep in America Poll: Average Number of Hours of Sleep by Age (for Previous Two Weeks)			How Much Sleep Children Need: National Sleep Foundation and American Academy of Pediatrics's Recommendations	
Age	Total Hours of Sleep (Average)	Total Hours of Nighttime Sleep	Total Hours of Daytime Sleep	Recommended Hours of Sleep by Age (Total Daytime and Nighttime) National Sleep Foundation Pediatric Task Force	Recommended Hours of Sleep by Age (Total Daytime and Nighttime) American Academy of Pediatrics
0–2 months	13.2 hours	7.8 hours	5.4 hours	14–15 hours	16–20 hours
3–5 months	13.1 hours	9.3 hours	3.8 hours	14–15 hours	16–20 hours
6–8 months	12.8 hours	9.7 hours	3.1 hours	14–15 hours	14–15 hours
9–11 months	12.1 hours	9.3 hours	2.8 hours	14–15 hours	14–15 hours
12–17 months	12.5 hours	10.1 hours	2.4 hours	12–14 hours	10–13 hours
18–23 months	11.6 hours	9.7 hours	1.9 hours	12–14 hours	10–13 hours
2-year-olds	11.4 hours	9.6 hours	1.8 hours	12–14 hours	10–13 hours
3-year-olds	10.8 hours	9.5 hours	1.3 hours	11–13 hours	10–12 hours
4-year-olds	10.5 hours	9.6 hours	0.9 hours	11–13 hours	10–12 hours

Note: There was considerable variation in the number of hours of sleep in a 24-hour period any individual child recorded during the National Sleep Foundation's *Sleep in America Poll* (2004). Infants ranged from 11 hours or less to 15 hours or more; toddlers ranged from 11 hours or less to 13 hours or more; and preschoolers ranged from 9.9 hours or less to 11.1 hours or more. The study was based on a random sample of 1,473 adults with a child aged 10 years in their household.

Sources: Sleep in America Poll (Washington, DC: National Sleep Foundation, March 2004); George J. Cohen, *American Academy of Pediatrics Guide to Your Child's Sleep* (New York: Random House, 1999); Jodi A. Mindell, *Sleeping through the Night*, rev, ed. (New York: HarperCollins, 2005).

sensitive, you may want to limit your preschooler's exposure to anything that might be scary or overly stimulating at bedtime. (Dad may want to hold off playing the "I'm a monster and I'm going to eat you" chase-and-tackle game until the following morning!) See Chapter 8 for more on dealing with these and other common preschool sleep rites of passage. In Chapters 4 and 8, we'll talk about how a wired, hyperactive preschooler may actually be an extremely overtired preschooler, and why we parents need to stress the importance of healthy sleep habits as our little ones move into the exciting but busy preschool years.

Solutions Central—The Last Word

HOPEFULLY, THIS QUICK trip to the sleep science lab has helped you to understand why your child's sleep patterns are the way they are and how they are likely to evolve as she moves from the newborn to older baby to toddler to preschool stage. And, with any luck, reading this chapter has helped to ease some of the pressure to do something about your child's sleep "problem," which, after reading this chapter, you may now see as less of a problem.

CHAPTER 4:

Winning at Sleep Roulette

"I found that every time I decided on a technique, I would read another book that would scare me into thinking that the initial technique was wrong and that my child would be scarred for life if I should decide to use it. I was really confused by each book."
— KARYN, 31, MOTHER OF ONE

EVERYTHING ABOUT SLEEP can seem frighteningly high-stakes at 3 a.m. Make one tiny misstep on the sleep front and your child will either end up waking in the night well into his high school years or dragging you on some future episode of *Dr. Phil* to expose your nighttime parenting faux pas. And with every sleep expert offering slightly different advice on the ideal timing and method for sleep training you may be unsure about who to believe, how to proceed, or which sleep training camp you should be signing up for. That's where this chapter fits in. I'm going to help you separate sleep fact from sleep fiction by:

- zeroing in on strategies that have been proven to promote healthy sleep habits in babies and young children

- showing you where commonsense factors like your child's temperament and your parenting style and intuition fit into the equation

- giving you some basic facts about the major sleep training schools of thought that form the basis of many of the best-selling sleep books on the market today so that you'll have some tools to help you make sense of the abundance of sleep information that is likely to come your way.

One of the key points that I'll be making time and time again (both in this chapter and the chapters which follow) is this: You're unlikely to find an off-the-shelf sleep solution that fits your baby or your family's needs perfectly. The most effective sleep solutions are those that are designed by you, the parent, with your baby's needs in mind. That means playing sleep detective (gathering clues about your baby's sleep problems so that you can figure out what types of solutions might work best) and sleep scientist (coming up with a sleep plan for your baby that you can test in your very own in-house sleep "lab").

Eight Best Sleep Strategies: What Every Parent Needs to Know

Sleep scientists have identified eight sleep strategies that are effective in encouraging healthy sleep habits in babies and young children:

1. Learn to spot and respond to your child's sleep cues at each age and stage—during the baby, toddler, and preschool years. You want to ensure that your child is benefiting from adequate sleep.

2. Teach your baby to distinguish between night and day and expose your baby to sunlight to help reinforce your baby's natural circadian rhythms (the body's built in sleep/wake "clock").

3. Establish a consistent, predictable, soothing bedtime routine during the newborn phase, and allow this routine to evolve as your child becomes an older baby, toddler, and a preschooler. You will find this easier to accomplish if you provide a sleep environment that is sleep-enhancing.

4. Let your newborn practise falling asleep on his own (instead of rocking him, patting him, or nursing him to sleep after each feeding).

5. Learn to differentiate between the normal noises your baby makes in his sleep and bonafide "pick me up" crying.

6. Treat daytime sleep as a priority as long as your child needs his naps. Children who nap well during the day sleep better at nighttime.

7. Recognize when your child no longer needs to be fed in the night and use non-food methods to soothe your baby back to sleep so that he'll be more likely to sleep through the night.

8. Remain as calm and relaxed as possible when you're dealing with your child's sleep issues. If you become stressed, your child will pick up on how you're feeling, and his own feelings of stress will escalate.

While it's best to work on these strategies when your child is a baby it's never too late to get with the sleep program. In other words, if your child is a toddler or a preschooler and has picked up some less-than-great sleep habits along the way, you can use this information in this section of the chapter to analyze your child's sleep habits and come up with a plan for helping your child to develop healthier sleep habits. You'll also find additional information on dealing with baby, toddler, and preschooler sleep problems in Chapters 6, 7, and 8.

1. Learn to Spot Your Child's Sleep Cues

LIKE THE REST of us, your child has a sleep window of opportunity, a period of time when he is tired, but not too tired. If that window closes before you have a chance to tuck your child into bed, his body will start to release chemicals to fight the fatigue and it will be much more difficult for you to get him to go to sleep.

Baby Sleep Cues

So how can you tell if your baby is getting sleepy? It's not as if your one-month-old can say, "Mom! Dad! Enough with the funny faces and peekaboo games, puhleese!" Here are some sleep cues that your baby is ready to start winding down for a nap or for bedtime:

- **Your baby is calmer and less active.** "The most obvious cue for me is when Emma gets really still and stares off into space," says

Christine, the mother of nine-month-old Emma. "She is usually really active, so I know she is tired when she is really calm."

- **Your baby may be less tuned-in to her surroundings.** Her eyes may be less focused and her eyelids may be drooping. "I can tell when Amanda is getting tired. She rubs her eyes, does what we call the 'slow blink'—with every blink, her eyes stay closed a little longer," says Jennifer, 30, mother of one-year-old Amanda.

- **Your baby may be quieter and less chatty** (e.g., make fewer vocalizations). If your baby tends to babble up a storm during his more social times of the day, you may notice that the chatter dwindles off as he starts to get sleepy.

- **Your baby may nurse more slowly and less vigorously.** Instead of sucking away with great gusto, your baby will tend to nurse more slowly as she gets sleepy. In fact, if she's sleepy enough, she may even fall asleep mid-meal.

- **Your baby may start yawning.** And, of course, if your baby starts yawning, that's a not-so-subtle sign that he's one sleepy baby.

MOTHER WISDOM

Don't think of your newborn as bad or difficult if he has a total meltdown because he's gone from being tired to overtired. What you're dealing with is bad timing: not a bad baby. Simply launch into your repertoire of baby-soothing techniques (e.g., swinging, rocking, swaddling, "shush-ing," offering the breast or the pacifier, or whatever seems to work best with your little one), and focus on keeping own stress level down. And if your newborn happens to be one of those babies who deals with over-stimulation by shutting down and going to sleep, rather than simply assuming that you've been blessed with a great sleeper who can fall asleep anywhere, anytime, make sure that you're cluing in to what's really going on. Your baby isn't winding down to sleep in a relaxed and gentle manner: he's zonking out as a result of total exhaustion.

Either way, you'll want to try to spot your baby's signs of sleepiness a little sooner the next time around so that your baby gradually learns to associate falling asleep with feeling calm and relaxed—something that will help to set the stage for a lifetime of healthy sleep habits.

MOTHER WISDOM

Tuning into your baby's sleep cues also means making your baby's sleep a priority. Ideally, you want to ensure that your baby is able to get the sleep she needs at the times when she needs it—and in an environment that is as sleep-friendly as possible. In other words, you don't want all of your baby's naps to take place in the car seat while you're zipping to and from the grocery store. Sure, things won't work out perfectly all of the time—we're talking about parenting in the real world, after all—but you'll probably find that life runs a little more smoothly for both you and your little one if you have a reasonably well-rested baby and you tame your to do list at least a little.

When your baby is very young, you should start his wind-down routine within one to two hours of the time when he first woke up. If you miss his initial sleep cues and start to notice signs of over-tiredness (e.g., fussiness, irritability, and eye-rubbing), simply note how long your baby was up this time around and then plan to initiate the wind-down routine about 20 minutes earlier the next time he wakes up. (The great thing about parenting a newborn is that you get lots of opportunities to practise picking up on those sleep cues—like about six or seven times a day!)

Learning to read your baby's own unique sleep cues is the first step to a more rested and more content baby, says Sharlene, the 34-year-old mother of five-month-old Makenna. "The first thing I figured out was how long Makenna can be awake before she starts to get tired or overstimulated; she's generally only able to be awake for an hour or two maximum, especially in the morning. I know that if she wakes up at 8:30 a.m., then by 9:30 a.m. we should start thinking about putting her down for a nap. Then I looked for signs like rubbing her eyes, crankiness, and burying her head in my chest while making whiney, sheep-like noises."

Here's something else you need to know about babies' sleep cues, something that can toss you a major curve ball if you're caught off guard: Babies tend to go through an extra-fussy period when they reach the six-week mark. The amount of crying that babies do in a day tends to increase noticeably when babies are around six weeks of age. You aren't doing anything wrong and there isn't anything wrong with your baby. It's just a temporary stage that babies go through.

Of course, some babies tend to be more difficult to settle *period*. (We'll discuss temperament elsewhere in this chapter, at which point I'll give some tips for soothing your difficult-to-soothe little one.) You may also notice that your baby goes through an extra-fussy period whenever she passes through a growth spurt—something that typically happens as babies reach the three, six, twelve, and eighteen week marks, although the exact timing of these growth spurts varies from baby to baby.

Toddler and Preschooler Sleep Cues

Toddlers and preschoolers demonstrate a lot of the same sleep cues as babies (becoming calmer and less active, becoming less talkative, and yawning) before they reach the point of being overtired. And as your child becomes more verbal, you can encourage her to let you know when she's starting to get sleepy.

From Tired to Overtired

If your child becomes overtired, your child is likely to behave in one or more of the following ways (results may vary, depending on your child's age, personality, and preferred modus operandi):

- Your child will get a sudden burst of energy at the very time when you think she should be running on empty.

- You'll start seeing "wired" and hyperactive behavior, even if such behavior is totally out of character for your child at other times of the day.

- Your toddler or preschooler will become uncooperative or argumentative.

- Your child will be whiny or clingy or she'll just generally fall apart because she simply can't cope with the lack of sleep any longer.

You will probably find that your child has his or her own unique response to being overtired. Some children start to look

MOM'S THE WORD

"We thought she was suffering from colic or gas, but in reality, her regular evening hysterics were probably just overtiredness. She was only getting about 10 hours of sleep a day before we clued in."

—*Laura, 29, mother of 11-month-old Madeline*

pale. Some young babies start rooting around for a breast and will latch on to anything within rooting distance, including your face or your arm!

"The main cue for tiredness in Jesse is crankiness," says Johanna, 28, mother of 13-month-old Jesse. "When nothing seems to be wrong (he's fed and clean), but he's just whining about everything and wants to be held all day, he's overtired and needs help to get to sleep."

2. Teach Your Baby to Distinguish between Night and Day

BECAUSE OUR CIRCADIAN rhythm (our internal time clock) operates on a 24-hour and 10-minute to 24 hour and 20-minute cycle (everyone's body clock ticks along at a slightly different rhythm) and all of our rhythms are slightly out of synch with the 24-hour clock on which the planet operates, we have to reset our internal clocks each and every day. Otherwise, we'd slowly but surely stay up later and sleep in later each day until we had our cycles way out of whack. (See Chapter 3 for more about the science of sleep.)

Daylight is one of the mechanisms that regulate our biological cycles. Being exposed to darkness at night and daylight first thing in the morning regulates the body's production of melatonin, a hormone that keeps our bodies' circadian rhythm in synch so that we feel sleepy and alert at the appropriate times of day. By exposing your baby to daylight shortly after she wakes up in the morning and keeping her environment brightly lit during her waking hours, you will help her circadian rhythm to cue her to feel sleepy at the right times. She'll also start to associate darkness with sleep time and bright light with wake-up time. You'll find that it works best to take advantage of sunlight (as opposed to artificial light) whenever possible. (Obviously, you'll want to take steps to protect your baby's ultra-sensitive skin. See Appendix A and Appendix B for links to numerous pediatric health websites.)

Sleep researchers also offer some additional tips that may be helpful in teaching your baby the difference between night and day:

- If your baby happens to doze off during one of his daytime feedings and he's just started his feeding or he just got up from his nap, try to wake him up. You want him to finish his feeding before he goes down for his next nap as opposed to eating and sleeping in little "snacks." (Note: Some very young babies tend to fall into a pattern of short, frequent catnaps that tends to mirror their snack-style eating patterns. As their tummies grow bigger and they become capable of eating more food at each meal, they don't need to eat as often and the length of each nap tends to stretch out as well.)

- Expose your baby to daylight—ideally sunlight (remember to protect your baby's skin) as opposed to artificial light. Studies have shown that exposing your baby to daylight between noon and 4:00 p.m. will increase the odds of your baby getting a good night's sleep.

- Teach your baby that daytime is for playing and nighttime is for sleeping by emphasizing the difference between your family's daytime and nighttime routines. Here are a few tips:

  ○ Interact with your baby as much as possible during her daytime wakeful periods (e.g., by singing to her or playing peek-a-boo while you're folding a load of laundry; talking to her or reading to her while you are nursing).

  ○ Dim the lights and keep the household noise and activity level lower in the evening (a time of day when your baby is making the transition between daytime and nighttime).

  ○ Try to make your nighttime interactions with your baby fairly low-key (e.g., changing her diaper in the night only if it is dirty or if you think she's going to be really wet by morning; resisting the temptation to turn on the television or a light so that you can read in the wee hours of the morning; and minimizing the amount of chit-chat and play with your baby in the middle of the night so that she gets the message that nighttime is for sleeping; the fun and games are on hold until after daybreak).

3. Establish a Consistent, Predictable Bedtime Routine during the Early Months of Your Baby's Life, and Allow This Routine to Evolve as Your Child Moves from Stage to Stage

SOME PARENTS RESIST the idea of instituting a bedtime routine because they have the mistaken belief that taking an "anything goes" approach at bedtime will make life easier for them. After all, if they don't become a slave to their baby's bedtime routine, won't they be able to take their baby out in the evening—or have other people put their baby to bed—without worrying about any possible disruption to their little one's bedtime routine?

Having a predictable bedtime routine will make life easier for you and your baby in the long run. Once your baby figures out that bath time is followed by a feeding and a cuddle (or whatever is part of your pre-tuck-in ritual), she'll start mentally winding down once her toes hit the water. Of course, this isn't likely to happen overnight. Not only is there a learning process involved, some babies greet the arrival of the Sandman a little less enthusiastically than others. But if you persevere and come up with a routine that works for you and your baby, you will find that tucking in your little one becomes easier and that, over time, you'll have more flexibility in your evening plans. Once your baby is an old pro at this bedtime thing, you may be able to experiment with putting her to bed in a safe sleeping spot while you're visiting friends or relatives, delaying her bedtime a little if you're out in the evening (the experts suggest keeping your baby's bedtime within a predictable one-hour range), or allowing a trusted friend or family member to babysit so that you can enjoy the occasional baby-free evening

MOM'S THE WORD

"I think routines are helpful because they are familiar and comforting and provide a bridge from wakefulness to nighttime slumber, and help to differentiate nighttime sleep from a nap. Even for the parent, they're helpful because there are some parts you can do on autopilot. But the routines should be flexible enough to travel with, and you should be able to perform them at any time. You have to observe your child to make them work. Will a bath wake her up or make her sleepy today? Will one more story allow her time to babble a little and get situated? Can she rub her own cheek with the edge of the blanket to soothe herself, or shall I do it tonight because it feels lovely? Does she need to see me read the book, or can I recite it from memory while I close my own eyes and rest?"

—*Marla, 36, mother of one*

without having to worry about your little one missing out on some much-needed sleep. (Other people who are babysitting for you don't have to use the exact same bedtime routine as you do—just a reasonable facsimile.)

And, of course, the baby who falls asleep easily at bedtime tends to be the baby who falls asleep a little more easily at naptime (although most parents find that getting a baby to fall asleep at naptime initially tends to be more of a challenge than getting a baby to fall asleep for that nighttime sleep). However, as you'll see later in this chapter, babies who nap tend to sleep better at nighttime, so most sleep experts feel that naps should be a priority for young children well into the preschool years. For now let's talk about what types of bedtime rituals might calm and soothe your baby so that she can wind down to sleep and how to make bedtime routines work for you and your child.

Here's what parents and other bedtime experts have to say:

Don't start obsessing about bedtime routines too soon. When your baby is a newborn, focus on maximizing his and your opportunities for sleep. Don't worry about any bad sleep habits you may be teaching him at this stage. He's too young to start forming any lasting sleep associations. You'll just make life harder for yourself and your baby—and for no good reason—if you make the bedtime routine too complicated too soon. (See Chapter 3 for more about the science of sleep and the major sleep milestones.) Jen, 30, has some very wise words for parents who, like her, may feel pressured to focus on bedtime routines before they or their babies are ready: "I felt a lot of pressure to start a bedtime routine early, but I honestly don't think it's possible until three months or so (or at least, it wasn't possible for our baby). You need to get past the "sleeping-eating-briefly awake-sleeping-eating" pattern of the early days, and into a period when baby goes down at night for at least several hours—i.e., a time when bedtime is different from the other times of day that he/she goes to sleep. When we did start a routine, it was pretty basic: bath, PJs, special music, and nursing."

Putting a bedtime routine in place for your baby may require making some changes to your own evening routines. "I didn't really know anything about bedtime routines when my daughter was a newborn, so we didn't do anything special for the first two to three months," recalls Cathleen, 32, mother of seven-and-a-half-month-old Miyoko. "Part of the problem was that we as parents didn't have a routine—everything seemed so chaotic all of the time, there was no organization to our lives, so we never sat down and thought about how to provide a routine for the baby." Schedule-free living may be an appealing lifestyle in your double-income-no-kids days. It's not so great when there's a baby who'd really like to go to bed sometime this evening. And if your family has an extremely erratic routine—two parents working rotating shifts, for example—you may find that you have to keep your child on a consistent sleep schedule, even if that means that your child ends up going to bed before you get home from work when you're working certain shifts.

Create a sleep-enhancing household environment in the evenings. Reduce the light level in the house and try to reduce the overall noise and activity level in the household (use a white noise machine or play soothing music to drown out noise). "I swear by the sound machine," says Renay, a 35-year-old mother of one.

"Rachael can sleep through a fire alarm, but if you turn on a table lamp, she wakes up!"

Accept that bedtimes vary from baby to baby. Your best friend's baby may be off to Dreamland by 8:00 p.m. each night, roughly the time your baby is just starting to show the first signs of sleepiness. Console yourself with this mantra: my *very* smart baby isn't ready for bed yet because her *very* bright brain is too busy learning. If you repeat it often enough, you may even forget about the lines under your eyes. Maybe.

Bedtime doesn't have to be at the exact same time every day for babies, toddlers, and preschoolers who are still napping. Varying your child's bedtime by up to an hour may actually make more sense, some sleep experts note, because doing so allows you to respond to your child's sleep cues as opposed to simply watching the clock and putting your child to bed at the exact same time every evening, even if he's not actually sleepy yet. If your child had an extra-long afternoon nap that ended later in the day than usual, he may not be ready for bed as early as he normally is. (Of course, you'll want to prevent those late-in-the-day naps from becoming too much of a problem by waking your child up if he's still sleeping at 4:00 p.m. or 4:30 p.m.) And the sleep experts tend to agree on this point: Once a child stops napping, a consistent bedtime becomes more important because you no longer have the naptime wild card affecting evening sleepiness to the same degree. If your child is getting up at the same time each day or being woken up and eating his meals at roughly the same time of day, he will feel sleepy at roughly the same time of day. Some sleep experts warn that keeping children up too late at night leads to overtiredness, something that affects not only the quality of nighttime sleep but the quality of naps the next day, too. And many parents report that the later their baby, toddler, or preschooler stays up at night, the earlier that child wants to start his day the following morning: "One thing I've learned, keeping them up later just makes them get up earlier," insists Brandy, a 32-year-old mother of two children, ages two-and-a-half and four-and-a-half. "My kids have a very consistent bedtime as a result."

Lori Anne, 34, and her husband decided that having a consistent bedtime for their five-and-a-half-month-old son Milo had to be the priority while he was still very young: "Both my husband and I have made a commitment to have a consistent bedtime for Milo," she explains. "This means that Milo doesn't stay up late if I'm going to be home from work a little later. This might mean that I don't get to see Milo at all some evenings, but I think it is more important to maintain his sleep routine. That said, I make an effort to get into work early and to work through my lunch so that I can usually leave the office by 5:00 p.m. This is how our bedtime routine works in the real world."

Jennifer and her husband opted for a slightly more flexible approach. "We want to maintain a fairly regular routine, but we're not the kind of people who gave up everything when we had kids, and we do go out for dinner or to other events occasionally, and we want her to be able to enjoy them with us," the 30-year-old mother of 12-month-old Amanda explains.

Realize that there's no such thing as a one-size-fits-all bedtime routine. What settles the average baby may not work for your baby. The very same wind-down rituals that your cousin's baby adores—gentle rocking and a soothing lullaby—may have your free-spirited little one arching her back and wriggling in an effort to make a late-night getaway.

MOTHER WISDOM

Young babies have sensitive skin, so you might not want to overdo it with the pre-bedtime baths, particularly if your child is prone to rashes. Some parents with natural-born water babies who find a bedtime bath extremely relaxing, but who have highly sensitive skin, find that it works well to limit soap use to every second or third day, or to switch to a mild soap that's designed for children with extra-sensitive skin. Bathing your child in lukewarm (rather than very warm) water; patting her gently to dry her off; and applying a moisturizing lotion can also help to minimize skin irritation.

MOTHER WISDOM

Continue to make physical activity a part of your child's day as he moves into the toddler and preschool years. And as he reaches these ages, think about including a bedtime snack that is sleep enhancing rather than sleep disturbing. (See Chapter 2 for tips on the types of foods that tend to promote rather than disrupt sleep in adults and give foods that are age-appropriate for your child.)

Focus on activities that your baby is likely to find soothing. For some babies that's a pre-bedtime bath. For other babies, that bath would have them doing the baby world equivalent of cartwheels for hours. You know your baby best, so you'll know whether the bath is best reserved for dawn or dusk.

Active play is a good thing earlier in the day. A rousing game of "where's the baby?" or "this little piggy" is a lot of fun for everyone, but it's best to reserve the wild and crazy play for earlier in the day rather than right before bed. Your baby will get all revved up and will be understandably confused and/or outraged when you switch gears and try to tuck her into bed: "One minute we're playing "peek-a-boo" and the next minute I'm being whisked off to bed? *I don't think so!*" The solution is obvious. Make active play part of your baby's daytime routine. You want her to get plenty of physical activity so that she can practise her emerging skills and be genuinely tired by the time naptime or bedtime rolls around. And given that it can take an hour or longer for her to wind down from the adrenaline burst that accompanies active play, those wild and crazy pre-bedtime games don't do much to help chase your little one off to Dreamland.

Don't overlook the magic of massage. Massage improves the quality of sleep for many babies and a lot of adults. It can also be very soothing for babies who are colicky (babies who cry for more than three hours a day at least three times a week during the period between three weeks and three months of age). If you decide to massage your baby, avoid nut-based oils for allergy reasons and traditional clear baby oils, which are mineral based, contain a lot of additives, and will not be absorbed well by your baby's skin. Most massage therapy professionals now recommend grape seed, wheat germ, olive, or sunflower oil as "best bets" for massage oils for babies. Massage oils should be edible because babies can easily get massage oil on their fingers and then put their fingers in their mouths. See the Appendices for resources related to infant massage and colic.

Make your baby's bedtime routine a family affair. Get your partner, your baby's grandparents, or your baby's older siblings in on the act whenever it is practical and appropriate. That way, your baby will be open to the idea of someone other than you putting her to bed.

Teach your baby to speak the language of sleep—literally. You may also find that it works well to use some predictable sleep words that your baby will eventually associate with bedtime as you use them night after night—words like "sleepy time" or "bedtime" or "nighttime" or "tuck-in time"—whatever works best for you.

Consider lulling your little one to sleep with a lullaby. Mothers and fathers have been singing lullabies to their babies forever. And why not? Most babies find it tremendously soothing to have someone sing to them as they drift off. Combine that lullaby with motion and swaddling you may have a totally irresistible baby-soothing technique.

Realize that your baby's bedtime routine will evolve as he moves from stage to stage. "When he was just a newborn, the routine was entirely breast-feeding-centered," explains Rachel, a

---

📢 **MOM'S THE WORD**

One challenge that developed out of the "Daddy puts baby to bed" sleep ritual was that Makenna would only go to sleep at night for Daddy. This made things incredibly hard for me when Chris was working evenings. When he wasn't there, I struggled to get her to fall asleep because I didn't have the "master baby calmer" touch. It was so bad that at one point I ended up sitting on his side of the bed, wearing one of his t-shirts and doing everything that he did to put her to sleep. Of course she wasn't fooled.

—*Sharlene, 34, mother of one*

33-year-old mother of one. "Byron nursed to sleep for nighttime and naps. At about four months we started introducing elements like reading a story, and finally putting him down awake. Now it's the same every night—change diaper, pick up toys, brush teeth, read story, sing song, lights out. He really likes routine as a toddler, but if we're traveling or there's some other interruption, he's reasonably flexible as well. The most important things are the story and song."

4. Let Your Baby Practise Falling Asleep on His Own So That He Can Learn How to Soothe Himself Back to Sleep

SOME SLEEP EXPERTS recommend that you put your baby to bed in a sleepy-but-awake state whenever possible from the newborn stage onwards so that he can practise some self-soothing behaviors; others say that you should give your baby at least one opportunity to try to fall asleep on his own each day; and still others say that there's no point even bothering to work on these skills until your baby reaches that three-to-four month mark (when your baby's sleep-wake rhythm begins to mature so that some sleep learning can begin to take place).

Some sleep experts claim that the sleep-association clock starts ticking at around six weeks. They claim that *this* is the point at which your baby begins to really tune in to his environment as he's falling asleep. So if he gets used to falling asleep in your arms while you rock him and sing to him, he will want you to rock him and sing to him when he wakes up in the middle of the night. That's the only way he knows how to settle himself to sleep. This is because he has developed a sleep association that involves you: You have become a walking, talking sleep aid!

Some parents decide that it makes sense to take a middle-of-the-road approach to sleep associations during the early weeks and months of their baby's life. They decide to make getting sleep the priority for themselves and their babies and to take advantage of any opportunities to start helping their babies to develop healthy sleep habits (e.g., taking advantage of opportunities when baby

 MOM'S THE WORD

"Huge mistake number 1: Putting baby in a bassinet that vibrates.

Huge mistake number 2: Putting baby in a bouncy seat that vibrates.

Huge mistake number 3: Putting baby in a swing.

And then expecting baby to sleep in a flat, motionless crib."

—*Patricia, 31, mother of one*

---

seems drowsy enough to be put in bed sleepy but awake rather than feeling that it's always necessary to rock baby to sleep), but not to allow themselves to get stressed over baby's sleep habits. After all, according to some experts at least, she may still be too young to "get with the sleep program."

Regardless of *when* you start paying careful attention to the types of sleep associations your baby may be developing, at some point you will want to consider whether your baby could be starting to associate any of the following habits or behaviors with the process of falling asleep:

- nursing to sleep or falling asleep during a bottle-feeding
- being rocked to sleep (in your arms or in a vibrating chair, a swinging cradle, or by some other means that provides motion)
- having you rub or pat his back, sing a lullaby, say "shhhhh", or otherwise play an active role in helping your baby to fall asleep
- having you in the room until your baby falls asleep
- relying on a pacifier (something that the American Academy of Pediatrics is now recommending for babies over the age of four weeks, but that forms a sleep association nonetheless; see the material in the sidebar which follows for more on this controversial recommendation)
- relying on some other sleep aid to fall asleep, something that the sleep experts suggest you think about introducing when your baby reaches the four- to five-month mark (see Chapter 5 for important safety information on comfort objects such as special blankets or stuffed animals).

 PILLOW TALK

The American Academy of Pediatrics recently recommended that babies sleep with pacifiers after age four weeks because pacifiers are believed to help reduce the risk of sudden infant death syndrome (SIDS). Groups such as The Academy of Breastfeeding Medicine have argued that pacifiers should only be offered to infants who are not being breastfed: "As exclusively breastfed infants feed frequently through the night, breastfeeding is thought to reduce SIDS by the same proposed mechanism as supine [back-lying] sleep and pacifiers, namely less deep sleep and frequent brief awakenings. Breastfed babies do not need artificial pacifiers to get stimulation since they already have the protective effect of suckling during the night." There are also concerns that increased pacifier use could cause some breast-fed babies to develop nipple confusion and reject the breast (while this is less common after four weeks of age, it can still be an issue); or to request feedings less often as a result of pacifier use (which could diminish the mother's milk supply). And then there's the fact that some babies don't want anything to do with pacifiers, and they're unlikely to accept one willingly, whether or not the AAP wants them to or not—something that could result in added bedtime stress for parents and babies.

(See Table 4.2 for more about the impact of many of these sleep associations on the long-term sleep habits of babies.)

Here's something important to keep in mind, particularly since we tend to fall into an "all-or-nothing" trap when we're dealing with the subject of sleep. You can reduce the strength of any particular sleep association by making sure it is only present *some of the time* when your baby is falling asleep. If, for example, you nurse your baby to sleep *some of the time*, rock your baby to sleep *some of the time*, and try to put your baby to bed just *some of the time* when she's sleepy but awake, she'll have a hard time getting hooked on any one sleep association.

Sleep experts stress that the feeding-sleep association tends to be particular powerful, so if you can encourage your baby to fall asleep without always needing to be fed to sleep, your baby will have an easier time learning how to soothe herself to sleep when she gets a little older.

Table 4.1

National Sleep Foundation Data on Babies and Toddlers and Sleep Aids

	Usually/Always Has a Pacifier When Sleeping	Sucks Fingers or Thumbs	Sleeps with a Soft Object Like a Teddy Bear
Babies	28%	16%	46%
Younger toddlers	25%	14%	69%
Older toddlers	18%	10%	63%

Source: National Sleep Foundation, *Sleep in America Poll* (Washington, DC: National Sleep Foundation, March 2004).

While wind-down techniques such as rocking, swaddling, shushing, (i.e., making a shushing sound) and nursing your baby to sleep can be very effective at soothing newborns and young babies who have not yet developed the self-soothing skills to get themselves to sleep, you should think of these techniques as a stop-gap measure that should be used while you wait for your baby's self-soothing skills to emerge. After the newborn stage, there will be a transitional period when your baby is mastering the all-important art of soothing himself to sleep. With some gentle encouragement from you and plenty of opportunities for practice, your baby will gradually learn how to get herself to sleep and back to sleep when she wakes up in the night.

Just realize that you have to provide your baby with these opportunities for learning if you want her to master this very important skill (as opposed to being so afraid of exposing her to any frustration that you deprive her of the opportunity of learning the art of self-soothing at a time when she is developmentally primed to learn it). Of course, you don't want to jump the gun by trying to teach her to self-soothe before she's ready (and not all babies are ready to master this skill at exactly the same time). That will only set up you and your baby for frustration, so your best bet is to let your parenting intuition help you decide whether your baby is ready to start practising her self-soothing skills.

Most babies are ready to start practicing these skills around the three- to four-month mark. (If your baby is already showing signs of being able to self-soothe at an earlier age, of course you can take advantage of that.) Once you decide to let your baby practise her self-soothing skills, you will need to determine whether to stay with your baby to provide gentle reassurance (either hands-on comfort or reassurance without any actual touching) or let her learn to settle herself on her own by leaving the room for a few minutes.

Practising Your Baby's Self-Soothing Skills

If you're not quite sure how to let your baby practise self-soothing skills, here are a few ideas.

Option 1: Parent Stays in the Room

If you decide to remain in the room when she's trying to get herself to sleep at this point, one of two things are likely to occur:

1. She may fall asleep on her own without any help from you.

2. She may agree to go to sleep either

    (a) with some hands-on help from you or

    (b) simply by being comforted by your presence.

    (If this becomes a regular part of her bedtime routine, she could begin to associate you with her wind-down-to-sleep routine.)

3. She may launch into a full-blown protest.

Option 2: Parent Leaves the Room

The second option assumes that you're either putting your baby to bed in a crib or in another sleeping environment where it will be possible to leave her on her own (e.g., a co-sleeping arrangement in a completely baby-proofed room).

If you put your baby to bed when she's drowsy but still awake, and leave the room, one of three things are likely to happen, provided that you give her a moment or two to try to settle herself on her own:

1. She may settle down to sleep immediately.

2. She may briefly protest as you leave the room (not actually crying, but mildly fussing or whining for a moment), only to settle down to sleep within a minute or two.

3. She may launch into a full-blown protest.

All too often, the sleep-training experts get divided into the cry and no-cry camps, and forget that there's some sensible middle ground to be staked out before you start thinking about sleep training. I'm talking about when your baby is doing a lot of informal sleep learning, thanks to all the great things you've done to create a healthy sleep environment for her, teach her the difference from night and day, and so on. In fact, the more and better sleep groundwork you lay for her, the greater the odds that you may never need a formal sleep-training program at all. One night your baby may start sleeping through the night. And if she starts waking up again in the night at some future point—as many children do—you'll have the knowledge and skills required to troubleshoot those issues as they arise. (See Chapters 6, 7, and 8 for more about that.)

- **Some babies find it easier to fall asleep when there is a parent in the room. Others do not.** If your baby falls into category B, your presence in the room can actually interfere with your baby's ability to get to sleep. And if you are using the variation of this method which has the parent physically present in the room, but not picking the child up, your baby may be frustrated or upset that you're standing right there, but not responding to his cries to be picked him up. Pay attention to your baby's reactions as you decide whether your baby will find it easier to settle down to sleep with you standing right there or with you close by, but not in the room. Then follow your baby's lead.

- **Understand that there's a world of difference between the wind-down fussing that some babies do as they settle down to sleep and the "Come and get me: I'm wide awake!" wail.** It takes most of us 15–20 minutes to fall asleep, babies included. If you pick up your baby when she's doing her final bit of wind-down fussing (a noise that some sleep researchers have compared to the sound that a battery-operated toothbrush makes when it's running out of batteries!), you interfere with her ability to get herself to sleep and you have to start the bedtime routine all over again, something that's just as frustrating for *her* as it is for you. (You know how tortuous it is for you when you're almost asleep and the telephone rings? That's what it's like for your baby when her eyes are closed, she's in the final stretch of her wind-down fussing, and you suddenly scoop her up out of bed to soothe her.) You may notice this mild wind-down fussing before your baby goes to sleep and sometimes when your baby wakes up in the middle of the night. Listen to your baby before you pick her up. She may be almost asleep—or still asleep! (Some babies make these tired whining sounds in their sleep.) If you can learn to spot the difference between the fussy "I'm almost asleep" or "I'm still asleep" sound and the "Pick me up now! I'm wide awake and I'm not going to go to sleep anytime soon" cry, you'll save yourself and your baby a lot of frustration.

- **Don't let other people make you feel guilty about how you handle your baby's wind-down-to-sleep routine.** This is one of those situations where you really can't win, no matter what type of parenting decision you make. If you're actively involved in settling your baby to sleep, rocking her or staying in her room until she's found her way to Dreamland, people will give you unsolicited lectures about the unhealthy sleep associations you're creating. (It's your choice to make, not theirs. If you make those sleep associations, you'll simply have to find a way to break them down the road. Some parents decide that's a small price to pay to make bedtimes less stressful for themselves and their babies during the early months.) And if you give your baby a chance to learn to settle herself by engaging in some mild wind-down fussing, you're likely to have some people stick you with the "cruel parent" label.

5. Learn How to Understand the Noises Your Baby Makes in His Sleep

A FINELY TUNED parental ear is one of the most powerful tools you have at your disposal as you help your baby become a good sleeper. If you can learn to differentiate between the sounds that your baby makes when he's still sound asleep from the sounds he makes when he needs some nighttime parenting, you'll be providing your baby with some additional opportunities to learn how to soothe himself to sleep.

"If I leave Sadie alone for too long, she'll wake up completely, and then that's it for a couple of hours," says Samantha, 31, the mother of eight-month-old Sadie. "So now I go in quickly so that I catch her while she's still mostly asleep."

"Rose has a certain cry that we must respond to," notes Jennifer, 28, the mother of 18-month-old Rose. "She won't stop crying until we do."

Cries like Rose's don't leave any room for parental second-guessing. It's a cry in the night that says, "I want my Mommy and Daddy and I want them right now!" But not all nighttime cries fall into that category. There are peeps and middle-of-the-night cries that a baby makes when she's not even fully awake.

The sleep experts say that overparenting—trying *too* hard to anticipate and meet your baby's every need, in an effort to spare her frustration—can interfere with sleep learning. If you respond to your baby at the first sign of any middle-of-the-night tossing and turning (which may merely be your baby's efforts to settle back into a more comfortable sleeping position or a noise that she makes as she moves from one sleep stage to another), you may wake up a sleeping baby. And if you automatically assume that she's hungry and proceed to offer the breast, you may train her to start waking up for food at a time of night when she was neither hungry nor awake—something that some experts would argue interferes with her natural sleep learning that needs to occur if your baby or toddler is to master the art of self-soothing and makes motherhood harder for you. (See Chapters 6 and 7 for more on this issue.)

MOM'S THE WORD

"I think many parents are afraid to help their child build independence in going to sleep. They feel that children always need to be with the parent, cuddled to sleep, responded to immediately. I think that this doesn't give the child a chance to learn to soothe herself and can foster routines that are very difficult to sustain as the child gets older."

—*Laura, 37, mom of one*

---

6. Make Daytime Sleep a Priority: Children Who Nap Sleep Better at Nighttime

RESEARCH HAS SHOWN that babies who nap during the day sleep better and longer at nighttime. While you might think that skipping babies' daytime naps might make it easier to get them off to bed come evening, babies typically end up being so overtired that they have a very difficult time settling down at bedtime and they don't sleep particularly well during the night. And rather than sleeping in so that they can catch up on the sleep they didn't get the day before, they tend to start the next day too early and they have a difficult time settling down for their naps, as well.

The sleep experts sum this phenomenon up nicely: Sleep begets sleep. The corollary, of course, is "Poor sleep (or no sleep) begets poor sleep," a phenomenon Sharlene, 34, the mother of five-month-old Makenna, has observed firsthand: "If Makenna has had bad naps during the day, night sleep is torturous."

It is important to make your child's daytime sleep a priority, just as you make a point of ensuring that he receives nutritious meals and snacks on a regular basis. Your child needs nutritious "sleep snacks" during the day in addition to his main nighttime "sleep meal" in order to be at his best. (Babies, toddlers, and preschoolers who nap are generally in a better mood and have an improved attention span as compared to their age-mates who don't nap.)

7. Recognize When Your Baby No Longer Needs to Be Fed in the Night and Start Using Non-food Methods to Soothe Your Baby Back to Sleep

YOUR BABY MAY continue to wake up in the night out of habit even when he's outgrown the need for a middle-of-the-night feeding. If your baby is going without that nighttime feeding some of the time or doesn't seem particularly interested in nursing once he gets up in the night (he seems more interested in cuddling and hanging out with you!), it might be time to eliminate that nighttime feeding and use non-food methods to soothe him back to sleep.

Eventually, of course, you'll want to encourage him to assume responsibility for soothing himself to sleep, but the first hurdle is to work on breaking that powerful food-sleep association. With some children, it happens quickly. With other children, it's a much slower process. Once you break that association, he may stop waking as often in the night and may be ready to start working on acquiring some self-soothing skills. (See Chapter 6 for a detailed discussion of specific techniques for eliminating nighttime feedings.)

8. Remain as Calm and Relaxed as Possible about the Sleep Issue

IF YOU ARE frustrated and angry when you deal with your child in the night, your child will inevitably pick up your vibes, even if you're trying hard to hide your feelings.

Accepting the fact that some babies take a little longer to learn the sleep ropes and feeling confident that you can solve your child's sleep problems will make it easier to cope with the middle-of-the-night sleep interruptions. Studies have shown that parents who have realistic expectations about parenthood and who feel confident in their own abilities to handle whatever parenting curveballs may be coming their way find it easier to handle the challenges of nighttime parenting.

Sleep Survey Says ...

SLEEP SCIENTISTS HAVE mulled over the data from sleep study after sleep study, hoping to zero in on (a) the factors that explain why some babies seem to arrive on the planet programmed to sleep well while others seem to view giving in to sleep as a major sign of weakness, and (b) what specific sleep behaviors parents should be encouraging or discouraging. And here's perhaps the most important sleep statistic of all: *Sleep problems don't go away on their own.* Forty-one percent of children who were getting up at age eight months were still getting up in the night at age four years, so if your baby is well into the second half of the first year of her life, you may want to come up with a plan for promoting healthy sleep habits in your child. Some of the factors that make for a healthy sleeper are firmly rooted in nature (we are hardwired with genes and, to a certain degree, our own temperament) while others are much more a product of nurture (the parenting we receive and other environmental factors).

How Temperament Affects Sleep

IF YOU'VE BEEN making your way through mountains and mountains of generic sleep advice and thinking, "This would never work for my baby," temperament may be the reason. Not all babies come "wired" the same, so not all sleep advice will work equally well for all babies.

MOM'S THE WORD

"My mother-in-law was most reassuring when she told me that none of her three kids went to sleep until almost 10 each night, and none of the three slept through the night until after three years old. That made me feel like our daughter was merely exhibiting a familial tendency. It was such a relief."

—*Marla, 36, mother of 16-month-old Josephine*

"Some kids require a great deal of sleep even at two to three years of age in comparison with their peers," adds Nathalie, 34, mother of five-year-old Chloe and three-year-old Bradley. "Others seem to thrive on less. Some children cannot fall asleep unless they are in a quiet and dark environment, while others can fall asleep in their lasagna with chaos going on around them." Given those individual differences, how could any off-the-shelf sleep solution work for every child regardless of temperament?

It can't, insists Marie, 35, the mother of nine-month-old George. "I have considered my baby a 'high-needs' baby and this carries over to his sleep patterns. As a small infant he always wanted to be held and required a lot of attention in this way. He wanted to nurse a lot and be close to me. When he sleeps he wants to do the same—nurse a lot and be close to me! He was always happy if he had these two things and would loudly protest when he did not. The same for sleeping! High-needs babies are high-needs 24 hours a day."

Sleep Researchers: Meet the Parents!

Sleep researchers have discovered what many parents know intuitively. Temperament has a key role in determining how well a particular child is likely to sleep (see table 4.2). Researchers at the University of Reading, U.K., have found, for example, that parents who have children with more challenging temperaments need to be more persistent in encouraging such positive sleep behaviors as:

- consistent bedtime rituals
- consistent bedtimes
- consistent wake times
- self-soothing behaviors.

If you are the parent of a high-needs or spirited baby, toddler, or preschooler, it will likely take your child longer to master basic sleep skills and you will likely have to put more effort into helping him learn how to be a good sleeper. The good news, of course, is that it can be done. A child with a challenging temperament isn't destined to be a poor sleeper forever, even if it feels that way to you some days.

Who's Calling Who Temperamental?

Just in case you're wondering who gets classified as "easy" or "challenging" these days, this is how the lines tend to be drawn (see Table 4.2 for definitions):

- children with easy temperaments are those who are mild in intensity, positive in mood, and high in initial approach and adaptability
- children with challenging (a.k.a. difficult or spirited) temperaments are those who tend to be "intense and negative in mood; low in approach and adaptability; rhythmic"

The key issue to bear in mind when you're thinking about temperament is what psychologists call "goodness of fit"

- how well your child's temperament fits your expectations of what your child would be like
- how compatible your temperament is with your child's temperament.

Researchers have found that when a mother and her baby share similar temperamental characteristics, it's easier for the mother to respond to her baby's needs with greater sensitivity. When there isn't the same fit, it's more difficult for mothers to be sensitive and responsive. So how much of a difference can this issue of fit make to the child's long-term health and well-being and the mother's effectiveness as a parent? One study found that the high-needs babies who exercised the best self-control at age two were those whose mothers had learned to accommodate their difficult temperaments—in other words, to work with and not against their children's temperaments. However, a mother who chooses to follow her

mothering intuition and disregard friends and family members'
advice that she try a particular sleep training method that
worked with their children can receive a lot of criticism. Unless
she's confident that she's chosen the right parenting path for herself
and her child, she may second-guess her nighttime parenting
decisions and even override her parenting instincts in an effort
to solve her child's sleep problem and quell the criticism of her
parenting choices, something that can lead to guilt, regret, and
frustration after the fact.

What can make the comments from other people particularly
hard to take is the fact that babies who sleep well are often
described as good babies, which can leave you wondering if your
less-than-terrific sleeper is, by default, a bad baby or if you're a
bad parent.

Lose the labels, suggests Rachel, 33, herself the mother of a two-
year-old who, as she tells it, was blessed with his *father's* great sleep
genes. "Parents should definitely not feel guilty if their kid won't
sleep. I did nothing to deserve my good fortune, and they certainly
don't *deserve* to be losing sleep either!"

MOM'S THE WORD

"I think we need to move past the idea of 'good' and 'bad'
because I don't think those judgments do anyone much good. Let's instead
look at if this particular family is getting the sleep they need and if not, put
our energy into fixing it (not worrying about it, labeling it, feeling guilty about
it, etc.) if we are the parents or making them feel like failures if we are on the
outside looking in. Sleep is for the baby parent set what little league scores
are for the school-age parent set and what college admissions are for the
teenage parent set and I think it is unfair to the kids and the parents."

—*Sarah, 32, mom of one*

Table 4.2

Temperament and Sleep

Temperament Characteristic	What It Refers to	How It Affects Your Child's Sleep	Working with Your Child's Temperament to Promote Healthy Sleep Habits
Activity level	How physically active your child is	Your child may be totally wired at bedtime—so full of energy, in fact that you may not ever realize that he's tired until he's overtired. This can make it difficult for him and for you to get a good night's sleep. Highly active children are likely to be more active, even when they are sleeping. Your child may end up banging his head against the side of his crib, ramming his head against you (if he's sharing your bed), or falling out of bed (if he's a toddler who is new to the world of big-kid beds).	Learn to spot your child's tiredness cues so that you can get him off to bed before he has a total meltdown. Make his sleeping environment as safe as possible so that he is less likely to get hurt. Provide reassurance if he wakes up upset after one of his nocturnal bumps in the night.
Distractibility	How easy it is to distract your child from a particular activity	Children who are highly distractible are more difficult to soothe because anything can disrupt their bedtime routine when they are trying to get to sleep.	Minimize distractions at bedtime so that your child will find it easier to wind down and go to sleep. Make sure that your child's sleeping environment also minimizes distractions (e.g., a dark room without any sound/light mobiles).

continued on p. 116

Temperament Characteristic	What It Refers to	How It Affects Your Child's Sleep	Working with Your Child's Temperament to Promote Healthy Sleep Habits
Distractibility	How intensely your child responds to situations, how loud your child is	Children who are highly intense may have more difficulty in falling asleep and may need more time and more help from you in learning how to get to sleep. A highly intense child may become over-stimulated, something that can make it more difficult for the child to wind down at bedtime.	Watch out for signs of overstimulation and overtiredness, minimize distractions at bedtime, develop a soothing bedtime routine that will help your child to fall asleep.
Regularity	The predictability of your child's biological rhythms, such as eating and sleeping	A child with irregular biological rhythms will have more sleep difficulties than a child with more regular biological rhythms.	If your child's patterns are highly irregular, look for sleep patterns as they emerge and work with—not against—your child's patterns. Gradually encourage your child's sleep/wake schedule to become more regular, while recognizing that his schedule may still get thrown off quite easily and quite often. It becomes easier to help children regulate their eating, sleeping, and other biological rhythms as they get older, so if you've got a baby with wildly unpredictable sleep patterns, don't assume that your child's sleep patterns will always be as challenging as they are during the baby stage.

Sensory threshold (sensitivity)	How sensitive your child is to noise (e.g., if he startles easily in response to certain sounds), textures (e.g., if he can't tolerate being in contact with certain fabrics or hates tags on his clothes), temperature changes	Sensitive children may have a more difficult time getting to sleep and staying asleep. She may resist bedtime rituals that other children find soothing (e.g., infant massage) or become fussy for reasons that aren't immediately apparent to you (e.g., the tag or zipper or fabric on her pajamas are making her uncomfortable). Toddlers and preschoolers who are highly sensitive may hear every little sound and find it impossible to go to sleep while the bathroom tap is dripping or the wind is blowing. Sensitive children are more prone to waking in the night due to their increased sensitivity to their environments—everything from noises to temperature changes to feelings of wetness or hunger.	If your child's patterns are highly regular, make your child's love of routines work to your advantage. A child who feels more secure when there's a predictable bedtime (bath, toothbrushing, story, cuddle) routine will have an easier time going to sleep. Accept the fact that your child is extra-sensitive and try to eliminate as many sources of irritation as possible (e.g., uncomfortable clothing, waking up in the night due to a wet diaper). Consider running a white noise machine or a fan at night to mask household creaks and bumps that may wake up your child. Sensitive children are also quite tuned into how their parents are feeling: If you're stressed, your child may pick up on your stress level, too. As your child becomes more verbal, make sure she has a chance to discuss any worries/concerns that may be chasing the Sandman away. You may find that your baby prefers a firm touch to a light, repetitive touch. Swaddling (to prevent self-startling) can be helpful in soothing some newborns.

continued on p. 118

Temperament Characteristic	What It Refers to	How It Affects Your Child's Sleep	Working with Your Child's Temperament to Promote Healthy Sleep Habits
Approach/ withdrawal (initial reaction to a new situation)	How your child responds to new situations or strangers (e.g., quick to warm up vs. hesitant to warm up); most babies experience stranger anxiety during the second half of the first year of life.	A child who doesn't respond well to new situations may have difficulty sleeping in different surroundings (e.g., when you're on vacation or visiting relatives); adjusting to the time change; getting used to her big-kid bed, and so on.	Promote the use of a familiar comfort object like a special blanket, crib sheet, or white noise machine so that something about her sleep environment will be familiar while you're away from home. Encourage other self-soothing behaviors so that your child will have tools to rely on if she's feeling scared or unsure.
Adaptability	How readily your child adapts to changes in routines or transitions	A child who has difficulty with changes to his routine may have difficulty coping with the time change, the transition from a bassinet to a crib, etc.	Make changes in stages as opposed to all at once whenever possible. Accept that change is difficult for your child and that you may be in for some rough nights whenever she's trying to make a sleep transition or deal with some other change to her regular sleep routine. Realize that other changes in her life may spill over into her

| | | nighttime behavior. For example, when she changes day-care providers, she may start waking in the night again. Encourage self-soothing behaviors so that your child will have tools to rely on if she's feeling scared or unsure. On a day-to-day basis, make your child's love of routines work to your advantage. A child who feels more secure when there's a predictable bedtime (bath, toothbrushing, story, cuddle) routine will have an easier time going to sleep. | Realize that it may take a little longer for your child to wind down and give in to sleep. Minimize distractions and use wind-down rituals. Establish a clear and consistent bedtime routine early on, and stick to it as much as possible. As your child gets older, be fairly consistent about the bedtime rules and to spell out your expectations in advance to discourage your child from bargaining to stay up late. |
| Persistence | How long and how hard your child works at getting his needs met. Will he react strongly if you aren't able to meet his needs immediately? | A child who is highly persistent can be a challenge on the sleep front because he can refuse to give in to sleep or, as he heads into the toddler and preschool years, insist on "just one more story" or "just one more glass of water" until it's almost time for Mom and Dad to go to bed! | |

continued on p. 120

Temperament Characteristic	What It Refers to	How It Affects Your Child's Sleep	Working with Your Child's Temperament to Promote Healthy Sleep Habits
Mood	Whether or not your child tends to be a naturally pleasant and easygoing or more difficult to please and somewhat moody and temperamental	A child who tends to be moody or to cry a lot tends to be more difficult to settle down at bedtime than a child who is more easygoing. Being frustrated, over-tired, or having her favorite pair of paja-mas in the laundry can totally throw her off her bedtime game.	Do your best to anticipate potential bedtime disasters and to head off trouble. Use some wind-down rituals that work for your child. Accept that it may take a while to get your baby (or toddler or preschooler) off to bed. He needs to feel emotionally okay in order to drift off to Dreamland and that can take considerable time, energy, and creativity on your part.

Note: These nine traits were first identified by child psychiatrists Alexander Thomas and Stella Chess, who are famous for conducting the New York Longitudinal Study of 133 children. They wrote about the various ways in which these traits could match up and concluded that there were three basic types of children: easy children, "slow to warm up" children, and "high-needs" or "difficult" children. More recently studies about temperament have focused on the countless combinations of traits of temperament and how they play out in individuals: e.g., if you're sensitive and moody, persistent and regular, and so on.

Sleep Training: The Mother of All Hot Topics

SURE, THOSE DISCUSSIONS at childbirth class about pain-relief options, breast-feeding vs. bottle-feeding, and immunization sometimes got a little heated. Chances are at least one mama-to-be was offended enough by another's take on the hot topic *du jour* to mutter something snarky under her breath when she thought no one could hear her. Well, those pre-birth discussions were a mere appetizer designed to whet your appetite for the sleep-training debate main course.

For starters, many parents (myself included, I must confess) aren't that crazy about the term sleep training. ("I don't like to think I am training Lilith to sleep well as much as teaching and encouraging her to do so," explains Sarah, 32, mom to 14-month-old Lilith. "After all, as good as a climber as she is, she is not a little circus monkey to be 'trained.'") However, since everyone else is using the term and there isn't a particularly mainstream alternative— sleep learning sounds as awkward and politically correct to my ear as the incredibly annoying toilet learning!—I guess we'll have to live with it for now.

Sleep training—as you probably know—is the term used to describe a formal and prescribed method of teaching babies to sleep through the night. It's most commonly applied to cry-it-out methods, in which babies are allowed to cry for either fixed intervals of time or until they stop crying, but some people apply the term more broadly and also use it to describe so-called gentle or no-cry methods (e.g., methods in which no crying is tolerated or a small amount of crying is tolerated, but a parent remains with the child to provide comfort) as well as putting babies on sleep schedules.

MOM'S THE WORD

"You can't argue baby advice. It's like religion and politics. I found that I had to listen to my gut and follow my daughter's lead."

—*Patricia, 31, mother of one*

(See Sleep Tool 2 for a basic overview of each of the major sleep-training methods, including a summary of what parents typically like and dislike about each method.) Most experts feel that sleep training should be left until a baby is at least five to six months of age (although some extreme baby scheduling methods have promised to have babies sleeping through the night by age six weeks—an approach that has been severely criticized by pediatric health authorities).

Why It May Be Difficult to Talk Sleep with Even Your Very Best Mom Friends

When one of my favorite mom bloggers initiated a sleep discussion on her blog recently, she jokingly noted that she was likely to lose about half of her on-line friends by daring to come out of the sleep closet—in other words, by stating her particular sleep camp allegiance in public (in her case, cry it out). Bloggers have been flamed, after all, for far less. But by some miracle, she managed to escape relatively unscathed. Perhaps it's because she hosts an exceptionally popular blog and most of the momosphere would have jumped to her defense. (Or at least I hope they would have, even if they didn't necessarily share her sleep philosophies. After all, if a mom can't turn to other mommy bloggers for support when she's going through sleep hell with her child, where is she supposed to turn for support, advice, and cyber sympathy?)

Moms' groups (virtual or otherwise) do, after all, tend to be less judgmental than your average impromptu gathering of women. Some function as group problem-solving teams, determined to arrive at the sleep answer on behalf of their members. After all, as even the most savvy researcher-moms quickly discover, there isn't one sleep answer to any sleep question. "Every baby is so different and I really don't believe any one method will work for every baby," notes Jennifer, 30, the mother of 12-month-old Amanda. "For that reason, I try not to be judgmental of other parents who choose cry it out. It's really none of my business and everyone has to do what's right for them, taking into account their own ability to parent when

MOTHER WISDOM

"When mothers feel uncertain they can be easily intimidated by 'expert' advice. Listening to a mother, it can often sound as though there are three people in her home: herself, her baby, and whichever 'baby expert' she is trying to follow. Expertise is invaluable in exceptional circumstances. But mothers can be pressured into supposing that they need someone to tell them how to run their everyday lives."

—Naomi Stadlen, What Mothers Do: Especially When It Looks Like Nothing (2004)

---

tired, how the lack of sleep is affecting their marriage/relationship, and what other effects the lack of sleep is having on their life (e.g., a partner who needs to be well rested for their job)."

That's not to say that moms don't end up feeling severely judged by other parents (particularly moms) from time to time. Nathalie, a 34-year-old mother of two, has thought long and hard about why some mothers feel such a powerful need to defend their own mothering choices and to judge other mothers so harshly. "I think that motherhood is such an earth-shattering experience in terms of our identities and confidence that whatever choices you make as a new mother, you feel that you have to defend to the death because that is the only sense of self you have to hold on to at that point. To have potentially made the wrong decision as a parent—whether it be in your eyes or the eyes of others—is devastating to admit because it equates to having failed as a parent, a role that, as you look around you, others seem to carry out so successfully and effortlessly."

The Expert's Not the Boss of You

Adding to the problem is the fact that many new mothers are quick to turn to the experts for advice. And, of course, if you happen to consult a handful of experts, you'll get conflicting sleep advice, which can leave you feeling confused and overwhelmed.

"I find it ironic that it's up to me to solve her sleep problems when experts in the field don't even agree on techniques. In fact, they fundamentally *disagree* on many points and methods. How am I supposed to know what to do if they don't?" asks Laurie, 38, the mother of 19-week-old Edie.

"I found that every time I decided on a technique, I would read another book that would scare me into thinking that the initial technique was wrong and that my child would be scarred for life if I should decide to use it," recalls Karyn, 31, mother of a nine-month-old. "I was really confused by each book."

"I am a researcher by nature, so I decided to read everything there was on the subject," adds Michele, mom to three-year-old Mikaela and one-year-old Xander. "I learned that actually I am better off to choose one piece of literature to read—one highly recommended by fellow mamas, not doctors. I ended up confused. I found a piece of literature that would back any strategy I came up with. On nights when I had resolve, Ferber and Weissbluth and I were steadfast. On nights when I was tired, we were all miserable. I found Sears, who said we could all sleep together forever. He knew it was okay for my daughter to only sleep while latched, being held, and in my right arm."

And even if you *do* decide to put your faith in a single expert, you may find yourself feeling dissatisfied with the off-the-shelf sleep solution, whether that came via a book, a DVD, a half-hour TV show, a magazine article, something you read on a website, or a sleep course you took in your community.

"It bothers me that so much of the parenting information out there is black and white when we live in such a gray world," says Tanya, 36, mother of five-year-old Zachary and three-year-old Hayley. "How can we be so naive to think that if all babies and families are so different that one solution will work for everyone? What seems to be missing is the empathy or the reality check for the mother and father—that this is just one reality. Each baby is going to be different, and you don't know what sleep plan you are signing up for. We need to be more flexible in our approach."

As valuable as all of these sources of information may be, they can't necessarily deliver all the answers to your child's sleep problems despite all the promises on the book jacket or the DVD package.

PILLOW TALK

Seventy percent of parents are able to solve their child's sleep problems by reading books, talking to friends, or picking up tips from TV shows and magazine articles. The other 30 percent require help from doctors, sleep experts, and other professionals to help themselves and their babies to get the sleep they need.

And, unfortunately, a lot of sleep products prey on vulnerable parents by over-promising sleep results that they simply can't deliver in the short run or perhaps even in the long run.

One-size-fits-all sleep solutions can also fail to take into account your parenting philosophies and your family's situation, notes Jennifer, 28, the mother of 18-month-old Rose. "Rose slept in our room until she was six months old. That worked for us. My sister's babies slept in their own room right from the get go, and she was a firm believer in 'cry it out.' None of them are permanently traumatized. Parents are too concerned with 'the right thing.' They need to find 'the right for me' thing. That's the only thing that's going to work."

And whatever you do, don't fall into the all-too-common trap of assuming that the mismatch between your family's situation and a particular sleep program means that you are doing everything wrong when it comes to sleep.

"I tried all the sleep programs, but I could never get past the 'all or nothing' feeling that I got from them," says Laura, a 32-year-old mother of two (ages five and three). "I always cheated and gave in on some small detail. Then I would feel like a failure and move on to the next technique."

Sometimes it can be helpful to think of sleep books and other related resources as resources, not prescriptions: that should help to eliminate any guilt you feel about "cheating" on your baby's sleep program, and will instead free you up to combine the best ideas from all the books, articles, and other resource materials you've consulted. "The different sleep philosophies are merely tools you have at your disposal to adapt to your situation, says Lisa, a 28-year-old mother of one. Love 'em or leave 'em, in other words, with no morning-after-sleep-program regrets.

Sleep Nirvana: You Can Get There from Here!

"We need to keep expert advice in perspective," writes Bonny Rechert in her wonderfully wise book *In Search of Sleep: Straight Talk about Babies, Toddlers, and Night Waking.* "The pediatrician who tells you you need to let your baby cry at night, the sleep clinician who advocates a special program with a timer and a chart, and, yes, the sleep researcher who promotes the benefits of co-sleeping—these professionals know something about kids and sleep, but they don't know the whole story. Not the way you do. ... No sleep expert has your intimate sense of the quirks and characteristics that make your little one different from every other child on the planet." Most parents who've test-driven their fair share of sleep-training techniques would agree with Reichert—well, maybe not initially, but after going a few rounds with the sleep experts *du jour*. They find that there's this sudden breakthrough moment when they realize that they are the true experts, and they need look no further than their own parenting intuition for the wisdom needed to deal with their child's sleep problems. Kimberley, 31, says: "I feel like every resource or person that I've turned to in the past year has offered me conflicting advice on everything from how long my daughter should sleep to how often she should sleep to how she should fall asleep to where she should sleep to when she should sleep," the mother of a 12-month-old explains. "Friends whose babies slept through the night at two months of age all had different techniques; the various books all claimed to have the right answer. Even the different doctors at our pediatrician's office offered me wildly different advice. After months of tearing my hair out while we struggled with my daughter's less-than-ideal sleep habits and reading every sleep expert out there, I finally realized that the person I needed to be listening to was my daughter. From my research, I had a sense of the average range of hours a baby her age needed to sleep and an idea of what normal sleep patterns

> **MOM'S THE WORD**
>
> "It's not babies who need sleep training, but parents. We need to know our babies and to learn what will work for them and for us."
>
> —*Jennifer, 28, mother of one*

might be. From observing my daughter, I realized that she was not sleep-deprived and that she did have a sleep pattern, however little it resembled the ideal. I decided that we would work on finding a sleep style that was comfortable for all three of us, however that might look."

"Perhaps the most important lesson I'm learning is to trust my own instincts," confirms Cathleen, the 32-year-old mother of six-month-old Miyoko. "Everyone has an opinion on baby sleep and for me, I find it very easy to feel guilty or doubtful about my parenting choices. But when I take a moment to think about it, I know what works best for me and my baby."

The Sleep Plans of Which Dreams Are Made

So you've decided to come up with your own homegrown baby, toddler, or preschooler sleep plan made up of the best elements of every sleep program you've ever read, tried, or heard about. Here are some of the key questions to ask yourself:

Are your child's sleep patterns a problem in the opinion of the sleep experts (see Chapter 3 for some sleep milestone guidelines) and, more importantly, are her sleep patterns a problem for you? "I think some people are too quick to label a normal sleep pattern as a 'problem' and that some people have excessively high expectations of babies," says Christine, 32, mother of two. "I also think it is important not to treat all babies with the same methods (e.g., I believe some babies do need extra nighttime feedings even if they 'shouldn't'). Jennifer, 28, the mother of 20-month-old Rose, agrees and adds that it's the parent—not the parent's best friend, sister-in-law, neighbor, or mother-in-law—who gets to decide whether or not there's a bonafide problem. "Don't let anyone else define sleep problems for you," she stresses.

Are you missing out on so much sleep that your ability to function or to be an effective parent is affected? If you feel like you could fall asleep at the wheel while you're driving or that you're so tired that you don't enjoy being a parent, obviously you're no longer dealing with a sleep problem. You're dealing with a sleep crisis. It's time to call for backup, call your family doctor, get some sleep, and come up with a game plan for dealing with your child's sleep problems.

Are there any health issues that could be contributing to your baby's sleep problems? It's important to deal with any underlying health issues first. Otherwise you'll be treating the symptoms (disrupted sleep) rather than the underlying problem (your child's medical condition). If your child's sleep problems are long-lasting or particularly severe, a thorough physical may be in order. Talk to your child's doctor.

Can you come up with a sleep plan that you and your partner can both live with? It has to be something you both can stick to otherwise it will be game over before you even begin. Bear in mind that coming up with a parenting game plan by day is easier than carrying out that plan at night. *Note:* The section which follows provides a list of sleep talk questions that may help spark a dialogue between you and your partner about whether the sleep status quo is acceptable for the two of you and, if not, which sleep-training methods might best meet the needs of your family.

The Big (Sleep) Talk: Discussing Sleep Issues with Your Partner

The following are some of the issues to consider when discussing your child's sleep habits with your partner. Some of these questions also focus on issues that relate to you alone. You may also want to share this information with your partner and/or to consider if any of these could be issues for your partner, too.

Your parenting values/your child-rearing beliefs/your relationship with your partner

- What sleep-training methods would you and/or your partner feel comfortable trying? (See Sleep Tool 2.)

- What sleep-training methods would you and/or your partner not feel comfortable using? (See Sleep Tool 2.)

- Are you and your partner basically in synch when it comes to parenting values and child-rearing beliefs? If there are areas where you aren't in synch, how can you deal with that reality and still function as an effective parenting team?

- Is one of you doing most of the nighttime parenting at this point?

- How would you describe your relationship with your partner at this time?

- How would your partner describe his/her relationship with you?

- If you are currently experiencing any relationship difficulties, would either of you say that your child's sleep issues are adding to those difficulties?

Your work/family realities

- How important is it that you and/or your partner get a full night's sleep on a regular basis?

- What are the realities of your living situation? Are you living with family members who can't tolerate any crying from your child? Are you living in an apartment with paper-thin walls? Do you have an ill or aging relative living with you? Do you have other young children?

- What else is going on in your life and your partner's life? Is your stress-o-meter already maxed out? How is your partner feeling/coping these days?

- Are you coping with any physical or mental health conditions that make it important for one or both of you to get a full night's sleep? What about your partner?

Your schedule (rigid or flexible)

- Can you and/or your partner work around your baby/child's erratic schedule for many months/years to come?

- Under what circumstances would you and/or your partner be willing to encourage your baby/child to modify her sleep schedule to be more in synch with your own?

Your lifestyle

- Do you and/or your partner travel/visit friends frequently? If so, how will you teach your baby/child to adjust to sleeping in different surroundings?

- Will your baby/child be cared for by her grandparents or childcare providers from time to time? If so, how can you prepare your baby/child to adapt to this situation?

Support systems

- What sources of support are available to you and/or your partner in the community? (Don't forget to include any employee-assistance benefits that may be available through your workplace or your partner's workplace.)

- Do you or your partner have family members or friends who can pitch in and relieve you of some of your responsibilities or provide some hands-on help on the weekend so that you can catch up on some sleep?

- Would you be able to hire a postpartum doula or night nurse to help you catch up on your sleep? (Don't forget that it may be possible to barter for these services, in some situations, or to ask for them as a gift.)

Are you ready to deal with your child's sleep problem?

- If your child has a sleep problem, but you can't deal with it at this point, what might be making it difficult for you or your partner to deal with the underlying issue?

Examples:

o Fear about something happening to your baby in the night

o Sadness at not being able to spend more one-on-one time with your baby during the day

o A desire to hold on to the baby stage just a little longer (particularly common if you have the sense that this is your last baby)

o Not wanting to deal with the problem because you're too tired

o Anxiety about what dealing with your child's sleep problem might involve for one or both of you

Is this the right time for you to make major changes to your family's sleep routines? We've already talked about what makes sense in terms of timing from your baby's perspective. You also need to ensure that you're implementing your sleep plan at a time when you can afford to lose a little extra sleep (bear in mind that things are likely to get worse on the sleep front before they start to get better) and when you're not likely to be dealing with too many other major life curveballs (to the extent that you can predict them, of course). The type of sleep-training method you choose and how quickly your child responds to the sleep-training method will affect how much sleep you miss out on, but it's hard to predict just how much, so it's generally best to err on the side of caution. There will never be a "perfect time" to deal with your child's sleep issues, however. At some point, you may have to simply take the plunge.

Are you keeping a sleep log? If not, start keeping one before you start making any changes so that you can identify any negative sleep associations that could contribute to your child's sleep problems. Note such things as your child's waking time, bedtime, the starting time and ending time of your child's naps, what—if anything—you had to do to get your child to go to sleep (or back to sleep) anytime he woke up in the night, and so on.

(See Sleep Tool 5 or simply jot some notes on a calendar or in a notebook.) Don't make the note-keeping too much work or you simply won't bother, or you'll stress yourself out trying to remember if your baby woke up at 1:07 or 1:17 a.m. Keep a notebook and a pen close to where your baby sleeps so that you can scrawl a few notes down in the middle of the night. You can always reconstruct your notes in a more coherent fashion in the morning.

Are you prepared for the fact that changing established sleep habits takes time and patience? I mean really prepared. Like crash diets, "quick-fix" sleep programs don't work. Think about how dramatically you are affected each time the clocks shift backwards and forwards. Sleep affects all of us in pretty powerful ways. According to Kim West, author of *Good Night, Sleep Tight: The Sleep Lady's Gentle Guide to Helping Your Child Go to Sleep, Stay Asleep, and Wake Up Happy*, bedtime problems are easier to solve than napping, early rising, and night wakening, but none of them are a cakewalk, so patience is a decided virtue—no, let's make that a necessity—when you're encouraging your child to make some changes on the sleep front.

Can you deal with the two steps forward, one step backward sleep facts of life? There will inevitably be backslides. If your child comes down with an ear infection, you move to a new house, or plan a week-long visit to a friend or relative, or your child achieves a major developmental breakthrough like learning how to pull himself to a standing position, all bets may be off on the sleep front for a couple of days. Of course, some kids are ultra-flexible. They may be able to handle any and all (or at least most) disruptions to their sleep routines. These are those highly portable kids that parents used to lug around suburbia in generations past. They'd simply curl up on the sofa or on the spare bed in the guest room if they happened to get tired before Mom and Dad finished their bridge game, and then they'd get carried home to bed at the end of the evening. Maybe you were one of these kids. ...

Is your sleep-support team in place? What you ideally want is a posse of parents who share your parenting philosophies and who can help to bolster your confidence (and pour you strong cups of coffee) on days when the going gets tough. It would also be really nice if they'd pop over and offer to fold the occasional load of laundry, bring you a homemade lasagna, and chase you to your room for a nap while they take over baby-cuddle duty. Choose your friends wisely, moms and dads. You want to have an all-star team in place at times like these.

If Plan A Fails ...

Most parents zero in on a particular sleep philosophy that works for them on both a philosophical and a practical level. (See Sleep Tool 2.) Initially, philosophy can have the upper hand, but that can change as the reality of parenting hits the road and as your child's nighttime parenting needs evolve over time.

"When my baby was around four months of age, she was waking every hour and a half," recalls Erin, 30, mom of 11-month-old Fiona. "I was feeding her each time she woke up, and she was no longer falling asleep nursing at that age, so we had to rock her back to sleep every time, which took about half an hour. That left me with about 45 minutes to sleep before she was up again. Needless to say, it only took a couple of weeks for me to reach the breaking point, when we decided to let her cry it out a little at a time."

"We realized that staying with her in her room—and holding her especially—was making it more difficult for her to go to sleep," says Jennifer, 30, mother of 12-month-old Amanda. "Once she was older—nine months or so—there were a few times that, out of desperation and the need for a brief respite, we would put her down after struggling with her for an hour and, after a minute or two of hysterical crying, she would promptly fall asleep. We started to realize that this was simply her pattern, and that the longer we worked against it, the longer it drew things out. Now we go through her bedtime routine and then I put her down pretty much asleep. Usually she will stay asleep, but if she's cranky—teething or overtired—she may insist on one of us staying with her while she falls asleep. We just rub her back for a few minutes, say, 'Try to go to sleep. I'll be back if you really need me. I love you," and then quietly leave the room and close the door. Within a couple of minutes, she is almost always asleep. If she's not, we go in and comfort her for a few minutes without picking her up and then leave again and she does go to sleep without too many problems."

"I was totally opposed to the idea of 'cry it out' until I had a baby who wouldn't sleep," says Dani, 36, mother of two. "Now I am a strong proponent of 'cry it out'—adapted to what you can tolerate and what's best for your baby's personality—but only for babies older than six to nine months."

Marla, 36, agrees with Dani's take on the timing of sleep training: "I do believe children need sleep training, but when they're older," the mother of 16-month-old Josephine explains. "When my daughter was so new, and needed to suckle often and nurse through the night, it was easier and more comforting for both of us for me to be right there. For almost the first year, her cries at night never escalated to the point of waking her up entirely because I was so close by. Then, at the point when she could go through the night without needing to nurse, I was right there to soothe her back down quickly as we dropped feedings one at a time. Then, when it was time to put her down in the crib to sleep, it was only a few nights of having to get up to soothe and pat her back down to sleep. But at this point, just after a year old, she was able to understand what 'sleepy time' meant. She may not have liked it, but she understood. Before then, it was just upsetting screams. Even now, at almost 16 months, I understand that she's a little person who might need comfort during the night, not training. But it was my need to sleep more and my understanding that we were keeping her from sleeping better that hardened my heart enough to see it through. Before that, my hormones and tender emotions just made me want to keep her close to me."

Of course, many parents who go the no-cry route find that there's a tremendous payoff for themselves and their children for sticking to the slower but gentler route. Bonnie, the 35-year-old mother of four-year-old Lauren, believes that her daughter is the person she is today because her parents have always treated her with love and respect, whether she needed her parents in the bright of day or the middle of the night.

"Lauren is one of the most compassionate children I have ever met," she explains. "She is the first one there if someone is crying. She's concerned about every ambulance going by. She's gentle beyond belief. And her devastation at the recent loss of our pet canary made me realize that she sees animals as beings with feelings— not just objects—which is quite a mature concept for her age. I think her depth of compassion is directly related to how we parented her at night. We treated her fears with respect and compassion, not annoyance and dismissiveness."

Solutions Central—The Last Word

WE'VE COVERED A lot of turf in this chapter—everything from baby sleep cues to practices that promote healthy sleep habits in young children to research on which children are likely to be the best sleepers to what the major sleep philosophies have to offer tired parents. (Whew!)

In the next chapter, we'll focus on where baby should sleep— co-sleeping (both bed sharing and room sharing), having siblings share rooms with babies, and having babies sleep on their own.

CHAPTER 5

Bedroom Politics: Where Will Your Baby Sleep?

"I was amazed at how interested people were in my 'sleeping' life after I had kids. No one ever asked how I was sleeping before I had kids!"
—KERRI, 39, MOTHER OF SEVEN

THE ALWAYS-HOT debate about where babies should sleep threatened to turn into a raging inferno as I was writing this book. The American Academy of Pediatrics released a new statement on sudden infant death syndrome (SIDS) that gave bed sharing a definitive thumbs-down. (The AAP did, however, follow in the footsteps of both the Canadian Paediatric Society and the United Kingdom Department of Health by recommending that babies share the parents' room, just not the parents' *bed*.)

And that was just *one* of the AAP's SIDS recommendations that had the entire pediatric health community and most parents talking sleep for weeks on end. (I'll be summarizing the other key recommendations at relevant points in this chapter.) Who knew sleep could be so controversial and that the debate could get so nasty?

SIDS: Some Basic Facts

BEFORE WE GET into the specifics of the AAP's new SIDS recommendations, which will have major implications for your sleep decisions for your baby, let me define the term "sudden infant death syndrome." Sudden infant death syndrome is the sudden and unexplained death of a child under the age of one year that remains unexplained after a thorough medical investigation, including an autopsy. SIDS is the leading cause of death in infants aged one month to one year. Typically, an apparently healthy baby is tucked into bed and then never wakes up. To determine that a baby has died of SIDS, the medical examiner rules out other causes first. In the past, SIDS was also used to describe unexpected deaths of children over the age of one year. These deaths are now referred to as sudden unexplained deaths of childhood (SUDC). (See www.sudc.org for more information about SUDC.)

Here are some other noteworthy facts about SIDS:

- Approximately 60–70 percent of babies who succumb to SIDS are male.

- Eighty percent of babies who die of SIDS are younger than six months of age (the peak risk period is age two to four months).

- Twins and triplets face an elevated risk of SIDS (2.5 times that of singletons).

- SIDS is also more common in babies who are born prematurely (before 37 completed weeks of pregnancy) and/or at low birth weight (babies who weigh less than 5 lbs, 8 oz at birth).

- SIDS occurs two to three times as often in members of the American Indian and Alaskan native populations.

- Teen mothers are five to fifteen times as likely to experience a SIDS-related risk than other mothers.

The Bedrooms of the Nation

WHEN FORMER CANADIAN Prime Minister Pierre Elliot Trudeau said that the state had no business in the bedrooms of the nation, he must have been talking about the bedrooms of people other than parents because the state (in Canada, the U.S., and the U.K.) has been spending a lot of time focusing on the bedrooms of the Moms and Dads lately, or at least the sleeping habits of parents and babies.

In 1999, a much-debated U.S. Consumer Product Safety Commission study recommended that parents avoid sleeping with children under the age of two. The study was controversial because, in the minds of many people, it failed to make an adequate distinction between babies who became entrapped in the furniture and suffocated in their parents' beds, almost always while sleeping alone, and babies who actually succumbed to SIDS. Since then, the American Academy of Pediatrics (along with the Canadian Paediatric Society and the United Kingdom Department of Health) have been taking an increasingly negative view of bed sharing. Here's what the AAP's Task Force on Sudden Infant Death Syndrome had to say in its policy statement entitled *The Changing Concept of Sudden Infant Death Syndrome: Diagnostic Coding Shifts, Controversies Regarding the Sleeping Environment, and New Variables to Consider in Reducing Risk:*

> Bed sharing, as practiced in the United States and other Western countries, is more hazardous than the infant sleeping on a separate sleep surface and, therefore, [the AAP] recommends that infants not bed share during sleep. Infants may be brought into bed for nursing or comforting but should be returned to their own crib or bassinet when the parent is ready to return to sleep.

The AAP argues that while there are some obvious breast-feeding and bonding advantages to bed sharing, the risks outweigh the benefits. The APP noted that bed sharing appears to be a particularly risky proposition:

- for infants under age 11 weeks (whether or not the mother smokes, a finding that appears to refute some earlier studies that had indicated bed sharing was a less risky proposition for non-smoking mothers)

- when there is more than one person sharing the bed with the infant, e.g., parents and baby; parents, baby, and sibling(s)

- when the person sharing the bed with the infant has been drinking or is overtired (and may not be easily aroused from sleep if he or she accidentally rolls over the baby, which could allow stale air to accumulate around the baby's face and/or for the baby to suffocate

- when the baby sleeps for a longer stretch of time in the parents' bed (e.g., the greater the number of hours a baby spends in the parents' bed, the greater the risk)

Instead of sharing your bed with your baby, share your room, suggests the APP. The AAP notes in its recommendations that parents in the U.K. are now advised to have their babies sleep in a crib in the parents' room for the first six months of life. (The Canadian Paediatric Society also made the same recommendation to Canadian parents in its 2004 policy statement *Recommendations for Safe Sleeping Environments for Infants and Children*.) The AAP recommends that parents put baby to bed in a crib, bassinet, or cradle that meets the safety standards of the Consumer Product Safety Commission. (In Canada, parents will want to read the Canadian government's *Cribs and Cradles Regulations*, published in the *Canada Gazette*.) When the Canadian Paediatric Society issued its sleep guidelines in 2004, it recognized that some parents will continue to take their babies to their beds. The CPS noted: "The recommended practice of independent sleeping will likely continue to be the preferred sleeping arrangement for infants in Canada, but a significant proportion of families will still elect to sleep together."

MOM'S THE WORD

"I'd like to see a campaign similar to the Back-to-Sleep campaign that teaches parents how to co-sleep safely with a child."

—*Marcelle, 33, mother of two*

PILLOW TALK

Sleep anthropologists like James McKenna, PhD, have noted that bed sharing with Mom seems to prevent babies from drifting into an overly deep sleep (a sleep that, for some babies, is so deep that they may fail to arouse themselves if they run into difficulty while they are sleeping). While some pediatric health authorities (most notably the American Academy of Pediatrics) don't agree with McKenna's argument when he makes the case that having mothers and babies sleep together is the best way to reduce the risk of SIDS, other leading health authorities—including the Canadian Pediatric Society—are open-minded enough to stress the need for more research in this area. The CPS's recently revised *Recommendations for Safe Sleeping Environments for Infants and Children* state: "Bed-sharing is different from solitary sleeping, especially for young infants, because of the complex . . . stimuli resulting from the close proximity of the parent. According to the arousal deficiency theory, mother and infant bed-sharing promotes infant arousals, which may be protective to infants at risk of SIDS. While bed-sharing, infants have less deep sleep than when they sleep alone. The responsiveness of the mother to infant arousals during bed-sharing might also be protective. These hypotheses need to be researched further."

Unfortunately, the AAP fell short of acknowledging this reality when it issued its new SIDS guidelines even though the number of parents who bed share on a full-time basis has increased significantly in recent years. The National Infant Sleep Position Study (NISP) (U.S.) found that the bed-sharing rate more than doubled during a seven-year period in the late 1990s. While 5.5 percent of babies were sleeping with their parents in 1993, that number had shot up to 12.8 percent by 2000.

Making Bed Sharing a Safer Option: Some Unofficial Tips and Suggestions

IN THE ABSENCE of any official safe bed-sharing recommendations, parents who bed share must exercise common sense and piece together sleep rules from various information sources. That can take a lot of work and may mean that important safety information falls between the cracks as parents make all-important sleep decisions for themselves and their babies. (As James J. McKenna and Thomas McDade recently noted in the medical journal *Paediatric Respiratory Reviews*, "While bedsharing can never be publicly recommended, due to its complexity, blanket recommendations against bedsharing and eliminating safety information for bedsharing families cannot be justified either.") If, after doing thorough research into the pros and cons of bed sharing and discussing this issue with your baby's health care provider, you decide to take your baby to bed with you for all or part of the night, consider these important safety points, which will make the sleeping environment as safe as possible:

Note: The material in this section should not be interpreted as permission or a recommendation that you consider bed sharing, but rather as information to be discussed with your baby's health care provider as part of your research.

- **Do your homework.** Research the bed-sharing issue carefully before you start bringing your baby to bed.

- **Strive to create the safest possible sleep environment for your baby.** While there are no guarantees with any sleep environment (babies die while sleeping in "perfectly safe" cribs, too), given that the current research seems to indicate that there are specific risks associated with bed sharing, do what you can to minimize those risks.

- **Remember that it is not safe for a baby to sleep on any soft sleeping surface.** If you sleep on a waterbed, a pillow-top mattress, or a mattress that is any less firm than a crib mattress, you cannot provide a sufficiently firm sleeping surface for an infant. And allowing a baby to sleep on a comforter, quilt, duvet, sheepskin or other type of thick blanket is dangerous. A baby may bury his face in the soft material and re-breathe exhaled air—something that can trigger a series of biological catastrophes that can result in a SIDS-related death.

- **Consider the rolling risk.** Babies are at risk of rolling out of beds that are raised off the floor. Even babies who are "too young" to know how to roll over have wriggled over to the edge of the bed or learned to roll on their own in bed one night. For this reason, you should never leave a baby alone on an adult bed.

- **Be aware of the risk of entrapment.** Babies can suffocate or strangle to death as a result of becoming trapped between the mattress and the bed frame, the bed and the wall, or the bed and another piece of furniture. If entrapment is a possibility, you need a sleeping alternative. Your bed should be at least a foot away from the closest piece of furniture to eliminate the risk of injury or strangulation in the event of a fall. That may mean packing your night tables away for now.

- **Guardrails designed for older children pose a significant threat to babies.** Guardrails designed for toddlers and preschoolers are not safe for babies because babies are much smaller and can become entrapped in these devices.

- **Remove all pillows and blankets from your bed while your baby is sleeping with you.** That means relying on your pajamas to keep yourself warm. You may want to dress in layers and wearing cozy sock-style slippers to bed. Elizabeth Pantley, author of *The No-Cry Sleep Solution*, suggests wearing an old turtleneck or t-shirt with a vertical cut from waist level to the neckline underneath your pajamas. Moms in cooler parts of the country may want to sleep in a full set of long underwear (including a long-sleeved undershirt) and some extra-warm socks. (Hit the local work wear store and buy the warmest outdoor wear they sell. If it's warm enough to keep hydro crews toasty warm while working in −30°F weather, hopefully it will keep you toasty warm when you're camping out in your bedroom with baby.)

- **Make sure that you're sufficiently tuned into your baby's sounds and movements in the night.** Brandy, a 30-year-old mother of two boys, ages five years and one-and-a-half years, says, "I think as a mother, I have always been extremely aware of where my baby is when in bed with me. If his breathing pattern changes, I am instantly awake. I sleep more lightly than I ever have and am acutely aware of his movements. I am not sure this would apply to a father sleeping in the bed with a baby. My husband, by his own choice, decided to sleep in the guest bed rather than accidentally bumping our son in the night. He felt he might not be as aware of our son as I was."

- **Three in a bed may be too many.** Some SIDS studies have pointed to the dangers of having a baby sleep between two large adult bodies, due to the risk of overlying. In this case, it may be safest to have Mom and baby sleep alone.

- **Young siblings don't make safe bedmates for babies.** According to most safety experts, it's not a good idea for very young babies to share a bed with siblings who are still quite young themselves. Not only are there SIDS-specific risks associated with bed sharing, most young children simply don't know what is and isn't safe for babies. You'd hate to check on your six-month-old one night, only to find that your three-year-old had piled stuffed animals all over the bed as a surprise. (A very dangerous surprise indeed.)

- **Don't bring your baby to bed if you're overtired, intoxicated, taking sleeping pills, or under the influence of a prescription or over-the-counter medication that makes you less responsive to your baby (e.g., cough medicine or cold capsules).** And ask your partner to sleep elsewhere (or pop your baby in the crib for the night) if your partner is extra groggy at bedtime.

- **If you smoke or your partner smokes, or you smoked during pregnancy, bedsharing is not a safe option.** Exposure to tobacco smoke is harmful to babies, period. A study conducted by researchers in New Zealand concluded that exposure to tobacco smoke before birth may affect a baby's ability to respond to the nightly mother-baby interactions that occur during bedsharing—something that can leave that baby at an increased risk of experiencing a SIDS-related death.

Safe Sleep Strategies: What Every Parent Needs to Know

ALL BABIES ARE at risk of SIDS, whether they share a bed or a room with their parents, or sleep across the hall in a room of their own. And, contrary to some myths, babies born to non-smoking, non-drug-using moms are not immune to SIDS, and bed sharing has not been proven to protect babies against SIDS. (According to the AAP and other leading health authorities, bed sharing actually increases the risk, but this point is still being hotly debated.) Sometimes parents get a little fatalistic when it comes to following the SIDS recommendations. They point out that, in the SIDS world, there are no guarantees. You can play by the SIDS rules and still lose a baby to SIDS. That may be true, but by following the latest SIDS recommendations, you can sleep a little easier at night, knowing that you've done everything within your control to reduce your baby's risk.

What follows is a summary of the key SIDS recommendations that were in place as this book was going to press. Because information in this field is constantly changing, you should consult with your baby's health care provider and visit the websites of leading pediatric health associations for updates on ongoing research and recommendations in this field. See Appendix A and B for some suggested links.

The back-sleeping position is the only sleeping position recommended by the American Academy of Pediatrics and the Canadian Paediatric Society. The single most important thing you can do to reduce your baby's risk of SIDS is to put your baby to bed on his back rather than on his tummy or his side (unless, of course, your baby's health care provider has specifically recommended otherwise). The SIDS rate dropped from 1.2 deaths per 1,000 in 1992 (two years before the Back-to-Sleep campaign was launched in the U.S.) to 0.56 deaths per 1,000 live births by 2001. SIDS researchers have calculated that 73.7 percent of all SIDS deaths could be prevented if all babies were put to bed in the back-sleeping position. While scientists are still trying to identify all of the reasons why the tummy-sleeping position poses a greater risk to babies, they've zeroed in on one of the key factors: When babies sleep in this position, they tend to spend a significant percentage of their sleeping time in the face-down position. This effect is particularly pronounced if they happen to be sleeping on soft bedding (as opposed to a firmer surface) or if their faces feel cold (they may

PILLOW TALK

Researchers still don't fully understand all of the causes of SIDS, but they suspect that a combination of factors are at work. One highly respected theory, the triple-risk model for SIDS, argues that there may be three key pieces to the SIDS puzzle.

Researchers believe that babies who succumb to SIDS may have some sort of malformation or developmental delay with the part of the brain stem that is responsible for arousing the baby when a problem occurs during sleep (the first part of the puzzle). This brain stem malfunction becomes more of an issue if a problem occurs during a period of infant development when that baby is particularly vulnerable (the second piece of the puzzle). And exposing an infant to additional external risks (e.g., bedding in the crib, tobacco smoke, putting the baby to bed in the tummy-sleeping position) only adds to the risk (the third piece of the puzzle). If all these factors converge, you are looking at a maximum risk situation—the so-called triple-risk scenario. As a parent, you want to do what you can to minimize the risk factors over which you have some control—those that are associated with the third piece of the puzzle.

---

tend to burrow their face into the bedding). When babies sleep in this position, they breathe greater quantities of stale air, which they have already breathed in before and that therefore contains higher quantities of carbon dioxide and lower quantities of oxygen. If a baby does not pick up on the fact that he is not getting the correct amount of oxygen by repositioning himself or altering his rate of breathing, a dangerous cycle can begin and that baby can eventually run into trouble and become overheated. Becoming overheated can, in turn, increase the risk that the baby won't be able to arouse himself as he breathes in more and more stale air.

The tummy-sleeping position may also pose a risk to babies due to:

- an increased risk of suffocation, particularly in babies ages 13 to 24 weeks, the peak risk period for SIDS. Babies this age are able to move their heads around better than younger babies, but they may not necessarily be able to get themselves out of a potentially deadly situation in their sleep: e.g., burying their face in a soft mattress or a blanket or being pressed up against a person who hasn't noticed that the baby is in trouble (e.g., an intoxicated or overtired parent).

- the greater number of episodes of quiet sleep (the deeper type of sleep, which may not necessarily be the safest type of sleep for young babies) that occur when babies sleep in this position.

- the longer periods of sleep with fewer arousals when babies sleep in this position (again, not necessarily the healthiest pattern for babies, given that waking frequently may be a survival mechanism during the early months of life); and

- the fact that the baby can't regulate his body temperature as effectively while sleeping in this position as he can when he is in the back-sleeping position, which increases the risk for over-heating, a major SIDS risk factor. The risk of overheating will be increased if the baby's sleep environment is too warm, the baby is dressed too warmly, or the baby has an illness or a fever.

So, given that leading health authorities have been urging parents to use the back-sleeping position for their babies for more than a decade, why would some parents deliberately put their babies to bed in the tummy-sleeping position, something that dramatically increases their babies' risk of a SIDS death? (A recent article in *The New York Times* noted that 42 percent of the 24,000 respondents to a BabyCenter.com poll indicated that they were using the tummy-sleeping position for their babies. And Sarah Gilbert, an editor at BloggingBaby.com, stated in the same article that she had been using the stomach-sleeping position for her children and that "The Web consensus is that it is okay to do so.")

 PILLOW TALK

The fact that babies drool, spit up, and otherwise dampen the bedding around their faces may also help to explain why babies run into more trouble when they sleep on their tummies (and for much of their sleeping time the face-down position). Wet bedding tends to cling to a baby's face more than dry bedding, something that increases the likelihood of stale air pooling around the baby's face.

 PILLOW TALK

Research has shown that babies who are used to sleeping on their backs but who are suddenly placed in bed on their sides or their tummies face a very high risk of SIDS. (This risk factor jumps from the standard incidence rate of 0.56 deaths per 1,000 live births to 6.9 per 1,000 for the side-lying position and 8.2 for the tummy-sleeping position.) This is why the American Academy of Pediatrics stresses the importance of "every caregiver using the back sleep position during every sleep period."

Note: Some parents worry about positional plagiocephaly (a flat spot that can develop at the back of your baby's head as a result of spending so much time lying on his back). You can reduce the risk of this becoming a problem by giving your baby plenty of tummy time while you play with him on the floor and cuddle time while you hold him in an upright position in your lap.

And don't keep your baby in a car-seat carrier, stroller, or infant seat for too many hours of the day, which places pressure on the same part of your baby's head that receives pressure as when your baby is on his back.

Some parents are choosing to disregard the "back-to-sleep" message because their babies are sleeping more soundly and for longer stretches—and hence the parents themselves are getting more sleep—when their babies use the tummy-sleeping position. Unfortunately, more sleep for Mom and Dad comes with a potentially deadly price—an increased risk that the baby will succumb to SIDS. So are parents truly left with this terrible choice: Be sleep deprived forever or put your baby to bed in a riskier sleeping position because you're so desperate to get a decent night's sleep?

What *The New York Times* article failed to point out is that there is some sensible middle ground to be staked out. You can make the back-sleeping position more baby-friendly by swaddling your newborn (just be cautious about loose wraps and the risk of overheating), by using soothing sounds to help lull him to sleep, by using motion to encourage your baby to fall asleep until he develops his own repertoire of self-soothing skills, and so on. (See Chapter 6 for more baby-soothing tips and techniques.) You can also ask other people in your life to support you through this difficult and exhausting phase of parenthood. The situation doesn't have to be

PILLOW TALK

The American Academy of Pediatrics does not recommend the use of sleep positioners, sleep wedges, and other baby sleep products that are designed to ensure that babies remain in a particular sleeping position. They also suggest that parents steer clear of products that promise to help reduce the risk that a baby will rebreathe stale air. None of these products have been tested adequately to prove their safety or their effectiveness, according to the AAP.

---

nearly as black or white as the article made it appear. One final point: Part of being a parent is making decisions that are in your child's best interest, but that your child might not necessarily like. Your baby might not like being in a car seat, but you can't give your baby the option of riding around town in your arms instead. Likewise, your baby might not like sleeping on his back, but if that's the safest position for him (as it is for the vast majority of babies), that's the position you should be laying him down in until he's old enough to make up his mind for himself. (Once your baby can roll over on his own, you can stop sweating about your baby's sleep position. There's no need to flip him back to the back-sleeping position.)

- **Place your baby to sleep on a firm sleeping surface.** It's not safe for babies to sleep on quilts, comforters, sheepskins, or pillows. A firm crib mattress covered by a crib sheet is the recommended sleeping surface for babies.

- **Be aware of the risk posed by bedding.** Don't use comforters, pillows, or other bedding to create a bed on the floor or to pad the area around a crib mattress that has been placed on the floor (something you may be tempted to do if you're visiting friends or relatives). And don't add blankets to your baby's crib to keep your baby cozy while the air conditioner cools the rest of the family off on a hot summer day. According to the Canadian Foundation for the Study of Infant Deaths, both scenarios put babies at risk.

- **Ensure that your baby's crib or cradle complies with current safety standards.** The mattress should fit tightly (if you can squeeze more than two fingers between the frame and the mattress, the mattress is too loose) and the crib sheets should be equally snug-fitting. Ensure that they'll remain flat and in place no matter how much your baby wriggles around in her sleep. Plastic mattress covers should not be used on babies' mattresses. They pose a suffocation risk.

- **Give careful thought to where you place your baby's crib.** Make sure it's away from windows, window blinds, cords, and draperies (to eliminate the risks of falls and strangulation). And keep the crib out of direct sunlight to reduce the risk of your baby becoming overheated during naptime.

- **Check your baby's crib regularly for signs of wear and tear.** Ensure that there aren't any loose parts or sharp or missing pieces.

- **Continue to lower the crib mattress as your baby grows.** You don't want your baby to tumble out once she learns how to pull herself into an upright position.

- **Keep soft objects—including loose bedding, stuffed toys, and comforters—out of your baby's crib.** Using soft bedding in your baby's crib increases your baby's SIDS risk by 10 times. Using soft bedding and placing your baby to bed in the tummy-sleeping position increases the risk by 42 times.

- **Avoid pillow-like bumper pads.** According to the American Academy of Pediatrics, pillow-like bumper pads are not recommended due to the risk of rebreathing. You may want to take a pass on bumper pads, period. The slightly firmer style that the AAP recommends as an alternative becomes a hazard as soon as your baby is able to stand. If they're firm enough to stand up on, a baby who's determined to make a crib breakout can climb on top of them and tumble head first out of the crib. If you do decide to use them, keep an eye on your baby's ever-changing abilities and think about removing them if it looks like your newly standing baby is going to use them to make a "jail break."

CRIB NOTES

Don't forget to check the safety of the cribs that your baby sleeps in when your family is away from home. A study conducted by the National SAFE KIDS Campaign in 2000 found unsafe cribs and playpens in 80 percent of the U.S. hotels and motels it visited. And, of course, hotel and motels aren't the only sources of unsafe cribs for families on the move: Well-meaning friends and relatives may produce cribs that haven't been considered safe for well over 20 years, or they may offer your baby an air mattress, foam mattress, soft mattress, or some loose bedding to sleep on. None of these are safe sleep options for babies. Finally, if you're bringing a portable crib with you, make sure that the locking devices on the portable crib are securely locked before you place your baby in the crib. Babies have been suffocated when portable cribs have collapsed on them while they were asleep. There have been a number of recalls on portable cribs manufactured during the 1990s. To find out if the crib your child is sleeping in is affected, and to find out more about crib safety in general, visit the U.S. Consumer Product Safety Commission website at www.cpsc.gov. Canadian parents can find out about Canadian crib recalls by visiting the Health Canada website (Consumer Product Safety—Children's Products): www.hc-sc.gc.ca/cps-spc/index_e.html.

• **If you want to tuck your baby in with a blanket, tuck the blanket around the crib mattress so that the amount of exposed blanket only reaches the level of your baby's chest.** This will make it more difficult for your baby to get her face under the blanket, which poses a risk due to rebreathing.

• **Know the facts about sleep sacks before you decide if they are the best option for your baby.** The Canadian Foundation for the Study of Infant Deaths (CFSID) specifically advises against the use of "sleep sacks" (a garment that looks like a combination sleeper and sleeping bag). According to the CFSID, loose-fitting sleep sacks may pose the same kind of risk to a baby as traditional bedding if the baby is able to wriggle inside the sleep sack so that his face ends up being covered by the sleep sack. The risk is particularly high for a baby under 10 lbs. A safer alternative, according to the CFSID, is to swaddle your baby in a lightweight cotton receiving blanket. If you choose to swaddle your baby, don't swaddle the baby too tightly and make sure that your baby's head remains uncovered (to avoid over-heating your baby). Child health advocates have raised a couple of other health and safety concerns related to the use of sleep sacks:

o   Parents tend to overdress their babies when they are using sleep sacks, something which can lead to overheating.

o   Sleep sacks are typically classified as bedding rather than as sleepwear, which means that they don't have to meet the same highly rigorous standards for flammability that apply to sleepwear.

o   If a sleep sac starts to burn, hot air can pool within the sleep sack, causing more severe burns and tissue damage than the actual flames.

Note: The U.S.-based organization First Candle/SIDS Alliance has endorsed one particular brand of "wearable blanket" (that organization's preferred term for this type of product). The product in question—the Halo Sleep Sack—complies with U.S. Consumer Product Safety Commission standards for flammability. The product was also designed with a sleeveless, sack-like design to keep fabric away from baby's face and head. See www.halosleep.com for more information about this product.

• **Don't let your baby nap in a car seat or infant seat carrier unless you are providing direct supervision.** If a baby tumbles forward in one of these products, an upper airway obstruction can occur as a result of pressure from the harness straps. That's why safety experts (and even the manufacturers of these products) say that you should place your baby in a car seat or infant seat carrier only when you are right there to keep an eye on your baby. (That means you have to stay awake, something that's easier said than done some days!)

• **Put baby to bed with a pacifier.** The AAP is now recommend-ing that parents offer babies a pacifier at bedtime. There appears to be some sort of protective effect associated with pacifier use. SIDS researchers suspect that babies who use pacifiers may not sleep as deeply as other babies. (Once again, lighter, more active sleep appears to be healthier than deeper, quieter sleep for young babies.) Here are the important tips to bear in mind if you decide to follow these recommendations (which, by the way, generated just as much controversy as the co-sleeping debate).

- **Hold off on introducing a pacifier until your baby is one month of age.** This will help to ensure that breast-feeding is firmly established and minimize the risk of nipple confusion (having your baby confuse the techniques used to get milk out of a breast and the sucking motion required to suck on a pacifier).

- **Give your baby the pacifier when she goes to bed, but do not reinsert the pacifier once your baby has fallen asleep.** (That's the AAP talking, not me.) Given what we know about sleep associations—how babies like to recreate their falling-asleep sleep environment when they wake up in the middle of the night—it will be interesting to see how this plays out in the real world as millions of parents implement this recommendation—just how many millions of parents end up scrambling for missing pacifiers in the night.

- **Don't use a ribbon to keep your baby's pacifier in place all night.** Your baby's hands, fingers, or neck could become entangled in the ribbon. Likewise, don't try to prop the pacifier in place with a receiving blanket or other object. Keep your baby's face clear of bedding and other soft objects while she's sleeping to keep her from rebreathing stale air.

- **Don't coat your baby's pacifier in anything sweet.** Not only is this a bad habit to get into, babies aren't ready for anything other than breast milk or infant formula when they are very young. Giving a young baby honey can even result in botulism. Besides, children get introduced to sweets soon enough. Why jump the gun?

- **Check your baby's pacifier for signs of wear and tear, and replace it often.** Pacifiers deteriorate over time, and babies can choke if they swallow pacifier pieces.

- **Keep your baby's sleeping environment cool (but not cold).** Aim for a comfortable temperature in the range of 68°F–72°F (20°C–22°C). Be particularly careful not to crank up the heat too high during the cooler times of the year. Babies can easily become overheated because they do not have the ability to regulate their own body temperatures during the early months of life. You can check your baby's body temperature by putting your hand on her bare tummy or on the back of her neck to see if she feels sweaty or too warm.

- **Don't nap on the couch or in an armchair while you're holding your baby.** She could roll off the couch and fall to the floor while you are sleeping or she could become entrapped in the couch or armchair and possibly suffocate.

- **Don't keep this important safety information to yourself.** Ensure that everyone who takes care of your baby—child-care providers, casual babysitters, friends, relatives, and the neighbor who offers to stay with your baby—is fully up-to-sleep on safe sleeping practices, particularly the importance of placing babies to sleep on their backs. One in five SIDS deaths occurs while babies are in the care of someone other than the parents.

Other Tips on Providing Your Baby with a Safe Sleeping Environment

THE RISKS WE'VE been focusing up to this point in the chapter specifically relate to sudden infant death syndrome. Now let's look at some of the other important issues you need to think about to provide a safe sleeping environment for your baby, whether your baby is sharing your room or not.

- **Toys and mobiles:** Remove any toys and mobiles that are strung across your child's crib as soon as your baby is able to push himself up on his hands and knees.

- **Infant sleepwear:** Make sure your baby sleeps in flame-resistant sleepwear. Look for styles that hug her body tightly (e.g., sleepers) rather than loose-fitting nightgowns. And never allow your baby to wear a hat to bed.

- **Baby gates:** Install wall-mounted baby gates at the top (and, if necessary, at the bottom) of each set of stairs. Once your baby is able to escape her room, you need to make sure she can't wander out of her room and fall down the stairs. Stairs are responsible for a large proportion of falls involving young children. You'll also want to block off the bathroom, either by installing another baby gate or by closing the bathroom door. (Once your baby reaches the toddler stage and needs to use the bathroom in the night, you'll need to toddler proof the bathroom thoroughly, but, for now, keeping her out of the bathroom, period, is probably the best solution.)

- **Door alarms:** Consider installing a door alarm so that you'll know if the front door opens in the night. You don't want your little one to find his way outside in the night.

- **Pets:** Keep pets out of your baby's sleeping area. "I just recently gave my girlfriend a suggestion about dealing with all the cats in her house," says Sonya, 37, mother of two boys, ages one and three. "She has now put up a screen door (a fancy one) on the baby's room to keep them out ... and out of the crib."

Location, Location, Location ...

THERE'S NO SUCH thing as a one-size-fits-all sleeping arrangement when it comes to babies. Some parents like to have their babies in the same room so that they can take care of their babies' needs quickly and easily in the middle of the night. (And given the latest research showing that room sharing may help to protect babies from SIDS, it seems likely that some parents who might not have considered room sharing otherwise will give this option a closer look.) Other parents find it works better for them to have baby sleeping in her own bedroom. The parents may be so tuned into each baby snuffle and snort that they simply can't get the rest they need. (Of course, room sharing doesn't have to be an all-or-nothing proposition. If you or your partner are getting particularly exhausted, you might take turns bunking out in the guest room—or in what will some day be the baby's bedroom—so that one of you can catch up on your sleep while the other is on "baby patrol." You sometimes have to get creative when it comes to sleep. See Table 5.1 for a quick summary of the key pros and cons of the various sleep options.)

It's important to talk through the various sleep options with your partner before your baby arrives and to come up with a rough game plan as to where everyone will sleep and for how long. Realize, however, that your thoughts and ideas about sleep may change once you're dealing with the reality of nighttime parenting as opposed to just the theory. And don't be surprised if you have to experiment a little to find a sleep solution that will work for you and your baby, say parents who've been there—and if you find yourself considering some possibilities that hadn't occurred to you before nighttime parenting went from being an abstract concept to a fact of daily life.

"Before we had kids, I really thought babies belonged in their own cribs in their own rooms," says Dani, 35, the mother of two boys, ages three years and 17 months. "When I was about 8½ months pregnant with my first, one day I suddenly had to have a bedside cradle. I looked into Moses baskets and bassinets and playpens, but finally fell in love with an old-fashioned-looking wooden cradle from IKEA. My eldest slept in it until he was six months, and when my second son was born, he slept in it so long we had to use a shoehorn to cram him into it at night. ... He was eight months before I finally put him down in a crib in his own room."

"I swore she would never sleep in the bed because I was worried about safety," recalls Jodi, 34, mother of 14-month-old Jayne. "And then, the first night home, I couldn't stand to be apart (even in the same room, in her bassinet) so we put her in the bed. That lasted two nights. None of us could sleep. I would hear her breathing and it would keep me up all night. She stayed in her bassinet in our room for three months. I only put her in her own room when she got too big for the bassinet."

"For the first year, my daughter and I slept in another room most nights," recalls Marla, 36, mother of 16-month-old Josephine. "I found it easier to manage her and my insomnia, and thought it let my sole-provider husband sleep better. He missed

Table 5.1

The Pros and Cons of Various Baby Sleep Arrangements

Baby's Sleeping Arrangement	Pros	Cons
Room sharing (baby sleeps in a crib or cradle in your room)	You get to have your baby nearby, but you don't have to lose sleep worrying about some of the risks associated with bed sharing. You can listen for those reassuring baby noises in the middle of the night and you don't have to walk very far to pick up your baby come feeding time.	Cribs (and some cradles) take up a lot of space, so unless you have an extra-spacious room, you may find that sharing your room with a baby cramps your style—literally. Middle-of-the-night feedings and diaper changes can't help but become a family affair when you're sharing a room with your baby, which may make getting a good night's sleep a bit of a struggle for the parent who has to get up early the next morning to head off to work. If the other parent starts missing out on a lot of sleep, having one of you spend some nights in a spare bedroom may be the solution.
Bed sharing (baby sleeps in your bed)	You may find it comforting to have your baby so close by, and you may find that sharing your bed with your baby helps you to tune in to her rhythms and needs. It's easier to breast-feed your baby in the night if baby's right beside you in bed. Consequently, you may be encouraged to breast-feed longer. (Moms who sleep with their babies typically breast-feed three times as long as other moms.)	You'll have to rule out this option if you're unable to provide a safe sleeping arrangement for baby: a firm, flat mattress that is free of pillows and bedding. You'll also need to consider some related safety issues: where baby will sleep on nights when you or your partner have consumed alcohol or medications that may make you a little extra groggy.

	Some moms report that both they and their babies get more sleep when they share a bed. Not everyone has this experience, however. Some moms (and dads!) find that the quality of their own sleep suffers when they sleep with a baby. This may seem like the only workable solution to parenting a baby who wants to be physically close to Mom 24/7.	If you're currently bed sharing with a toddler or pre-schooler, you'll have to rethink this option. It's not safe for young siblings to share a bed with a baby. This is not a safe option if you or your partner smoke or if you smoked while you were pregnant.
Bed sharing with baby sleeping in a sidecar attached to your bed (a sidecar is sometimes called a co-sleeper)	A sidecar bed (a separate baby bed that attaches to the side of the parents' bed) allows you to sleep with your baby without having to worry as much about rolling over on top of baby while you are asleep. Your baby is sleeping right beside you, which makes breast-feeding very convenient.	The American and Canadian governments have yet to develop safety standards regulating sidecars and similar products (e.g., co-sleepers that look like change pads and that are placed in the middle of the parents' bed). A sidecar bed takes up a fair bit of space, so you'll need to have a decent-sized bedroom. Like a bassinet or a baby basket, a sidecar is an extra piece of baby equipment that you'll be using for only a relatively short time.
Baby sleeps in a crib in her own room	Baby gets used to her bedroom right from day one. You don't have to worry about getting woken up at 3:00 a.m. by every little snuffle and snort (in theory). You and your partner don't have to sublet your space with another family member, something that could potentially cramp your sexual style. (Many room-sharing and bed-sharing parents insist that this is a non-issue if you can take your sexual imagination out of the bed or the bedroom, and that being forced to be a little more creative can do great things for your sex life.)	You may find it hard to sleep without hearing all those reassuring snuffles and snorts. In fact, you may be so eager to hear the reassuring sounds of your baby's breathing that you crank the baby monitor up so loud that it sounds like you've got an obscene phone caller on speaker phone. (So much for getting any sleep.) You may also find yourself walking across the hall to do middle-of-the-night baby checks, even if your baby is sleeping soundly, simply because she's out of eyeshot.

me, and finally said that we really needed to transition her to her crib so that we could be together again—that sleeping in the same bed was one of the things he liked best about marriage. His plain request and my already mounting guilt made it easier to initiate the transition, as did my need to sleep more soundly. We never disagreed, but both knew when it was time to make some changes. I'm sure he would have been happier if she had been sleeping in her crib from the start, but as her nighttime caregiver, and with my own needs to be met, that was what I felt I needed to do."

Solutions Central—The Last Word

Your family's sleep needs will continue to evolve as your child moves from stage to stage—from a tiny newborn who is nursing around the clock to a more independent older baby who is able to sleep for five hours or longer at nighttime to a busy toddler to an inquisitive preschooler. You'll find out about the types of sleep challenges that your child may encounter at each age and stage in the remaining chapters of this book.

CHAPTER 6

The Real-World Guide to Solving Your Baby's Sleep Problems

Babies are babies. They need to be cared for. On the other hand, there does come a time when enough is enough, but that's an individual choice. Sleep problems are only sleep problems when you, the parent, think you have a problem sleeper.
—JENNIFER, 28, MOTHER OF ONE

THERE'S NO DOUBT about it. Sleep problems are definitely in the eyes of the beholder. But there tends to be a point in every sleep-deprived parent's life when a moment of truth is reached. Suddenly there's a certain amount of urgency to the situation: you've *got* to figure out a way to solve your baby's sleep problems. "For a long time during those sleepless months, I told myself that it was just a phase—that it would pass—and that things would get better in time," recalls Wendy, 30, mother of 13-month-old Thomas. "Then I realized that I needed to take action—that the problem wasn't going to go away on its own and that I needed to do something to make the situation better."

Hush, Little Baby ...

IT'S NO WONDER that parents in every culture have produced their own repertoire of lullabies. Parents have always played an active role in soothing their little ones to sleep. This section offers parent-proven strategies for managing the major types of baby sleep problems—everything from getting baby to go to sleep to getting baby to stay asleep to getting baby to stay in bed until a decent hour of the morning.

Back to Sleep

"My three-week-old hates sleeping on her back, but I know this is the safest sleeping position for babies. What can I do to help my baby to adjust to the back-sleeping position?" Start out by experimenting with some of the baby-soothing techniques listed in Table 6.1, particularly swaddling. The September 2002 issue of *The Journal of Pediatrics* concluded that infants may be happier about sleeping on their backs if they are swaddled. If those techniques don't prove effective, ask yourself whether back-sleeping is really the key issue. Perhaps your baby has a beef with her sleeping environment. Sometimes newborns are less than thrilled with the idea of sleeping in the wide-open expanse of a crib after spending many months in the much cozier quarters of the womb. The solution? See if she'd be happier in a cradle or bassinet. If she's still extremely unhappy sleeping on her back, talk to your health care provider. It's possible that something else is bothering her, like gastroesophageal reflux (GER). (See the information on GER at the end of this chapter.)

PILLOW TALK

Rocking your baby to sleep in a mechanical swing can trigger a deadly attack by family dogs. The back-and-forth motion of baby swings may trigger a dog's natural instinct to chase prey, according to a report presented at the 2005 meeting of the *American Academy of Forensic Sciences*. Get your pet used to the baby swing before you use it with your baby. Place a doll in it. And never leave your pet and your baby unsupervised.

"My baby is colicky. His sleep patterns aren't like the sleep patterns of other babies. What can I do to reduce the amount of crying and help my baby sleep better?" Colicky babies aren't about to settle down for a snooze, no matter how hard you try to soothe them. They're pretty much inconsolable, and you may be feeling that way yourself some days, too. (Colic is crying that lasts for more than three hours a day, that occurs more than three days a week, and that lasts for longer than three weeks in an infant who is otherwise well fed and healthy.) Colic occurs in between 5 percent and 25 percent of babies. It reaches its peaks at around six weeks of age and most babies will outgrow colic by age four months. Techniques to reduce the amount of crying in colicky babies include the following:

- Carrying babies around even when they aren't crying (so that they don't need to cry in order to signal a need to be held).

- Offering the breast and/or a pacifier for comfort.

- Eliminating milk products, eggs, wheat, and nuts from your diet if you're breast-feeding. According to an article in the August 14, 2004 issue of the *American Family Physician*, these are the only maternal dietary changes that have been scientifically proven to make a difference. That doesn't mean that you shouldn't try eliminating other foods from your diet to see if they make a difference for your baby. You just don't want to end up on starvation rations or the blandest diet imaginable for no good reason.

- If you're formula-feeding, talk to your baby's health care provider before switching your baby from one infant formula to another. Colicky babies tend to have extra-sensitive tummies and playing formula roulette may cause your baby unnecessary misery. It's also not a good idea to switch from cow's milk-based formula to a soy-based formula without discussing this first with your baby's health care provider. Babies can develop allergies to soy and American Academy of Pediatrics' Committee on Nutrition does not recommend changing to soy formula in order to treat colic. Unless your baby is spitting up a lot or having

Table 6.1

Baby-Soothing Techniques: Your Best Bets

Baby-Soothing Technique	How It Works	Why It Helps	Other Things You Need to Know
Nurse your baby.	Offer the breast for comfort as well as nutrition.	Sucking is soothing to babies, and then there's that added benefit of being nestled in the arms of someone you love.	Breast-feeding is comforting to mothers as well as baby, thanks to the release of the breast-feeding hormones oxytocin, prolactin, and cholesystokinin, so you get some soothing, too.
Swaddle your baby.	Or check out Appendix B for a link to an online video clip featuring step-by-step instructions for swaddling your baby—specifically how to keep your baby from becoming unswaddled when you pick her up.	Babies are used to being in tight quarters. Real estate is rather cramped inside the womb! Many young babies find it comforting to be swaddled. Perhaps it reminds them of life before birth. Swaddling newborns and young babies with their arms down makes it less likely that they will startle themselves awake.	Swaddling is recommended only until babies become so active that they can unswaddle themselves. It's not safe to put a baby to bed with loose bedding, so the swaddle should fit your baby snugly but not so tightly as to be overly constraining or uncomfortable. Don't allow your baby to become overheated in hot weather. Overheating is a key risk factor for sudden infant death syndrome. See Chapter 5. Sometimes when newborns are tightly swaddled, they don't ask to eat as often, which

		can contribute to inadequate weight gain, so be careful how tightly your baby is swaddled.
Give your baby the chance to get naked.	Make sure that the room is warm enough and then take off all of your baby's garments, diaper and all.	Most—but not all—babies enjoy the sensation of being naked. Some find it upsetting. Read your baby's cues and you'll soon figure out whether your baby belongs to the nudist camp or the put-my-clothes-back-on please camp.	You may want to toss an oversized beach towel on the carpet in the area where your baby will be enjoying her bare bum time. That way, if nature happens to call while she's *au naturel*, your carpet won't be any the worse for wear.
Soothe your baby with sound.	Babies tend to respond very well to five basic types of sounds: • soothing sounds (a parent's lullaby, other soothing music) • white noise (vacuum cleaner sounds, static on the radio, white noise CDs/machines) • swishing sounds (your dish-washer or washing machine) • rhythmic sounds (a clock or metronome) • shush-ing sounds	Babies find these sounds soothing. The swishing sounds and the rhythmic ticking sounds are apparently remi-niscent of the sounds babies heard while they were in the womb. Perhaps this explains why parents have been successful at gently shush-ing their babies to sleep for centuries.	Rather than burning out all your household appliances, record the sounds of your baby's favorite symphony of household noises so that you can play them back time and time again, take your soothing sounds CD with you to Grandma's house, and so on.

continued on p. 164

Baby-Soothing Technique	How It Works	Why It Helps	Other Things You Need to Know
Soothe your baby with a combination of sound and vibrations.	As William Sears has pointed out, the "fathering down" technique of having a father talk or sing lullabies to his baby while his baby's head is nestled under his chin can be very effective.	The deeper vibrations of the male vocal cords can be highly effective at soothing babies to sleep.	This technique can be combined with rocking and swaying or it can be done in a sitting or standing position, whatever works best for father and baby.
Use the side-lying hold.	You can hold your baby in a side-lying position in your arms or in your lap. If your baby is a big fan of movement, as many babies are, you can gently sway him. You may find it easier to hold him in this position if he's swaddled.	Your baby is likely to find this position soothing because this was the position he spent a lot of his time in before birth. It also prevents your baby from repeatedly startling into wakefulness, in part because it helps to suppress the "falling" sensation that newborns experience when they "startle" while they are on their backs.	While babies find it soothing to be on their sides, *the side-lying position is not a safe sleeping position for babies.* (See Chapter 5.) That's why many parents give their babies some side-lying time during their fussy, wakeful times in the evenings. *Tip:* You can carry your sleeping newborn over to her crib if she has drifted off to sleep in the side-lying position on your lap and then gently ease her on to her back as you tuck her in. *Just remember: You want to make sure that your baby is sleeping on her back before you say goodnight.*

| Get your baby in motion. | Swinging, swaying, and rocking motions soothe most babies. Cradle your baby in your arms or carry your baby in a sling or front pack-style baby carrier and move your body in a gentle, swinging motion. Or you can pop baby into the stroller and take a walk around the block. If she loves—rather than loathes—her car seat, you can try soothing her to sleep with a car ride. (As an added bonus, you get to listen to the radio, your favorite music, or perhaps even a book on CD!) | Before birth, babies are often rocked to sleep by the swaying motions of their mothers' bodies. After birth, they continue to respond to this familiar and comforting motion. Some babies respond extremely positively to being carried around (particularly babies who may have been overstimulated during a busy day and who want some wind-down time in the arms of a loving parent). | Not all babies are big fans of baby swings, so you may want to test-drive a swing in a store or at a friend's house before you buy your own. Here are some other important points to bear in mind if you decide to purchase a baby swing or other mechanical swinging device:

You don't want your baby to always associate falling asleep with being in motion. Some ways to get around this problem are to use a swing to lull your baby to sleep only while your baby is a newborn, or limit its use to a particular time of day (e.g., fussy period in evening), or to stop the swing from swinging once your baby has fallen asleep (as opposed to constantly winding it up after he has fallen asleep). Because your baby needs to be supervised in his swing, you shouldn't be using the swing for nighttime sleep anyway unless you were planning to stay wide-eyed and awake all night long, of course! |

continued on p. 166

Baby-Soothing Technique	How It Works	Why It Helps	Other Things You Need to Know
Soothe your baby with your unique scent.	Wrap one of your baby's bottom crib sheets around you when you go to bed at night so that it can pick up some of your scent and then make his crib up with this bottom sheet the next time it needs to be changed. You may want to build up a stockpile of pre-scented crib sheets so that you always have a spare.	Your baby finds your scent familiar and soothing. He's been getting used to your unique fragrance since before he was born.	While it's a great idea to transfer your scent to sheets and other items, don't put your baby at risk by allowing him to sleep with a t-shirt or other item of clothing that could end up covering his face while he sleeps. (See Chapter 5 for more on safe sleep guidelines.)
That loving touch.	Sometimes it's possible to soothe a half-awake baby back to sleep or to calm a fussy baby by gently rubbing your baby's head or chest. Your reassuring touch says, "It's okay, baby! I'm right here."	As your baby starts to settle and drift back to sleep, slowly remove one or both of your hands. Watch your baby's reactions to see if she's ready to go back to sleep on her own. If she begins to stir again when you start to move away, put one hand back on your baby again and give her a few minutes longer to settle into a deeper stage of sleep.	Try to remain calm and patient while you're stroking your baby. If you're feeling frustrated with your baby, ask someone to give you a break, or put your baby in her crib and give yourself a brief break from parenting.

| Warm your baby's bed. | Preheat baby's bed with a hot water bottle filled with warm water. Remove it before your baby goes to bed and remember to check the area where your baby will be sleeping to make sure it's not too hot. Flannel sheets will hold the heat better than cotton sheets. | Your baby is less likely to notice the transition from your arms to his bed if the temperature shift is less dramatic. | Never put a baby to bed with a hot water bottle due to the danger of overheating and the risk of potential suffocation. And never use an electric heating pad with a baby. |
| Try infant massage. | A University of Miami study concluded that infant massage can encourage newborns to sleep better. The babies' sleep patterns were better organized and they experienced fewer night wakings. The babies were also calmer, happier, and less fussy. Massage can help to aid in digestion, which makes it easier for babies to relax and sleep, and promotes weight gain and growth. | Not only is infant massage effective at calming babies, it is soothing to parents. In fact, a U.K. study, reported in the *Journal of Affective Disorders* in 2001, has shown that infant massage can be helpful in the treatment of postpartum depression by promoting a healthy bond between mother and baby. | It's a good idea to take a weekend course in infant massage so that you can have an experienced instructor teach you the basic techniques. |

continued on p. 168

Baby-Soothing Technique	How It Works	Why It Helps	Other Things You Need to Know
Offer your baby a pacifier.	Some babies would gladly nurse all day long, if given the opportunity. These are the ones who, when newborns, start rooting for a breast the moment you hold them on any angle that even comes close to approaching the horizontal position!	Give your baby the pacifier when she goes to bed, but do not reinsert the pacifier once your baby has fallen asleep.	The American Academy of Pediatrics recommends that you hold off on introducing a pacifier until your baby is four weeks old, to ensure that breast-feeding is well established and minimize the risk of nipple confusion (having your baby confuse the techniques used to get milk out of a breast and the sucking motion required to suck on a pacifier). See Chapter 5 for some other important health and safety information on pacifier use.
Pat your baby's back.	Pat your baby's back when she is propped over your shoulder, sitting on your knee, or in a side-lying position in her crib or bassinet (just remember to roll her onto her back when she's ready to go to sleep for safety reasons).	Most babies find it very soothing to have their backs patted in a gentle, repetitive motion.	There's no need to thump your baby on her back. A gentle pat will do.

| Introduce a lovey, a comfort object/ transitional object. | Offer your child a lovey, an object that can comfort your baby when you're not around. | Start making the lovey part of your baby's pre-bedtime routine. You might place the lovey between the two of you during your pre-bedtime cuddle, for example, and then encourage her to take it to bed with her. | There's still a lot of debate about the correct timing for introducing a lovey. Some experts say that loveys should be reserved for the toddler years, when there's less danger of a stuffed animal or blanket accidentally covering baby's face. Others say it's okay to introduce a small stuffed animal and a miniature blanket once your baby is old enough to roll around freely in the crib. If you have concerns about the safety of loveys, talk to your child's health care provider about when to introduce one. If you introduce one too early, there may be some key safety considerations to think about. If you wait too long, your child may be less willing to accept one. |

extremely loose or bloody stools, your baby's health care provider is likely to recommend that you stick with your baby's original infant formula.

- Responding to crying quickly (so that the baby doesn't become too upset).

- Using gentle rocking or white noise to soothe the baby, and avoiding overstimulation (colicky babies tend to be very sensitive to stimulation).

- Using a colic hold that puts pressure on the baby's abdomen (hold your baby so that he is lying across your forearm with his tummy down, with your hand supporting his chest).

- Emphasizing the difference between day and night (see Chapters 3, 4, and 5).

- Over-the-counter anti-colic products have not been scientifically proven to reduce symptoms of colic. A prescription medication that was used in the past to treat colic is no longer available for babies under age six months because of reports of apnea (episodes when breathing stopped) and deaths.

Coping tips for you:

- Don't beat yourself up or convince yourself that you're doing something wrong because your baby is colicky. Colic happens.

- Take breaks from your baby. If friends and family members offer to step in and give you a break, let them. And if you are at home alone with your baby and you feel yourself becoming frustrated and angry, put your baby in her crib and then take a break from the crying for a couple of minutes so that you can regain your cool. Use that time to call for support. Ask someone to come over and provide you with some hands-on help so that you can recharge your parenting batteries and/or get some rest. Taking care of a colicky baby is frustrating and exhausting.

- Remind yourself that colic is a limited-time offer, (thankfully). You and your baby will survive this, although it may be hard to believe that some days.

MOM'S THE WORD

"A saving grace to soothe her while she was gassy was me bouncing with her on a giant exercise ball. She often drifted off to sleep with the rhythmic bouncing and it was good exercise for me too!"

—*Michelle, 36, mom of Kaylei, 19 months*

When my baby gets really fussy, I find that distraction works best. It seems to stop him mid-wail. Then, at that point, once I've got his attention, I can start trying to soothe him again. Do you have any good baby-distraction techniques to suggest? Forget the diamonds: distraction is a mom's best friend. Here are five baby distraction techniques that many moms swear by:

- Hold your baby up to a mirror so he can check out the baby in the mirror.

- Take your baby into the bathroom or kitchen and let him listen to the sound of running water—either the shower, the water in the sink, or the swishing "womb-like" sounds of the dishwasher.

- Switch on a ceiling fan.

- Take your baby into the bathroom when one of his older siblings is having a bath so that he can take in all the sounds and sights of bath time.

- Strap your baby into his car seat and place his car seat on top of the dryer. Turn the dryer on, all the while holding the car seat in place with both of your hands. Stand there for a few minutes and see if the noise of the dryer will help to lull your baby to sleep. Make sure you're drying a pair of jeans with a zipper or a pair of running shoes so that you get some satisfying and soothing clicks and thuds. That's the best part! *Important:* For safety reasons, you have to stay with your baby at all times. Otherwise, the vibrations from the dryer could cause the car seat—and your baby—to tumble to the ground, with potentially tragic results.

Nap Know-how

"What times should I be putting my baby down for his naps?"
It depends on the number of naps your baby is squeezing in each day. Here's what the experts recommend in terms of timing if your baby is on a three, two, or one nap-a-day schedule:

- when your baby is on a three-nap-a-day pattern, typical for babies up to age six months: mid-morning, early afternoon, and late afternoon (Note: Watch the timing of that last nap: a nap that ends after 4:30 p.m. will interfere with your child's ability to get to sleep)

- when your baby is on a two-nap-a-day pattern, typically from age six months to around age 18 months to two years: mid-morning and early afternoon

- when your baby is on a one-nap-a-day pattern, typically from age 18 months to two years to some time after age three: early afternoon.

Every baby's sleep patterns are unique, so not every baby falls into this "classic" naptime pattern. If your baby is in the habit of taking a series of small catnaps rather than the longer naps that are more typical for children his age, you may want to try to gently encourage him to combine two of those shorter catnaps together into one longer stretch of sleep. Be forewarned: You may go through a period when your baby is totally miserable while you're trying to tweak his nap routine. But, over time, you may start to see results.

It's also important to bear in mind that some children simply require less sleep than others. If you have a child like this, you want to savor any signs of progress on the nap front, rather than holding out for naptime perfection. After all, every baby step taken en route to Naptime Nirvana, however slowly or reluctantly, is a very big deal indeed. In the meantime, schedule regular breaks for yourself, since you're not getting the naptime reprieves that some other moms are able to count on.

PILLOW TALK

Morning naps tend to be rich in the type of sleep which has proven to play an important role in brain maturation. Afternoon naps tend to be important in reducing levels of cortisol, the hormone linked with stress. No wonder babies need more than one nap!

"My baby hates taking naps. What can I do to make getting her down for a nap less of an ordeal?" Just as a predictable, soothing naptime routine can help babies to wind down for bedtime at the end of the day, a regular pre-naptime routine can help them to make the temporary shift from playtime to naptime. Some parents find that it works well to borrow some elements from their baby's bedtime routine, such as the darkened room and the pre-tuck-in cuddle for example. You may also want to think about adding an element that's unique to naptime, just to cue her that naptime "sleep time" is different from nighttime "sleep time," perhaps playing quiet music while she enjoys her relaxing daytime siesta.

"Naptimes are a major challenge at our house because I have a toddler as well as a new baby. I can't leave my toddler unsupervised while I try to settle my baby, so sometimes my baby doesn't get the daytime rest she needs." There are a couple of ways to approach this problem. You can try to arrange it so that everyone has naptime or quiet time at the same time (e.g., right after lunch, when your toddler and your baby are both likely to feel sleepy). Try settling your toddler down for his nap first. (You might want to put on some soothing music or a storybook on CD for him to listen to so that he'll have something to focus on as he winds down for his nap.) Then *you'll* be able to focus on getting your baby down for her nap. With any luck, you might even be able to squeeze in a short nap yourself before one of the kids wakes up. (Hey, it can happen!)

"My baby takes only 20-minute naps. Does a nap that short even count as a nap?" Not according to the nap police. While you may find a 20-minute catnap wonderfully refreshing, a nap that's less than an hour long will merely take the edge off your baby's tiredness without delivering the truly replenishing benefits of a real nap. If your baby decides it's time to get on with her day 20 minutes after she started her nap, treat that premature naptime awakening as you would a middle-of-the-night awakening: Use your baby-soothing techniques to resettle your baby, thereby gently but firmly letting her know that it's not time to get up quite yet. That might mean topping her up with a quick nursing session, or giving her a quick cuddle and a few reassuring pats on the back, and trying to gently ease her back to sleep. If that doesn't work, you may want to look at her overall sleep/wake patterns to try to consider what may be preventing her from settling down for a nice long nap. Some possible culprits include a sleep environment that is not conducive to sleep, not being tired enough to need a real nap, being too tired by the time naptime rolls around (in which case the adrenaline rush associated with overtiredness may be making it difficult for her to sleep for long enough), and/or not having the self-soothing skills required to soothe herself back to sleep (when she is momentarily roused during her naptime sleep).

"What should I do if my baby misses out on one of her naps? Let her sleep twice as long at the next naptime period?" The sleep gurus say that you should resist the temptation to let your baby take an all-day siesta on days when she misses her morning nap. No nap should be allowed to last for longer than three hours or you could find your baby's nighttime sleep schedule thrown seriously out of whack, which would throw the next day's sleep schedule out of whack, too. If the missed nap turns her into a grumposaurus rex by dinnertime, pop her into bed by 6:30 p.m. so that she can get a head start on her beauty sleep tonight. That's the best way to ease her back into her normal routine, according to the sleep experts.

Bedtime Problems

"My baby is really grumpy in the evenings. We need to move her bedtime back by an hour or two. How do we do this?" Settling on the right bedtime for baby is largely a matter of trial and error, as you've discovered. If you think your baby is getting overtired because her bedtime is too late, try shifting her bedtime by 15 minutes at a time every two to three nights. When assessing her overall level of tiredness, look at her sleepiness cues, the times she wakes up in the morning, and her overall mood. When you find a bedtime that seems to catch her at just the right moment (just as she's getting sleepy) and that leaves her in a good mood the next day, you'll know you've found the right bedtime for her.

"I end up staying up late waiting for my baby to have her last feeding of the night. This seems kind of crazy. What do other moms do?" It depends on the mom. Some decide to hit the hay as soon as they start to feel tired, figuring that minutes of sleep banked are a bonus. Other moms who find it really frustrating to be woken up from a deliciously deep sleep right after they entered Dreamland may decide to either do what you're doing (wait up for baby) or to gently rouse baby and offer their half-asleep baby a feeding before they both call it a night. (Some sleep experts are firmly opposed to the so-called "dream feed" or "focal feed" before bedtime. Some give it a resounding thumbs-up, proof that you can't make all of the sleep experts happy all of the time, so you'll have to decide if this idea will work for you and your baby or not.)

"My baby won't let anyone but me put her to bed." It's nice to be the number one draft for anything in life, including the position of bedtime parent-in-chief. But even the sports all-stars have backups, and you need a backup, too, so that you can be away at bedtime or naptime on occasion. Being indispensable sounds a lot more glamorous than it is in real life. You may want to get your child attached to a lovey that can help to take the place of you when someone else is pinch-hitting for you at bedtime (see Table 6.1). Of course, not every child is willing to have anything to do with a comfort object, notes Sharon, a 42-year-old mother of two: "I was my children's security blanket. I tried getting them a blanket or a stuffed animal, but nothing but me seemed to work."

There's another practical way of dealing with this, of course, if you're raising your child with a partner. Turn bedtime into a family affair. Over time, you can gradually ease out of the bedtime trio so that your partner can develop his own unique variation on the put-baby-to-sleep bedtime theme. Contrary to popular belief, each parent can sing from a slightly different songbook. It does help, however, if your baby can figure out that the song has something to do with bedtime (you're playing "Taps" rather than "Cockadoodledo").

Night Waking

"My newborn tends to doze off during feedings in the middle of the night. Then a short time later, he's paging room service again. How can I get him to finish a full feeding so he won't be up a half hour later looking for more milk—and more Mom?" Dozing off before they have a full tummy, and then quickly awakening to ask for the next course, is a typical *modus operandi* for your average newborn. Here are some mom-proven strategies for rousing your dozy diner:

- Sit your baby on your knee and gently rub his back rather than trying to nurse him in the side-lying position. (It's more work for you, but apparently he can't seem to stay awake when feeding is such a warm and cozy affair. Of course, you could take the opposite approach and decide that you're just going to let him catnap through his feedings and not worry about how often you're up with him in the night. That works for some moms. But it sounds like you'd rather have the feeding be over with once and for all, and then settle down for a serious chunk of sleep.)

- Some lactation consultants recommend the burp and bother technique, which is designed to encourage your baby to have a full course meal all at one time, as opposed to an appetizer, a nap, the main course, a nap, dessert, a nap, and so on. Here's now it works. Once your baby stops actively swallowing, sit her up, pat her on the back until she's more alert, and then continue the feeding. Once she starts nursing more slowly again or seems to drift off, repeat the process. At some point, you'll decide that she's had enough to eat and you simply let her nurse the last time around.

- You can try undressing your baby until he's down to his diaper. (Just bear in mind that you'll have to get him dressed again if he dozes off during the remainder of his feeding.) You can also make gentle bicycle motions with his legs while talking and singing to him.

- Rub the bottoms of your baby's feet. This is highly stimulating to babies.

"My baby has started waking in the night since I went back to work. Any tips on dealing with this problem? I'm exhausted." Check in with your child's daycare provider to get a sense of his daytime sleep/wake patterns. Some babies who are particularly attached to mom and dad decide to "hibernate" during the day—sleep as much as possible—so that they can hoard their awake time for when they are reunited with their family. If your baby seems to be falling into this pattern, you may want to think about maximizing the time you spend with your baby during your non-working hours. That may help to ease the problem.

You should also at least consider the possibility that your baby could be waking in the night for reasons totally unrelated to your return to work (see Sleep Tool 4 for a list of other common causes of night waking in babies). To ease your mind, you may want to set up an appointment with your child's health care provider to rule out any physical causes for her sleep woes. Illness and certain medical conditions, including sleep disorders, and certain medications (both prescription and over-the-counter) could be making it difficult for her to get a good night's sleep.

Early Birds (a.k.a. Larks)

"My baby is waking up too early—at 4:30 a.m.!" Believe it or not, babies who wake up too early are generally overtired babies. If you move your baby's bedtime so it falls a little earlier in the evening, your baby might sleep in longer in the morning. (I know, it's counterintuitive, but it works.) Try shifting your baby's bedtime until she is no longer waking up before the birds. Then toast the dawn with non-alcoholic champagne and orange juice the first day she sleeps past 6:00 a.m. That's a decent sleep-in time for a baby. If that doesn't work, you may also want to consider whether something else could be responsible for your baby's early morning awakenings. (See the material at the end of this chapter.)

"My baby keeps losing her pacifier in the dark at night, and then crying because she can't find it." If your baby is old enough to find her pacifier on her own, you may want to send her to bed with more than one pacifier. Some parents have found it works well to either put a bunch of pacifiers all around their baby (so that there's a good chance that one will be within easy reaching distance) or to designate one corner as pacifier central (over time, baby will learn where to find the soother stash in the middle of the night).

Feeding to Sleep

My baby will go to sleep only if I nurse him to sleep. What can I do to start teaching him other ways of falling asleep? Look for opportunities in the day when you can nurse your baby after he wakes up as opposed to right before he goes to sleep. You will likely find that this is easier to do when he first wakes up in the morning and after his morning nap. What you're trying to do, of course, is to avoid running into a situation where your baby always gets nursed right before he goes to sleep. Help your baby to learn to fall asleep at naptime and at bedtime in a number of different ways (as opposed to always being nursed to sleep). You might rock him to sleep at one nap, nurse him to sleep at another nap, "*shush*-pat" him to sleep at another nap (making shush-ing sounds while you pat him to sleep), etc. When your baby wants to nurse before naptime or bedtime, look for signs that your baby is getting sleepy and that he has satisfied his need for food and is now nursing for comfort rather than nutrition. Then:

- **Gently break the seal between the baby and your breast.** Continue to hold your breast against your baby's cheek so that baby doesn't experience a dramatically different change in position or sudden loss of the feeling of warmth.

- **Remain in this position until your baby starts to get really drowsy (but is still awake).** Then transfer your baby to bed. What you're trying to do here is to get your baby used to the idea of falling asleep without a nipple in his mouth. Initially, you're creating a new sleep association—the idea of falling asleep in your arms—but this will be an easier sleep association to break because you can have your arms in contact with her when she's in her crib.

- **Once he's gotten used to falling asleep without having the nipple in his mouth, you then work on having him fall asleep in his bed while you pat him and "shush" him to sleep or use some other equally soothing technique that seems to work particularly well for your baby.** Then you progress to the point where you're simply laying him down in his bed and he's drifting off to sleep. (When you're coming up with a sleep plan for your baby, you may want to break your sleep goal down into a series of baby steps, and then work at achieving those goals one by one.)

"Do I need to encourage my baby to give up her night feedings or is this something she is likely to do on her own?" It depends. Some babies give up nighttime feedings on their own at a relatively young age (by age five to six months). Others need some gentle encouragement from their parents. If your baby is nursing only once or twice in the night and it's not a big deal for you (e.g., you've got your nighttime sleeping routine down to such an art that you're barely even aware of the fact that you're up in the night with your baby), you're probably not in much of a hurry to eliminate your baby's nighttime feedings. If, however, your baby is up repeatedly in the night, is growing well, doesn't appear to nutritionally need those nighttime feedings, and you're desperately craving sleep, you might want to encourage him to do his dining in the daytime rather than at night. Here's how:

- **Breast-feeding:** Reduce feeding times by a few minutes each night and feeding intervals by half an hour.

- **Formula-feeding:** Reduce the amount of liquid by 1 oz each night and increase the feeding interval by half an hour each night.

Important: Never allow a baby to take a bottle to bed. This practice can contribute to early childhood caries (baby bottle mouth). While you could allow your baby to take a bottle of water to bed (water isn't damaging to your baby's teeth), you might not want to create the bottles-in-bed association *period.*

"The moment I go in to settle my baby in the night, he wants to nurse no matter what." It's a lot easier to deal with this particular nighttime challenge if you've got someone else to pitch in on nighttime parenting patrol because, in the minds of most breast-feeding babies, Mom = milk. Since that person will need to bring baby to you if baby is insistent that nursing is the only thing that's going to do, they'll have to rely on some of the other methods outlined in Table 6.1 to soothe baby. This can help baby learn to settle back to sleep without being fed, which will help to ease that powerful nurse-to-sleep association and gradually teach baby not to expect food each time she wakes in the night.

If you have been blessed with an exceptionally spirited baby who knows what she wants and isn't going to settle for any substitute for Mom or Mom's breasts, you can opt for Plan B—decreasing the duration of each middle-of-the night feeding. Obviously, you'll do this only with an older baby or toddler who has gotten into a bit of a sleep rut: She's nursing frequently throughout the night because that's the only way she knows to get herself back to sleep. You would never want to cut back on the frequency or duration of feedings for a young baby because your baby needs those calories and your breasts need the stimulation in order to cue the milk factory to increase milk production so that there will be more milk on tap for the next day. (See my book *The Mother of All Baby Books* for more on this topic.) When you send in your sleep reinforcements, make sure they know that it's okay to come and get you if baby is really unhappy. You don't want them to feel like they have to put themselves or baby through a night of misery if it's clear that baby really can't cope without nursing.

"My baby nurses every hour on the hour all night long. What can I do to get him to ease up on the nighttime feedings?" Analyze the problem. Is this a temporary situation (e.g., a growth spurt) or could your baby be using you as a sleep aid in order to get back to sleep every time he wakes in the night? If your baby is going through a growth spurt (something that typically occurs at around age 10 to 14 days, 6 weeks, 3 months, and 6 months of age, and that lasts for 24 to 48 hours while your baby nurses often to build up your milk supply), try to persevere for a few more nights, and ask other people in your life to help you catch up on your sleep so that you can remain as well rested as possible. If your baby has learned to associate nursing with falling back asleep, try to teach him to fall asleep using methods other than nursing (see section above on teaching babies other ways of falling asleep other than nursing). Here are some other tips that can be helpful to moms who have babies who nurse frequently in the night, and some tips that may be specifically helpful to bed-sharing moms.

- Before you rush to pick up your baby and offer the breast in the night, make sure that your baby is actually awake and looking for food. Some babies stir in their sleep and make noises that resemble cries. Your baby may still be fast asleep when he's making these sounds. If you pick him up when he's sleeping restlessly and making these sounds, you're basically offering food to a baby who was sound asleep, which could eventually teach him to be hungry in the night. (See Chapter 4 for more on this issue.)

- If your baby nurses frequently in the night, gradually cut back on the amount of time your baby nurses during each feeding in the night. When you're nursing your baby, watch for signs that he's starting to get sleepy and that he's no longer nursing quite so vigorously. Then gently insert your finger to break the suction while he's nursing and hold him against your breast so that he can get used to falling asleep without a nipple in his mouth. If he protests vigorously and starts rooting around frantically, you can give him back the breast again and try again in another couple of minutes when he's a little more sleepy. Try this a few times. If you get worn out before baby does, you can try again at the next feeding. It's a learning process for you both. As he learns to fall asleep without the breast in his mouth, you can start to introduce a time gap between the end of the feeding and when baby goes to sleep (e.g., he's drowsy but still awake when you put him back in his crib or settle him down to sleep beside you). He may be happy to nuzzle up next to the breast or to have his hand on your breast—his way of knowing that the breast is there if he wants it.

• You can also start to make things a little less cozy for middle-of-the-night nursing. Try shifting your body position slightly (e.g., reclining on your back slightly) so that nursing isn't quite so convenient. Then you'll be able to differentiate between nursing because the breast is there and nursing because baby's tummy is rumbling. (It's up to you to decide whether to offer the breast in one or both situations, but you'll be making conscious mothering decisions.)

Baby's Not Sleeping through the Night Anymore

"My nine-month-old was sleeping through the night really well, but now she's up in the night crying at least once or twice. I've heard that separation anxiety can be an issue for babies around this age. Can you explain how this affects babies' sleeping patterns and what we can do to deal with it?" Your baby's knowledge of the world is growing by leaps and bounds. She's figured out that the two of you are separate human beings, but for her, out of sight means gone forever, which is why parting isn't sweet sorrow—it's sheer torture. This is why she wants to want to double-check that you're still there when she awakens in the night. This burst of separation anxiety may also coincide with any major change in baby's life—e.g., a new day-care provider, Mom re-entering the workforce, etc. She is likely to feel an extra strong desire to reach out to you for support and reassurance in the night. You can help to minimize your baby's separation anxiety by:

- Trying to keep her with you as much as possible when the two of you are home together (e.g., not sneaking off to the bathroom on your own just because it's quicker and easier to do so) but, when you do leave the room without her, talking to her from that other room so that she starts to learn that your temporary disappearing act is just that: temporary.

- Giving your baby lots of time and attention during the day/evening so that she's less likely to ask for this time and attention at night.

- Handing her to other people (e.g., child-care providers, grandparents, visitors), as opposed to waiting for these people to take her from your arms. (This sends the message that you're in control of the situation and that you trust the other person.)

- Encouraging attachment to a lovey that can serve as a stand in for you when the two of you are away from one another.

- Responding to your baby in the night so that she knows you're still there. Depending on this situation, you may decide to respond verbally ("It's okay. Mommy's here, but it's sleepy time for Kellie") or physically (walking into your baby's room so that she can see that you're still there, patting your baby, picking your baby up, nursing your baby, etc.).

MOTHER WISDOM

Having your child start waking in the night after sleeping through for a period of months can be a particularly frustrating (but very common) end-of-first-year parenting experience. Not only are you likely to be mystified by your baby's behavior (he's Mr. Independent one moment and Mr. Clingy the next), you may feel like all the progress you made on the sleep front during the early months has been lost for good. Naomi Stadlen explains what's really going on in her book *What Mothers Do: Especially When It Looks Like Nothing*: "When a nine-month-old baby seems to want her more at night, his exhausted mother wails that she feels as if they are both 'going backwards.' But they aren't. It's more like the swing of a pendulum: if it swings further out, it will return further back, too."

"**My baby keeps practising her standing-up skills in the middle of the night. I keep finding her stuck in a standing-up position at 2:00 a.m. She ends up crying for help because she doesn't know how to get back down! What should I do?**" In retrospect, this is one of the cutest baby sleep stages, but it's pretty frustrating and exhausting when you're living through it. Fortunately, because babies are so determined to master a particular milestone, they tend to pass through each of these milestones pretty quickly, so you'll have only a few nights of having your baby stuck in the sitting-up position and a few nights of your baby stuck in the stand-up position, and so on. So what can you do in the meantime? Give your baby plenty of time to practise her skills in the daytime. Show her how to get out of the position that's causing her (and you) so much grief in the middle of the night. "My husband had the amazing idea of showing our baby how to get down on her own by walking her hands down the bars of the crib," recalls Kristi, 27, who is currently pregnant with her second child. "What a concept! He showed her three times and then she got it. No more problems!"

Changing Spaces

"**My newborn wakes up every time I try to put her in her crib. She wants to sleep in the sling or in my arms. I'm hardly getting any sleep at all.**" Newborns look lost in a big, empty crib and sometimes they feel that way, too. Your baby may feel cozier if you tuck her into a bassinet or a cradle instead. Make sure it's been assembled properly so that it won't tip over if your baby burrows her head into one end. If you want to stick with the crib, try using some of the soothing techniques outlined in Table 6.1 to help your baby to feel more at home in her crib. And remember that she may be protesting the change of environment as much as the crib itself: she'd much rather sleep in your arms. So if you can make the transition from your arms slow and gradual, she'll be less likely to protest. Remember, you're trying to convince her that there's some merit to sleeping somewhere other than your arms. It can take time to negotiate such a deal.

"**My baby's outgrown the bassinet, but she hates her crib.
Now what?**" Change is tough for all of us, babies included. Your
baby may like the coziness of being nestled in the bassinet and may
feel lost in that giant crib. She may feel a bit more secure if you try
putting her to sleep in a horizontal position at one end of the crib,
so that she's surrounded by crib walls on three sides. It's also possible
that there was something about her bassinet that she particularly
liked, but that her crib environment doesn't replicate, as was the
case for Patricia's baby daughter Anna Catherine: "The bassinet
vibrated, and the crib did not," the 31-year-old mother of one
recalls. "She didn't appreciate this little glitch." You can also help to
ease the transition by doing it in stages. Start to establish a bedtime
routine for tucking her into her bassinet (e.g., nursing, turning on
some soothing music or white noise, cuddles, patting, *shush*-ing)
and then use the exact same routine when you tuck her into her
crib. For tips on transitioning your child from the family bed to
a crib, see Chapter 7.

"**How do we transition our baby from sleeping in our bed
to sleeping in her own crib?**" The strategies that work best for
you will be determined by your baby's age and temperament, how
you feel about the various sleep-training methods (e.g., see Sleep
Tool 2), and how soon you hope to move your baby from your bed
to his or her own bed (either a crib in your room or a crib down
the hall). If your baby is still quite young, you may want to consider transitioning your baby from your bed to his own crib in the
same room. The American Academy of Pediatrics and the
Canadian Paediatric Society recommend room sharing. If your
baby has a sensitive or otherwise challenging temperament, you
may wish to proceed slowly. A "cold turkey" sleep-training method is
likely to be traumatic for both you and your baby. Don't forget to
factor in your own parenting philosophies. You may feel no
amount of crying is tolerable, or you may feel that a small amount
of crying can be tolerated over the short run if the goal is to foster
better sleep habits. (A word to the wise: try to talk this issue
through with your partner *before* the two of you find get embroiled
in a heated discussion on the issue some morning at 3:00 am.)

Sleep Disruptions

"My baby has a cold. She keeps waking up crying in the night because her nose is all stuffed up. What can I do to help her sleep better?" The standard advice to adults who aren't feeling well is to drink plenty of fluids. The same advice applies to babies. Make sure that your baby is nursing frequently so that she stays well hydrated. You may find that nursing is a frustrating experience if her nose is really plugged up. Using a saline nasal spray that is recommended for babies and then suctioning her nose with a nasal aspirator can help with this problem. (Your baby's health care provider or your pharmacist can recommend some specific products.) Your baby will find it easier to breathe at night if the air in the room where she's sleeping is kept moist. Use a cool-air vaporizer with distilled water. Clean the vaporizer regularly to keep the vaporizer from becoming a breeding ground for bacteria and mold. (Note: Avoid using a warm-water vaporizer because of the potential for burns.) Do whatever you can to encourage your baby to sleep, even if it means taking a few steps backward in your plans to encourage better sleep habits. You can get back on track when your baby is starting to feel better.

MOTHER WISDOM

Your baby or toddler is getting too big to swaddle and she's making it clear that she's not going to let you use that nasal aspirator to vacuum out the insides of her nose. So how are you going to pull off this particular nose-clearing maneuver? Here's how. Lay your baby across your lap with the back of her head in the crook of your arm with her inside arm behind your back and your hand holding her outer arm down. (If she's kicking and wriggling and you don't have another person to help hold her still, gently hold her legs between your legs.) Hold your baby's head against your chest and, using your free hand, squeeze the bulb of the aspirator and quickly apply the aspirator to each of your baby's nostrils. She won't be impressed, but hopefully you'll be able to clear a lot of gunk out of her nose so that she'll sleep more soundly.

"My baby has an ear infection. The pain in his ears is making it difficult for her to sleep at night. What can I do to make her more comfortable?" An ear infection can be extremely painful. The pain is caused by a fluid buildup in the inner ear that can't drain away when your baby is lying down. Your baby should be seen by his health care provider in case treatment is required. Pain medication may help her to sleep more comfortably.

"My baby has just been diagnosed with gastroesophageal reflux (GER). What does this mean and how does GER affect a baby's sleep patterns?" Gastroesophageal reflux is a medical condition in which the muscle responsible for keeping food from moving from the stomach back up into the esophagus isn't doing its job properly. Babies with this condition can experience heart-burn-like stomach pains that are particularly acute when they are lying down, so—not surprisingly—these babies tend to have fairly severe sleep problems. (If the stomach contents that are being regurgitated make their way to the throat and larynx, the baby will wake up coughing and choking. If they only go as far as the lower esophagus, the baby will likely wake up crying, but there won't be an obvious clue as to why.) GER may be characterized by frequent vomiting or spitting up, sudden or frantic crying that sounds as if the baby is in pain, feeding problems (e.g., a baby who doesn't want to nurse even when he is hungry, or who eats too quickly, or who becomes extremely fussy after feeding), crying whenever the baby is placed in the back-lying position, and—in some cases—weight loss. You may find GER easier to manage if you reduce the size of your baby's feedings and feed her more often (whether you're breast-feeding or formula-feeding). Smaller feedings will be easier for his system to handle. Then make a point of holding your baby in an upright position for at least a half-hour after each feeding. Ask your health care provider if he recommends a medication (acid-reducing medications may be required to help your baby feel comfortable again) or an alternative to the standard back-sleeping position that is recommended for the majority of babies. And try to minimize your baby's crying because crying will only make your baby's GER worse. (See the list of suggested baby-soothing techniques in Table 6.1.) *Note:* Pacifiers may provide a great deal of relief to a baby with GER: as he sucks on the pacifier, he will be clearing acid from his esophagus at the same time.

"My baby was sleeping really well until she started teething. Now each time she starts to get a new tooth, her sleep patterns get thrown totally out of whack. What can I do to ease her discomfort when she has a new tooth coming in and to help all of us get more sleep?" If your baby is having a lot of restless nights and you're seeing a lot of the symptoms of teething (e.g., drooling, runny nose, rash around the mouth and chin, red cheeks, increased desire to nurse or a baby who suddenly doesn't want to nurse because it hurts to nurse, swollen gums, and a mild diaper rash that is caused by your baby's increasingly acidic digestive acids), your baby may be getting a new tooth. Here are some tips on managing her discomfort:

- Give your baby something to suck or chew on. If you're breast-feeding, offering the breast is a natural. Nursing for comfort or nutrition will help to ease babies' sore gums. During the day, she may get relief from biting down on a chilled teething ring or a refrigerated wet washcloth.

- Rub your baby's gums with a cold, wet finger. (Wash your hands first.)

- Keep your baby's chin dry and apply ointment to keep it from getting sore and red. That will only add to her misery and may increase the night wakings. (Note: Lanolin works well and it won't harm your baby if a bit ends up in her mouth.)

- If your baby is having a really tough time with a particular tooth, talk to your health care provider about the use of pain-relief medications. A mild analgesic like infant acetaminophen or ibuprofen may ease her pain and can also help with sleep. Some products that numb the gums can provide some relief, but some parents report that their babies are freaked out by the numb sensation in their mouths and these products carry a small risk of allergic reactions and a decreased gag reflex.

"How can I help my baby to adjust to the time change?"
You can either switch your baby's bedtime, wakeup time, and
naptimes right away (the cold turkey approach!) or you can help
her to adjust in stages: "I found that slowly adjusting her bedtime
in 15-minute intervals seemed to help," recalls Renay, 35, mother
of one. "Sometimes, I started adjusting Rachael's schedule before
the time change and sometimes I started adjusting after the time
change." No matter which approach you take, realize that there will
be a bit of an adjustment as your child gets used to the time
change, so try to leave a little extra slack in your schedule around
the time that the clocks move forward or back. Your child's sleep
schedule may be thrown out of whack, so you may be a bit more
sleep-deprived than usual.

Have Baby, Will Travel

**"My baby hates sleeping anywhere other than at home. The
last time we stayed in a hotel, she was up most of the night.
What can we do to help her feel more comfortable sleeping
in places other than at home?"** Ah, yes, the family *helliday*, the
stuff of which memories are made. Of course, you have to survive
them first, something that's easier said than done if your entire
family is in the same hotel room (or, worse, the same room at a
friend or family member's house); your baby is totally freaked
about sleeping in an unfamiliar crib or bed; you're in a different
time zone; your eating schedule is off; and you left "Mr. Bunny"
in the airport washroom yesterday. You can minimize upheaval
when you're traveling by:

- **Keeping baby's sleep schedule in mind when planning your
  travel itinerary.** "Red-eye flights work well if the flight is long,
  says Zaheeda, 33, mother of eight-month-old Arjun. "Once at
  the destination, help baby to adjust to the new time by keeping
  him busy in the daytime and spending as much time as possible
  outside, in the daylight. The exposure to sunlight will help
  adjust baby's biological clock."

MOTHER WISDOM

Not sure how to help your baby to cope with the time zone change while you're away on your family trip? Most sleep experts suggest that you switch to local time for bedtime and wake-up times, but that you allow naptimes to occur at times when your child needs them most, even if those naps are a little off schedule. Then reverse the process when you get home.

- **Considering what helps your baby to sleep well at home and trying to replicate that environment on your trip.** "Pack your baby's sheet for a familiar smell and feel," suggests Sarah, 34, mother of one. "Take something to darken the windows with," adds Laura, 29, mother of one. "Bring a small sound therapy machine," says Heather, 33, mother of one. We used one at home every day and then if we went traveling we would take it with us and the sound would at least be the same."

Seeing Double

"Should my twins sleep together or apart?" If your twins are both sleeping well, keeping them together is probably your best bet. One twins study found that twins who bunked together in the NICU grew faster, were healthier, and got out of the hospital sooner than twins who were separated shortly after birth. And parents of multiples find that until their babies become super-active, crib sharing generally works best after the babies come home. Parents who are worried about twin babies waking one another up in the night can generally rest easy on that front, says Nancy, 38, the mother of three-year-old fraternal twin boys Trevor and Ben: "They learned pretty quickly to sleep through one another's noises. We stuck with it and I think it has helped to this day. Ben can sleep through Trevor's snoring a mere six feet across the room when he can wake me up across the hall!" *Note:* See Chapter 5 for more on co-sleeping safety, including why it's never a good idea to have a baby sleep with an older sibling.

**"Should I wake up my other twin when I've finished feeding
my first twin in the night?** Or should I wait for that twin to wake
up on her own?" A lot depends on how much help you have in the
night and how similar your twins' feeding and sleeping patterns are.
If the twins are pretty much in synch in terms of their feeding and
sleeping patterns and you no sooner get your head on your pillow
after feeding twin number one before twin number two is looking
for you, you may want to make a preemptive feeding move. A big
advantage of breastfeeding is that you can feed both your babies at
the same time, minimizing the amount of sleep disruption. It's a
little trickier to pull this off when you're formula-feeding, but many
moms insist it can be done if you position yourself and both babies
appropriately. This is one of those situations where comparing notes
with other moms of twins can reap huge dividends—this time on
the sleep front. (Get in touch with the National Organization of
Mothers of Twins Clubs, Inc. at www.nomotc.org or Multiple
Births Canada at www.multiplebirthscanada.org to learn sleep-saving
moves from other moms of multiples.)

Solutions Central—The Last Word

EVEN IF THIS book rivaled the New York phone book in thickness,
it would be impossible to address the sleep problems of every baby.
The reason is simple: every baby, toddler, and preschooler is
unique. Sleep Tool 1 outlines a process you can use to solve whatever sleep problems the Sandman may send your way.

So at what age should you be thinking of sleep training anyway—
assuming you decide to go the formal sleep training route at all?
Most experts say you can start gently encouraging good sleep habits
once you emerge from the postpartum haze, but that a formal
sleep-training method shouldn't be used on a baby any younger
than five to six months of age (the age at which some babies first
begin to show an ability to sleep through the night without
requiring a night feeding). That "rule" doesn't apply to all babies,
however, so, once again, you'll have to be the judge where your

baby is concerned. In this particular area of parenting, patience can be a virtue, says Michele, the 30-year-old mother of two. "I think if you start sleep training too soon, you will not develop that necessary bonding that teaches your child security. Our children, while they may not have been champion sleepers, knew that we would come when they cried. They had faith that we could fix all."

The sleep buck stops with you. Only you can decide when the time is right to start tackling your baby's sleep problems or if, in fact, your baby even has a sleep problem. You may find it helpful to remember that the baby stage is actually made up of three mini-stages, and that your sleep expectations should reflect your baby's unique age and stage:

1. **The newborn stage** (officially the first four weeks of life, but when it comes to sleep stages, it is more useful to think of this period as the first four to six weeks): This is when your baby's sleep patterns are the most chaotic.

2. **The young baby stage** (age six weeks through five months): This is when your baby's sleep patterns start to become a little less erratic and more predictable. Daytime nap patterns and night-time sleep/wake patterns begin to emerge and some initial sleep learning can begin to occur.

3. **The older baby stage** (age five months to age one): During this period, most babies give up nighttime feedings and are capable of sleeping through the night most of the time. (Remember that "sleeping through the night" means sleeping for a minimum of five hours at a stretch.) Not all babies manage to achieve this milestone before age one, so there is a bit of a blurring together of the older baby and the toddler stages, when it comes to sleep.

CHAPTER 7

The Real-World Guide to Solving Your Toddler's Sleep Problems

For a long time during those sleepless months, I told myself that it was just a phase—that it would pass—and that things would get better in time. Then I realized that I needed to take action—that the problem wasn't going to go away on its own and that I needed to do something to make the situation better.
—WENDY, 30, MOTHER OF ONE

TODDLER SLEEP PROBLEMS tend to fall into one of two categories: sleep problems that are carryovers from the baby stage and sleep problems that tie into the exciting developmental breakthroughs of the toddler years. Your child's sleep-wake patterns are evolving along with everything else about her. And she is always looking for opportunities to be the one in charge, something that may mean deciding when or if she's going to take that afternoon nap. And, of course, those hardwired temperament traits that were apparent from the time she was very young will affect her sleep during the toddler years as well.

Depending on whether your toddler is newly one or on the verge of turning three, and where she's at developmentally, she may be exhibiting baby or toddler-like sleep behaviors (resisting the idea of going to bed, learning how to sleep through the night, experiencing middle-of-the-night separation anxiety, and getting rid of some of her daytime naps). Or she may have covered all that sleep turf by now (perhaps repeatedly!), and may be more a preschooler when it comes to sleep (experiencing bedtime struggles, bedtime fears, and a newfound reluctance to get out of bed in the morning). Not all kids hit the same developmental targets at the same time, so don't be surprised if your toddler exhibits a fascinating mix of baby-like, toddler-like, and preschooler-like sleep behaviors—or if she does a bit of backtracking from time to time. It's all to be expected in the Land of Toddlers.

The Truth about Toddlers and Sleep

SO EVERYONE ELSE'S toddler looks forward to naptime, hops into bed without any fuss at *all* at bedtime, and lets Mom and Dad doze until 7:30 a.m. each weekday morning—8:30 a.m. on weekends. That's the stuff of which parental fantasies are made. Sure, 60–70 percent of toddlers are able to self-soothe and get themselves back to sleep by the time they celebrate their first birthday, but that means that 30–40 percent of their fellow one-year-olds *aren't*. It's the sleep stat that no one talks about, however, except your most honest mom-friends. Now on to some other toddler sleep realities.

"At what point should I start worrying about my toddler's sleep problems?" There's no page in your child's baby book that will magically alert you to start worrying about sleep problems on such-and-such a date. That's because nothing about sleep is linear, predictable, or black and white. All that said, for most parents, there is a sleep moment of truth when you realize that your child's sleep problems are making life harder for him and for you, and the time has come to do something about the problem. "I knew it was time when I began to resent Mikaela," says Michele, 30, mother of two, recalling some of the irrational thoughts that ran

> **MOM'S THE WORD**
>
> "I agree that during the day and night, parents need to be patient, understanding, and loving, but I also think that you can take the idea of nighttime parenting too far. It's appropriate to teach our children to adapt to our lifestyle. I have a friend who chose to let her 18-month-old get out of bed and watch TV all night long while she tried to sleep on the couch instead of dealing with the problems and ending them."
>
> —*Julie, 29, mother of one*

through her head at that time. "I found myself thinking, 'What did she have against allowing me to sleep at night?' I felt terrible about having those emotions—guilty. I didn't admit it to anyone for fear it defined me as a terrible mother."

Some parents decide to take a laissez-faire approach to sleep problems, hoping that their child will develop healthier sleep habits and routines over time. But this approach, while well meaning, tends to reinforce poor sleep habits until they become firmly entrenched in the child's sleep routines, something that makes it unlikely that healthier, more sleep-friendly routines will develop spontaneously. In fact, research has shown that 41 percent of children who were getting up at age eight months were still getting up in the night at age four years. So if your toddler is still getting up frequently in the night—or having a hard time getting to sleep without a lot of hands-on help from you—you might want to explore some ways of dealing with the problem.

When you're considering your various sleep-training options, think about choosing a method (or blending a variety of methods) that emphasizes *teaching your child about sleep* as opposed to just *eliminating undesirable sleep behaviors* like crying in the night. (Remember, it can be helpful to think of the various sleep-training methods as a source of ideas rather than a sleep-solution blueprint.)

And here's something else you may want to mull over. You may want to take a two-tiered approach to tackling your child's sleep problems, e.g., helping your child to develop new self-soothing skills at the same time that you are encouraging him to reduce his dependence on the one soothing strategy that has served him so well up until now (crying for you). Otherwise, you're taking away his key soothing strategy and leaving him with nothing in return.

Bedtime Basics

"How do bedtime routines tend to evolve during the toddler years?" You may find that some of the bedtime rituals (e.g., turning on lullabies or the white noise machines) that helped your baby wind down when she was younger no longer play such an important role now that she's getting a little older. At the same time, you've likely introduced some new bedtime attractions, like bedtime stories, that have become treasured aspects of your toddler's end-of-day routine, and yours. Toddlers tend to be creatures of habit, so your toddler may give you some not-so-gentle prompting if you attempt to commit a major bedtime faux pas (brushing his teeth before he has his PJs on, not after) or if you attempt to fast-forward through his bedtime story, to skip one of his stories, or to read his story-books in the wrong order. *Note:* One thing you'll want to avoid introducing into your child's bedtime routine is TV-viewing. (A lot of parents think that TV viewing helps toddlers to wind down, but it actually revs kids up. And, besides, the American Academy of Pediatrics doesn't recommend allowing children under the age of two to tune into TV at all. The Canadian Paediatric Society suggests limiting TV viewing time to one hour per day for children under the age of four.)

"When I ask my toddler if he's ready to go to bed, he always says, 'No.' Then he ends up staying up later and later." Give your toddler choices about which pajamas he wants to wear, which bedtime stories he wants to hear, whether he wants you to tuck his favorite stuffed animal into bed before or after you tuck him in— just don't give him the choice of deciding on his own bedtime. If you get of the habit of announcing that it's bedtime rather than asking your child if he wants to go to bed, you'll sidestep this problem entirely.

MOTHER WISDOM

Make sure that your toddler's bedtime routine gives him something to look forward to. If your toddler loves a particular toy, and you decide that that it would be a suitable choice for bedtime (e.g., nothing that's going to encourage active play that will wind your child up rather than down; nothing that would be dangerous to take to bed, etc.), then you might make this a bedtime-only toy and spend a few minutes playing with your toddler and the toy as part of the bedtime routine. Then your toddler could take the toy to bed. In the morning, the toy would get tucked away to await the next night's tuck-in.

"My toddler won't go to bed unless I lie down with her until she falls asleep. I fall asleep, too, and half my evening is gone. How do I wean her off this habit?" Gently and with love—the same way you go about breaking any other habit, or at least that's the consensus of the parents I interviewed for this book. Most found that they were able to ease their way out of the stay-with-me-until-I-fall-asleep routine by suddenly finding something else that had to be attended to at bedtime. Trudy, the mother of two young children, didn't even have to come up with an excuse like washing the dishes or changing laundry loads or going to the bathroom (perennial favorites among other parents, it would seem): circumstances gave her the excuse she needed. "When our second child was about four months old, the company my husband works for went on strike," the 39-year-old mother of two recalls. "He's management, which meant he was working 12-hour days and simply couldn't be around for bedtime routines. I had to nurse the baby right at the time our toddler needed to go to bed, so I ended up explaining to Emily, the toddler, that Mommy had to feed Gracie, so we would do it sitting on the edge of Emily's bed. After a few nights I was able to move to the foot of the bed, then into a chair next to the bed. After a while I explained that Mommy was uncomfortable nursing Grace this way and was just going to be in the living room. Emily was fine with that. At first, she would

MOM'S THE WORD

"When my children became toddlers, the communication changed from a nod when asked if they are sleepy to utter denial."

—*Tracy, 35, mother of three*

---

still be awake when I put Grace to bed, but she didn't seem to need me to lie down with her. After a while, she would be asleep before I was done and now she goes to bed at 8 p.m. with a storybook and her lullabies and a pacifier. We must wean her of this habit, but that's another story!"

"When bedtime rolls around, our toddler fights us every step of the way. We never had trouble getting her to go to bed when she was younger. Help!" Bedtime resistance is extremely common among the toddler set (32 percent of toddlers kick up a fuss at bedtime). Toddlers are simultaneously expressing their distress at having to be away from you during the night and exercising their perceived right to say no to anything and everything. Add to that the fact that your toddler's bedtime may require some tweaking and you can see why bedtime resistance may be a problem at your place. Here are some questions that my help you to zero in on what could be triggering your toddler (or preschooler's) bedtime-resistance problems. (See also Sleep Tool 3 for a checklist of the most common reasons for bedtime resistance in toddlers and preschoolers.)

- **Is your child's bedtime routine still working as effectively as it once did?** Perhaps it's time to rework that bedtime routine. "As a toddler, Andrew seemed to do much better with a more structured routine," says Caroline, a 40-year-old mother of two. (See material in the section above as well as in chapters 4 and 6 for some thoughts on what aspects of your child's bedtime routine you might want to tweak.)

- **Does your child's bedtime need to be adjusted?** Bedtime fading is a technique that is often recommended when children are extremely resistant to going to sleep and it is obvious that their bedtime needs to be adjusted. (See Sleep Tool 2 and Chapter 4.) This technique involves putting your child to bed at a time when you know she will naturally be sleepy (even if this bedtime is, realistically speaking, far too late for her) to see if this helps to ease the bedtime battles, and then gradually shifting your child's bedtime earlier in 15-minute intervals until she is going to bed well *and* her bedtime is at a suitable time. Combining bedtime fading with positive bed-time routines (e.g., incorporating new routines into your child's bedtime routine that she is likely to particularly enjoy) seems to work particularly well, so you may want to take this two-tiered approach to troubleshooting your child's bedtime refusal problems.

Table 7.1

Before Tired Becomes Overtired: Spotting the Sleep Window of Opportunity

Your Child May Be Getting Tired If You Notice Her	Your Child May Be Overtired If You Notice Him
Losing focus	Becoming whiny
Becoming distracted	Acting clingy
Acting spaced out	Demanding your attention *right now*
Talking less	Wanting to be picked up and held
Rubbing her eyes	Getting really cranky when things don't go his way
Pulling at her ears	Becoming frustrated with his toys
Starting to yawn	Losing patience easily
Having watery eyes and heavy eyelids	Having temper tantrums
Sucking her thumb or wanting her pacifier or lovey	Running around in circles and acting wired or all wound up
Asking to nurse	Crying easily
Lying down as she plays with her toys	

- **Is your child's nap schedule contributing to the bedtime battles?** Is your child ready to give up a nap? (See the section on naptime solutions.) Is her final nap of the day occurring too late in the day (e.g., after 4:00 p.m.)? You can try moving your toddler's nap ahead by 15 minutes at a time to see if this helps.

- **Is your toddler trying to put off saying goodnight to you?** Separation anxiety can be a real problem for toddlers as well as babies. Maybe a lovey would serve as a suitable stand-in for you at night. It's a strategy that has worked really well for Irene, 30, mother of one: "Domenic picks a different buddy every night from his shelf of stuffed animals. Once he has done this, we first put buddy to sleep. Once buddy is sleeping, we do the exact same routine for Domenic." Some parents find that putting a toddler in with an older sibling can also work well. Just make sure that the older sibling is eager to take on this added responsibility (there will be some disrupted sleep and odds are at least a few of the older sibling's possessions will become casualties of the new sleeping arrangement, no matter now carefully you toddler-proof); that the sibling is old enough to understand how to be gentle with a toddler; and that you've got a game plan for getting siblings of different ages to sleep at different times in the same room.

- **Is your toddler becoming a master of the bedtime excuse?** Try to nip this not-so-great habit in the bud by anticipating all the items that usually show up on your toddler's post-tuck-in request list so that you can get through them all *before* you kiss her goodnight. That way, she'll have fewer reasons to call for you after lights out. You want her to get the message that bedtime is bedtime. Try making a pre-tuck-in checklist that both you and your toddler can refer to during her bedtime routine. If your list includes pictures, she'll be able to read it on her own, too. Don't make the list too fancy because you'll want to update it as your toddler thinks of new bedtime requests. You may want to print the list out on the family computer, using digital photos of your child brushing her teeth, reading a bedtime story, etc. Don't let the checklist become too long or you'll need to hire a personal assistant to help your child get through the bedtime tuck-in rituals.

PILLOW TALK

While you might be tempted to provide your toddler or pre-schooler with a pet fish or turtle so that he can enjoy a little middle-of-the-night companionship, stick with a plush "pet" rather than the real thing. Young children need to be supervised when they are around pets, both for their own safety and the well-being of the pet. You wouldn't want your child to try to kiss her new friend goodnight. Not only is that likely to be a little traumatic for the fish or the turtle, in the case of the turtle it could expose your child to dangerous salmonella bacteria.

- **Is your toddler's room likely to promote sleep?** Ideally you want your toddler's room to be dark, quiet, and kept at a temperature that is conducive to sleep (cool but not cold) and to contain a few toys, but not her entire toy collection. (See Chapter 2 for more tips on creating a sleep-friendly environment.) Make sure that the mattress on your toddler's bed is both comfortable to sleep on and safe for a child her age (see Chapter 5). And while you're doing a comfort check, check your child's nightie or pajamas. It's amazing how many pajamas come with irritating tags or itchy lace.

"Getting my toddler tucked in is easy. Getting him to stay tucked in is another thing entirely. What do other parents do to get their toddlers to stay in bed once they're no longer sleeping in a crib?" Some toddlers settle into their big-kid beds with minimal fuss. Other toddlers go a little crazy for a while, feeling an overwhelming need to test the limits of what they are and aren't allowed to get away with under the new rules of the bedtime game. If you think about it in those terms, your role is pretty clear—to teach your toddler the new sleep rules. Unless you let them know that running up and downstairs dressed in yellow fuzzy pajamas isn't going to cut it with you, they're doomed to spend the rest of their childhood operating under that unfortunate misconception. Obviously, your family's bedtime rules will be different from my family's bedtime rules. That's okay. What matters is that you and your toddler understand your bedtime rules, and that means being fairly consistent from one night to the next. (Obviously you'll cut your toddler some slack when she's sick or teething or otherwise out of sorts, but you can't make every night an exception or you really don't *have* any bedtime rules.)

Some parents will encourage their toddlers to call for them so that it's the parent who is doing the coming and going after tuck-in time. Others are fine with the idea of toddlers coming and going as many times as possible. Some parents use the idea of the bedtime pass, an idea that tends to work best with older kids, but that basically entitles the child in question to one trip to see Mom and Dad that has nothing to do with using the bathroom or other "legitimate" reasons for being out of bed. The idea is that once they've used up their bedtime pass, they're expected to stay in bed for the rest of the night unless they really need Mom and Dad, in which case, of course, they're free to go get them. Old membership points cards tend to work well as bedtime passes. So what do you do if your toddler comes out of her bedroom at, say, 45-second intervals? Try gently reminding her that it's bedtime and escorting her back to bed. Let her know that you're not far away and that you're going to sleep soon, too. If your toddler comes out again, let her know that you're going to close the door to her bedroom because she's having trouble staying in her bed. If she protests, let her know that you'll try one more time, but that if she comes out of her room, you will have no choice but to close her door because you need to make sure she gets her sleep so that she will feel happy and well rested tomorrow. It's your job as a parent. Then follow through if you have to. Sit outside her door for a few minutes and if you hear her getting back into bed, let her know that you're opening the door again because she's back in bed, but you will close it again and leave it closed if she comes out again. Then follow through. You may have to go through a few nights of the open-door/shut-door routine (and a few wails or shrieks of protest) as your toddler tests you to see if you really mean what you say, but once she figures out that you're serious, the bedtime yo-yo routine will become less of a problem. Or it should. If you're

MOM'S THE WORD

"I do anything it takes to get Jacob to sleep while he's teething.
When all the teeth are in (for now), we'll go right back to napping in the crib."

—*Julie, 29, mom of one*

---

patient, persistent, and basically kind, and you have some underlying
sleep rules, your toddler will eventually learn those rules and start
to follow them *some of the time*. And that means you'll start to get
some rest on a reasonably regular basis. And that, in the world of
toddler parents, is often as good as it gets.

Night Patrol

**"I thought babies were supposed to sleep through the night by
age six months or something. And yet my son is over a year and
he's still not sleeping through all the time. Is there something
wrong with him? Or with me?"** While you may feel like you're the
only parent who is up in the night with a toddler, the National
Sleep Foundation says otherwise. According to its 2004 *Sleep in
America Poll*, 47 percent of toddlers wake in the night and require
help from a parent in getting back to sleep. The first step in
helping your toddler learn how to sleep through the night is to
figure out what's causing him to wake up in the first place and why
he needs your help to get back to sleep again. Sleep Tool 3 lists
some of the most common reasons for night waking in toddlers
and preschoolers. You may also want to refer back to Chapter 4 for
information on what parents can do to promote healthy sleep
habits in their children.

**"My toddler is waking every few hours to nurse. I'm missing
out on a lot of sleep."** If you're looking for ways to reduce the
number of nighttime feedings or eliminate the nighttime nursing
sessions altogether, here are some practical strategies and suggestions
that have worked for moms with toddlers who are bed sharers and
moms with toddlers who are solo sleepers. If you're in the habit of
offering the breast every time your child makes the slightest peep

in the night, try to develop a repertoire of ways of responding to and comforting your toddler in the night. If you think your child might be thirsty and your child is in the habit of drinking from a sippy cup during the day, offer a sippy cup of water to your toddler to see if that takes care of the problem. (Note: Some parents find that it works really well to teach toddlers the sign for thirsty. It takes a bit of the detective work out of night-time parenting.) If you're sharing your bed with your toddler, start making a conscious effort to wake up and stay awake during feedings so that you can break the sleep-food connection for both yourself and your toddler. As a nursing mom, your breasts are your most convenient and powerful nighttime parenting tool, but you don't want to treat them like they are your *only* nighttime parenting tool. Like all moms, you've got a smorgasbord of other soothing skills at your disposal. You may find that you're less tempted to automatically pop out a breast—and your toddler is less likely to automatically ask to nurse—if your breasts are a little less accessible. So think about sleeping in a bulky sweater that helps to keep your breasts out of sight (and hopefully out of your toddler's mind!)

When your toddler is nursing in the night, watch for signs that he's switching from serious-business nursing to slow, leisurely I-could-fall-asleep-like-this nursing. (Remember, this is the habit you're trying to wean him off.) As your toddler starts to show signs of getting sleepy and nursing more for comfort than for nutrition, gradually ease the nipple out of his mouth and let him lean against your breast for a moment. Then position him so that he is snuggled up against you or your partner. He is likely to crave the physical contact while he's nursing less in the night, but you can wean him off this habit down the road. Eventually, you can get him used to having a lovey between the two of you. Over time, you'll find that he will wake less often in the night for hunger, and nurse for shorter periods, and, gradually, not nurse in the night at all. If this solution is taking too long for you, you can also speed the process along by increasing the interval between your toddler's nighttime feedings and/or decreasing the duration of each feeding. (See Chapter 5 for more on this technique.)

You and your partner can work together to wean your toddler off the habit of nighttime nursing. Since your toddler has learned to think milk when he sees you in the night, having your partner go in and soothe your toddler in other ways may be all it takes to get your toddler back to sleep *sans* milk. The secret to making this work is to cut your partner some slack. Do not hover. In fact, try to pretend you have been whisked off to another planet where moms are allowed to sleep without guilt. Let your partner know that he's welcome to get you if your toddler really and truly won't settle without a bit of nursing. This, of course, requires that you have total trust in your partner, that the two of you have thoroughly discussed your sleep philosophies, and that you've got a working game plan that you both can live with—and that game plan includes your partner coming to get you if the toddler is getting bent out of shape because she wants to nurse *right now.* The other approach—cold-turkey night weaning—is pretty hard on moms and toddlers alike (to say nothing of partners, siblings, and neighbors), so it's generally best to avoid it unless you're dealing with a family emergency that warrants an instant weaning. Sometimes slow can be a good thing in the land of parenting. And don't be surprised if you experience some feelings of sadness as your toddler's nighttime feedings come to an end—feelings that may take you by surprise if you were eager to phase out your toddler's nighttime feedings in the hope of getting a little more sleep. Weaning marks the end of a stage in your child's life as well as your life as a mother.

Is it really possible to teach a child to sleep through the night without any crying at all?

Maybe, for a very small percentage of kids. You may luck out and end up with one of those kids who hardly ever cries about any-thing—and who naturally starts sleeping through the night when he is ready. But if your toddler is more resistant to the process of learning to sleep and you have to play a more active role in helping her to learn how to soothe herself back to sleep when she wakes in the night—well, then there may be a few tears as she copes with some of the frustration of learning a new skill. There don't have to be a lot of tears, and those tears may be shed while you're providing comfort to your child (either constant comfort and reassurance or intermittent comfort, depending on the sleep training method that makes the most sense to you), but saying that you want to avoid any crying at all may be setting the bar pretty high for yourself as a parent. Maybe trying to minimize crying would be a more realistic objective to set for yourself than shooting for no crying period. After all, it's frustrating for your toddler to be denied what she wants (staying up as late as she wants at bedtime and getting up in the middle of the night if she feelings like it), and that may result in some crying.

"Ever since my toddler started sleeping in his own bed, his sleep habits have been getting worse, not better. He keeps toddling down the hall to see what we're up to—at 3 a.m.!" This can be one of the most frustrating sleep stages for parents— trying to figure out "what to do to stop the midnight raves in your bedroom when your child learns he is free to roam the house at all hours," according to Dani, 35, mother of two. So how should you respond if you find yourself being greeted by a tiny visitor in the night?

- Decide whether or not having a toddler hop up into your bed or camp out on your bedroom floor is a major deal for you. (Some parents who don't want their toddler bed sharing with them set up a separate sleeping area for their toddler in their bedroom so that the toddler has a safe spot to crash in the middle of the night, but that space isn't quite as cozy as sleeping with Mom and Dad.)

- The middle-of-the-night visits could become a repeat per-formance if you let them happen on too many occasions. If you're adamant that you don't want them to recur, sleep in your toddler's room instead of allowing her to camp out in yours if she's ill or upset from a bad dream. (You can sleep on an air mattress and a sleeping bag in a pinch, or plan ahead by putting a spare twin bed in her room if you suspect you'll be a regular visitor at Camp Toddler.)

MOTHER WISDOM

Sometimes parents start to feel like their toddler's sleep patterns have gotten worse since the toddler started sleeping on his own. Often, there's a simple explanation for this toddler-world sleep mystery: your toddler may have been waking in the night when he was in his own crib, but he was getting back to sleep on his own without calling for you. However, now that he's been "liberated" from his crib, he's decided to take advantage of that new-found freedom by coming to check on *you* when he awakens in the night.

- If you'd prefer that your toddler sleep in her own room rather than bunk in with you, provide gentle reassurance when she comes into your room in the middle of the night and guide her back to her own bed with minimal fuss.

No matter which game plan you decide on, it's important to let your toddler know that wandering around the house while everyone else is asleep is not okay: it's dangerous. Obviously, you'll want to back up your warning with some baby gates, door alarms, and other safety devices.

Little Ms. Early Bird

"My toddler is in the habit of getting up really early in the morning. Her rising time is definitely too early for me, but how do I decide if it's too early for her?" Most toddlers start their days sometime between 6:30 a.m. and 7:30 a.m. If your child is getting up earlier than that—say, at 5:00 a.m.—you may be able to convince her to go back to bed for another hour if you swing into action mode the moment you hear your early bird (a.k.a. lark) start to rouse. Then try to identify the cause of the problem as quickly as possible. Odds are she's waking up for one of the following reasons:

- **She's overtired.** It's that same sleep fact of life come back to haunt you yet again: Sleep begets sleep. If your child is not going to bed early enough, sleeping well at night, or napping well during the day, the biochemistry of lack of sleep can start conspiring against her and cause her to start waking with the birds—or before the birds—in the morning. Here's the clue to look out for: If your toddler gets up really early in the morning, and wants to go back to bed within two hours of getting up, that's a signal that she may not be getting enough sleep at night. She may be using that morning nap to catch up on her sleep. Try postponing her morning nap by 15 minutes each day until you've shifted that nap to mid-morning and she may start to sleep in a little later in the morning.

- **Her sleep-wake cycle needs to be reset.** This is most likely the case if she's the living embodiment of that old saying, "Early to bed and early to rise ..." The most effective ways of getting her back on track are to:

  - emphasize the difference between night and day by exposing your child to daylight (either sunlight or a lamp or light bulb providing artificial sunlight) first thing in the morning and again later in the day

  - emphasize the variations in household noise and activity levels in the daytime versus the evening and the night

  - offer your child meals and snacks at predictable times of day so that your child's body can develop a predictable rhythm and cycle

  - keep your child's sleep-wake times consistent on weekends as well as during the week. Otherwise all the hard work you've been doing to get her into a routine from Monday to Friday can be overturned on Saturday and Sunday.

  You may also want to try advancing her bedtime a little in the hope that she'll eventually shift her wake-up time, too. Sleep scientists recommend that you do this in small increments—no more than 15 minutes per night—until your toddler is waking up at a more appropriate time. Just make sure your expectations are realistic. Six a.m. is *not* an unreasonable hour for a toddler to be waking up. It just feels unreasonable to a parent who'd prefer a 7:00 a.m. wake-up call!

- **She is waking up early because she's used to having break-fast at the crack of dawn.** If your toddler is used to eating breakfast the moment she wakes up, see if you can distract her for a little while in the hope that her tummy alarm clock will eventually reset itself a little later, allowing her (and you) to start sleeping in a little later over time. Never allow your toddler or preschooler to have an early-morning snack in her bedroom unless you are there to supervise her when she is eating it, due to the risk of choking.

- **Something is waking her up.** She's cold, wet, or uncomfortable, or maybe your neighbor's noisy diesel car is acting like a 5:00 a.m. alarm clock. Some solutions: Experiment with diaper types and styles until you find the path to Sleep Nirvana. Ditto with ways of blocking out the noise and light from your least favorite neighbor's car. Maybe you might want to invest in room-darkening shades (which can be yanked up at a more civilized time of day) and pull out the white noise machine that you thought your toddler was finished with by now. The white noise machine can also be a godsend if you or your partner have to get up very early in the morning and the sound of early-morning showering or tooth-brushing tends to function as a wake-up call for your toddler. She can slumber on without even being aware that Mom or Dad is getting ready to go to work.

Once you've identified the problem, you have a decision to make. Are you going to treat this morning awakening as you would a middle-of-the-night awakening by taking care of the root problem, e.g., changing your toddler's wet bed and wet pajamas and tucking her back into her own bed or taking her back to bed with you for a cuddly morning slumber? Or are you going to decide that your odds of getting her back to sleep are slim to none, in which case you'll have to decide if you're ready to get up and start your day, or whether you'd prefer to supervise her in her bedroom, the family room, or some other child-safe area of your home while she plays with her toys? Over time, you may want to teach your toddler the morning rules: Morning starts when it starts to get light outside or morning starts when you hear Mommy's clock radio go off. But that's probably a lot to ask from a toddler. Better put that expectation on hold until your child heads into the preschool years.

Naptime Know-how

"How can I tell if my two-year-old is ready to give up his afternoon nap? I am starting to think he may be ready to give it up, but I'm not sure if I'm ready for him to give it up." Eighty percent of two-year-olds are members of the One-Nap-a-Day Club (see Table 3.3) and 19 percent of them are no longer napping at all, so you aren't the only mom putting out an all-points bulletin on a missing (or soon-to-be-missing) nap.

You'll probably find that there's this awkward period when your toddler is caught in a napping no-man's land: he sort of does and doesn't need that nap. You can use some of the same techniques that were helpful when your baby went from three naps to two (see Chapter 6). Other tips that work well with toddler nap transitions include moving the afternoon nap ahead a little (even if that means serving lunch a little earlier); having quiet time when you used to have naptime; and going to an every-other-day naptime schedule for a while to see how well your child functions without his morning nap. If you find that your child starts getting up really early in the morning (or is impossible to get out of bed in the morning), is extremely grumpy all day long, and is no longer sleeping well at night, she may not be ready to give up that nap quite yet. (See Table 7.2 for more tips on deciding whether or not your toddler needs her nap.)

Note: If your child is in daycare, this is one of those times when a lot of back-and-forth communication between you and your child's caregiver tends to really pay off. You'll be able to figure out what works in terms of promoting good sleep at night and keeping your toddler in a reasonably good mood during the day. A little bit of negotiating may be involved, particularly if your daycare provider needs to balance off the needs of some of the other children

 **PILLOW TALK**

Your toddler will sleep longer at naptime if you put him down for his nap in comfortable clothing and if you make sure that he had a sleep-friendly pre-naptime snack. Complex carbohydrates and protein are particularly effective, such as grilled cheese sandwiches on whole-wheat bread for lunch or some other toddler-friendly lunch that fits the bill. If you work outside the home during the day, you may want to see what's on the lunchtime menu at daycare and talk to his childcare provider about possible menu tweaks if you think his lunch is revving him up rather than winding him down.

---

in her care (e.g., she may not have time to cuddle your toddler on the couch for 45 minutes of uninterrupted quiet time or story-time, like you might do at home, if that's the time she has to feed the infant twins in her care).

Parental self-interest aside, you will want to encourage your child to continue to nap as long as he seems to need that daytime nap fix. Naps can function as a daytime elixir for toddlers by:

- providing them with an opportunity to catch up on any sleep they may have missed out on the night before

- improving their mood (something that will boost their popularity with those around them immeasurably)

- increasing their attention span (a real boon to learning new things) while giving them the opportunity to mentally file away everything they learned earlier in the day

- allowing them to release stress-busting hormones (yes, toddlers have stress, too), thereby making it easier for them to deal with the challenges of life in Toddlerland

- helping them to feel comfortably sleepy rather than overtired when bedtime rolls around

- giving them a break from their caregivers and their caregivers a break from them, which can result in wonderfully happy reunions after naptime.

Table 7.2

Does My Child Still Need a Nap?

	Your Child Probably Still Needs a Nap If ...	Your Child May Be Ready to Give Up Her Nap If ...
Your child's mood	Your child's mood nosedives as the day progresses. It's like living with Dr. Jekyll in the morning and Mr. Hyde in the afternoon.	Her moods are relatively stable most of the time. She's still going to have garden-variety meltdowns, but look for a reduction in the frequency of the "I don't really have anything to cry about except for the fact that I really need a nap" meltdowns. Bottom line? If she's in a generally good mood from dawn to dusk without taking a nap, chances are she's ready to be nap-free.
Your child's energy level	He starts showing signs of being tired or overtired. All of those telltale signs of sleepiness begin to show up. You see him yawning, rubbing his eyes, or staring into space. If he gets overly tired, he may get all wound up as the day progresses, running around the room in circles or yelling and acting hyper. And if you hop in the car to pick up milk and bread just before dinner, he's almost guaranteed to zonk out on the way to the grocery store.	On exceptionally busy days—the days when she's got gym-and-swim first thing in the morning and then the two of you of you decide to hit the grocery store right after that—she may be showing signs of tiredness by the time lunchtime rolls around. But on a typical day, she's still going to have some bounce in her step for most of the day. And if you encourage her to take a nap (at some point, this becomes a huge insult to a child who has become convinced that she's too big to have a nap), then she's likely to spend her entire time singing and playing (if you're lucky) or kicking up a fuss. At this point you may want to start encouraging quiet time, either in her own room (assuming she'll go for that option) or in the same room as you.

Coordination and ability to complete tasks	It's not just his mood that starts to fall apart because he's missed out on his nap. He starts to to lose it period. He begins to bump into walls. His feet get tangled up in one another. And tasks that he usually aces—like stacking blocks—become frustrating or downright impossible because he's lacking both the patience and coordination to tackle them.	Your child is getting enough sleep so she doesn't have to experience the frustration of losing her ability to accomplish a particular task with ease simply because she's overtired.
The daytime nap/nighttime sleep connection	Your child's nighttime sleep is worse on days when he misses one or more of his daytime naps, and *better* on days when he gets his naps. This makes you think he still needs his naps.	Your child has a hard time getting to sleep at night on those rare occasions when she actually takes a daytime nap. She seems to sleep better at night *without* the daytime naps.

Pacifier Partings

"My doctor has encouraged us to convince our two-and-a-half-year-old to give up her pacifier, but taking her pacifier to bed is a huge part of her bedtime routine. How can we break her of this habit and get rid of the pacifier?" If your toddler is in the habit of toting his pacifier around all day long, you may want to wean your child of his pacifier habit on a part-time basis (as opposed to expecting him to quit cold turkey). Here are some tips:

- Limit its use to naptime and nighttime: It gets handed over when your child steps out of bed and handed back over at tuck-in time. In between, it vanishes off the face of the earth as far as your toddler is concerned.

- When your toddler is not in bed, you'll have to be prepared to take on the role of distracter-in-chief. After all, whenever he's lonely, bored, or sad, he'll want to reach for old faithful, his pacifier. If you get tired of bursting into rousing rounds of your toddler's favorite song, you may want to encourage him to form an attachment to something else. It can be exhausting to be someone's substitute pacifier!

MOM'S THE WORD

"It has never been easy to get Daniel to nap. Once he hit two, it became a power struggle. He was not entirely physically ready to give up his nap, but he knew he didn't have to nap in the sense that I was powerless to actually make him sleep, so he'd resist. In the early days of this whole process, I'd spend three hours every afternoon trying to get him into his room or our room, or the couch—wherever, I didn't care!—to sleep. Neither one of us was happy; neither one of us willing to back down. Eventually, I realized this was just a waste of our time and with two kids in the house, a source of stress I just didn't need. So, I instituted quiet time: He could watch a video, read a story, or play quietly with a toy, but he had to do it in the living room for 45 minutes after lunch, a compromise we could both live with."

—*Marcelle, 33, mother of two*

MOM'S THE WORD

"We had a pacifier party. For months in advance we had told Mikaela that when you are three, there are no pacifiers. On the day she turned three, she awoke and we packed all the pacifiers into a box. We decorated the box together. The box was then 'sent' to the hospital so that new babies would have pacifiers. That night the pacifier fairy brought her Paci the Pig, a pillow stuffed-animal-type thing, for her to sleep with. This allowed her to go to sleep without her pacifiers."

—*Michele, mother of two*

- See how well your toddler is doing with the part-time pacifier program and then decide whether he (or you) is ready to go pacifier-free at naptime or at night. At some point, you'll have to decide whether to encourage him to give up the pacifier cold turkey or whether to let him take the pacifier to bed every other night, only on weekends, or on some other schedule.

- Give the pacifier to a friend who is expecting a baby. (Ask her to be a good sport and to accept the gift in the spirit in which it is intended—as a love offering—even if the thought of giving her precious baby-to-be a pre-owned pacifier makes her want to gag.) Remember, a pacifier is one of a toddler's most prized possessions. How can your friend *not* get weepy-eyed about that?

Musical Beds

"How can I tell when it's time to move my toddler out of the crib?" Most children make the move from a crib to a bed sometime between age two and three years. While 90–94 percent of toddlers under the age of 17 months and 77 percent of toddlers ages 18–23 months are still sleeping in a crib, by age two to three years, just 38 percent of children are still sleeping in a crib. It is probably time to move your child out of the crib if:

- He has reached three feet in height or the top rail or the crib is at the level of your child's nipples. (At this point, he is at risk of toppling out of the crib.)

- He has learned to climb out of his crib on his own or you are becoming concerned that he could take a tumble and injure himself.

- He is toilet trained and is starting to want to use the toilet at night, too. (Nighttime dryness typically occurs about six months after daytime dryness, so you don't have to worry about making the transition from the crib to the bed the moment your toddler is dry during the day.)

- He has expressed a strong interest in having his own big bed. (You might as well seize the moment.)

The *worst* reason to make the move is because you need the crib for another baby. It may seem like a practical solution to you, but it's generally best to wait until your toddler is ready. You can always start out with the new baby in a bassinet or a crib that you've borrowed from a friend or another family for a few months. Just make sure that the crib or bassinet meets current safety standards. (See Chapter 5.)

To help make the transition easier for your toddler, give her the opportunity to choose sheet sets for her new bed. If there's enough space in her room, set up the bed while her crib is still set up and let her decide when she's ready to make the move. You may find that she plays on the big bed for a while before she wants to sleep there—and that she possibly naps there on occasion—or you may find that there's no looking back as far as she's concerned once the big-kid bed with the snazzy new sheets has been set up in her room.

To eliminate falls out of bed, which could cause your toddler to become scared of her new bed, you may want to place her bed in the corner so that it is butted up against two walls. Just make sure that there is no gap between the wall and the bed where your child's head could become trapped. Place something soft and padded on the floor beside your child's bed in case she takes a tumble in the middle of the night. Other parent-proven tricks of the trade include the following:

- give your child plenty of opportunities to practise getting in and out of her new bed by the light of day

MOTHER WISDOM

Don't be in any rush to take the crib down. Make sure your toddler is well settled into her new sleeping location before you suggest that the two of you take her crib down so that she'll have more room to play in her bedroom.

- make sure that the bed rail is low enough so that your child won't trip and fall

- consider forgoing the box spring and bed frame until your child is a little older; place the mattress on the floor for now.

"We have been bed-sharing since our two-year-old was born. How can we ease him out of our bed and into his own room?" Basically, what you're working toward is your child's gradual move from sleeping in your bed to sleeping in his own bed down the hall. This is a big transition for him and for you, so you will probably find that it works best to break this transition down into a series of stages, e.g., toddler in our bed; toddler sleeping next to our bed; toddler sleeping across the room; toddler sleeping in own room with a parent in the room; toddler sleeping solo. You might also think in terms of the percentage of time that your toddler spends co-sleeping: full-time co-sleeper, part-time co-sleeper, occasional visitor, solo sleeper. This definitely isn't a cold-turkey or all-or-nothing proposition. Trust me!

Here are some strategies that tend to minimize stress for both toddlers and parents.

If you are transitioning your toddler from sleeping in your bed to sleeping in a crib, start by positioning the crib so that it is right beside your bed. That way, your toddler will still be sleeping beside you, but he'll have his own sleep space. Gradually move the crib a little farther away until your toddler is sleeping across the room. Then move the crib into your toddler's own room.

If you are transitioning your toddler from sleeping in your bed to sleeping in his own bed, start out with him sleeping on a mattress on the floor in your bedroom and then move the mattress down the hall to his room once he's used to sleeping on his own.

PILLOW TALK

Keep these important safety points in mind as you're helping your toddler to make the switch to her new bed:

- Don't offer your toddler a pillow until she's at least 18 months old. And when you *do* introduce a pillow, look for a toddler-sized pillow that is firm rather than soft in design.

- If you would like to offer your toddler a blanket for extra warmth and comfort at night, stick with a lightweight, child-sized blanket rather than a full-sized blanket, quilt, or duvet that might be difficult for your toddler to manage in the night.

- Bunk beds are not a safe option for children under six. Young children have been seriously injured—even killed—as a result of accidents involving bunk beds. Stick with a toddler bed (a great stop-gap measure, particularly since many feature built-in bed rails, but you'll have to replace it in a year or two as your child gets bigger), one of the new generation of extendable toddler beds (like the one made by IKEA) or a regular bed (a permanent sleep solution, but you'll need to purchase bed rails if you intend to raise your child's mattress off the ground).

Try to respond quickly to your toddler if he wakes in the night looking for you during his first few nights in his room. You want him to know that, even though he's bunking on his own now, you're nearby and available to him when he needs you. Chances are he'll test the "parental emergency-response system" a few times to make sure that it's working. Then, with any luck, he'll feel safe and secure in his new sleeping environment and he'll settle into his new sleeping routine. If you already have a "big-kid bed" set up in your child's room, you may want to switch him to his "big-kid bed" right away, but make yourself available to bunk in on a mattress or pad on your child's floor if your child needs some help in making the transition in stages.

Here are some other tips that can be helpful in easing your child's transition to his new room:

- Give your child a say in how his room is set up and decorated. Toddlers are natural-born control freaks. You might as well use that fact to your advantage.

Pillow Talk

According to the American Academy of Pediatrics, it's dangerous to pull your toddler's crib against your bed, keeping the rail that faces your bed at its lowest setting, or removing that crib rail entirely so that your toddler's bed is flush up against yours. Your child could potentially become trapped between the crib and your bed (which could lead to strangulation) fall through the gap and hit the floor, which could result in serious injury.

- Set up your toddler's bed before you help him make the move. Then give him the opportunity to take some of his naps in his future room, if he so chooses. (Napping in the new room is a less risky proposition for most toddlers than setting up permanent residence there.)

- Rather than trying to replicate the old bedtime routine in the new room, gradually ease into a new bedtime routine in the new room. That generally works better.

Solutions Central—The Last Word

UNDERSTANDING THE ROOT of most toddler sleep problems and what types of strategies are most effective in dealing with them are the keys to troubleshooting those problems. Hopefully, now that you've had a chance to apply the information in the numerous checklists, tools, and charts in this chapter, you'll be well on your way to designing a toddler sleep plan that is uniquely suited to your toddler's needs and that will soon have your entire family sleeping easy. Now, on to the world of preschoolers.

CHAPTER 8

The Real-World Guide to Solving Your Preschooler's Sleep Problems

We resigned ourselves to having wakeful nights forever, especially since friends of parents of teenagers are fond of saying, "Yeah, they wake you up now, but at least you know where they are."
—JENNIFER, 37, MOTHER OF THREE

I F YOU'VE GOT a preschooler who is still getting up in the night at least once a week, you're a member of the silent majority (silent because you're likely to be keeping this information under your hat because some people will assume that your child's sleep problems are your problem and a member of the majority because 64 percent of parents of preschoolers are awakened at least once in the night by their three- or four-year-olds).

Chances are when your baby first arrived on the scene, you had envisioned a few months of interrupted sleep—maybe a year's worth at the most. But now that year of very long nights has stretched into *years*, and you're still dealing with your child's sleep problems—and each person that you dare to mention your preschooler's sleep problems to is quick to offer advice on what you should be doing to fix the problem. (Naturally, each person offers totally contradictory advice, so you're quickly concluding that pretending to be well rested is perhaps the best strategy of all, at least when you're in the company of the more rabid advice givers.)

This is one place where you aren't going to be judged or offered pat solutions or patronized or treated in any of the 1,001 other annoying ways that you've no doubt already been treated as the parent of a preschooler who is somewhat resistant to sleep, so relax and read on. With any luck, you'll walk away with some fresh ideas on tackling your preschooler's sleep problems—either sleep issues that have been part of your child's life since he was a babe in arms or sleep issues that have arrived on the scene a little more recently.

Desperately Seeking Sleep Solutions

MOST PARENTS WHO have preschoolers with sleep problems find that their preschooler's sleep problems fall into one of the following categories: bedtime struggles, bedtime fears, nightmares vs. night terrors, or children who are reluctant to get out of bed in the morning. (That's a switch, huh?) We're going to be zeroing in on these types of problems and others in this section of the chapter. If I don't touch upon your preschooler's exact sleep problem (preschoolers are, after all, one of a kind, and their sleep problems can be completely out of this world), you may find it helpful to:

- read this chapter to glean sleep ideas and techniques that can be applied to whatever sleep problem is causing you and your preschooler grief

- review the basic facts about sleep science and what, statistically speaking at least, it takes to end up with a child who is a good sleeper (see Chapters 3 and 4)

- use Sleep Tool 1: "Sleep Problem Solver" to come up with a sleep plan that will work for your family

- review the information on the basic sleep-training techniques (see Sleep Tool 2) in case there are any ideas that might apply to your family's situation

- review the information in Chapters 1 and 2, which will help you to maximize your own opportunities for sleep, starting tonight.

Routines Revisited

"My preschooler can come up with more excuses to delay bedtime than any other kid on the planet. How do I get in touch with the folks from *The Guinness Book of World Records?*" Surf over to Guinnessworldrecords.com and tell the friendly folks there all about your preschooler's daring sleep-defying feats. (Keep me posted on your success with that, will you?) Meanwhile, I'm going to run through some strategies for dealing with preschool bedtime refusal (a.k.a. bedtime resistance) for other moms and dads with would-be record contenders. Here goes:

- **Start teaching your preschooler about the importance of sleep.** Help him to understand that everyone needs sleep to feel their best the following day. Read him books—both fiction and non-fiction—that talk about sleep, and help him to start paying attention to the different ways he feels on days when he's had enough sleep and days when he hasn't.

- **Keep your evenings calm, not frenetic.** When you're signing your preschooler up for activities, consider the time slot. An after-dinner soccer game could make it difficult for your pre-schooler to fall asleep for a couple of hours. Of course, in some communities you don't have much choice about soccer sched-uling. If you want your child to play soccer, you have to go with the time slot when it is offered and realize that your child is going to be bouncing even higher than a soccer ball every Tuesday night. Those are some of the tradeoffs we make when we're raising kids in the real world, right?

- **Keep a lid on the after-dinner craziness.** Erin, a 34-year-old mother of three finds that her kids tend to protest going to bed because that means putting an end to the wild-and-crazy chasing games with Daddy. ("Right before bed is exactly the time he wants to initiate a game of chase or monster, and then he complains when the kids don't settle nicely into their beds!")

- **Give your child choices at bedtime.** Just make sure they're the right choices. Let him decide which pajamas to wear, whether to brush his teeth before or after story time: just don't ask him *whether* he's ready to go to bed.

- **Provide your preschooler with some advance warning that the Sandman is on his way.** When preschoolers start dragging their heels or start coming up with excuses for postponing bedtime, more often than not it's because they're having a great time playing and they don't want to stop for something as blasé as bedtime. Giving your child a little advance warning that bedtime is coming can help to ease the transition for children who may find it hard to stop doing crafts just because bedtime has rolled around again. (See Sleep Tool 3.)

- **Let the Sandman take the rap.** Moms get saddled with enough blame, so let some cheap $5 alarm clock be the bad guy this time around. Let your child know that when the alarm goes off, he has five minutes to put his toys away and start getting ready for bed. It'll be the best $5 you spend this year.

- **Don't lose the bedtime routine too soon.** Sure your child is getting to be a really big kid, but she's not too big for a bedtime routine. You'll find that a bedtime routine that lasts between 20–30 minutes and that ends right in your preschooler's bedroom generally works best. Other tips:

  - Preschoolers love the same old, same old. That's why your child's favorite storybook is likely to be well worn by now, so err on the side of the familiar when it comes to bedtime.

  - Bedtime charts can be helpful in reminding preschoolers what's coming next. This tool can help to keep your older preschooler on board if or when he starts digging in his heels about going to bed. (Older preschoolers are more likely than younger preschoolers to drag out the bedtime routine, to want to go to sleep with the light on, to want attention after tuck-in, and to have a harder time getting to sleep than younger preschoolers.) You could stick with a straight to-do list or go with a sticker chart that allows your preschooler to earn rewards for so many nights of bedtime cooperation (e.g., the chance to choose a small prize from your in-house treasure chest or to earn an activity reward such as a trip to the park with you). The sticker chart idea can be used to encourage your preschooler to work on any sleep problem, e.g., staying in her own bed all night.

- **Go light on the liquids at bedtime and don't overdo it with the heavy meals and snacks either.** Offering too many liquids at bedtime can lead to more wet beds in a child who is prone to bed-wetting. ("We cut out the last bottle once toilet training started, as it's too much to expect him to last through the night with all that milk inside," says Julia, 35, mother of two.) And a heavy meal or a large snack right before bedtime can also interfere with sleep.

- **Make sure your child's bedroom continues to be a happy place.** Avoid sending your preschooler to her room as some sort of punishment. After all, you can't expect her to look forward to sleeping there if you regularly send her there for timeouts to punish her for hitting her baby brother.

- **Give your child an incentive to go to sleep by giving her a heads-up about what's on the agenda for tomorrow**. Of course, if you've got something mega-exciting planned for the morning, you may want to keep that news under your hat; otherwise your sleep incentive plan could backfire on you. Your child may be too excited to sleep at all tonight!

- **Keep television sets and computers out of the bedroom.** Not only do they represent a highly stimulating form of entertainment that can make it hard for a young child to wind down to sleep, your child could get up early or in the middle of the night and tune into some type of programming that is completely unsuitable for young children.

- **Find out if the bogeyman is getting in the way of bedtime.** Of course, if you've got a preschooler with a particularly vivid imagination, bedtime fears can also factor in to his reluctance to head upstairs and keep him up late defending himself and the rest of the household against the monster in the closet. (See the section below on preschooler fears.)

"My biggest problem was my son's desire to prolong bedtime by asking for story after story—a story about a mole; a story about a mouse; a story about a boy. Eventually I'd set out at the beginning how many stories he could have, and we'd stick to it."

—*Julia, 35, mother of two*

"My child is wired at bedtime even though he seems to be getting an age-appropriate amount of sleep. I'm starting to wonder if I should cut out his glass of chocolate milk at bedtime." It would definitely be worth trying that to see if it makes a difference. Caffeine and sugar can leave preschoolers wide-eyed and wired well into the night. And it's not just *your* preschooler who is developing a caffeine habit early in life, by the way: a typical preschooler consumes one or more caffeinated beverages each day. Common sources of caffeine in the diet of a typical preschooler include chocolate, chocolate milk, and caffeinated soda pop (many cola and citrus-flavored beverages). And realize that caffeine can be powerful stuff in the body of a small child. According to the Baylor School of Medicine, a 40-pound child who drinks one 12-ounce can of cola receives the caffeine equivalent of a 150-pound adult drinking two cups of coffee.

The Relaxation Express: The Top Relaxation Techniques for Preschoolers

Some of the relaxation routines that work well for grownups also work well for preschoolers. Here are a few techniques you may want to borrow from your own relaxation repertoire.

- **Reading:** If reading before you go to bed has been part of your own bedtime routine since someone read stories to you, you already know how relaxing this particular pre-tuck-in ritual is. Why not share the story magic with your child? If your preschooler would love story after story after story, pop in an audio book CD after you've finished reading a few books to your pre-schooler so that story time can continue after you leave the room.

- **Storytelling:** Don't overlook the time-honored tradition of storytelling. Some of the best stories come out of Mom or Dad's head—ideally the stories about funny, silly, or downright crazy things that you or your child did during his (or your) younger years. Just don't make the story too stimulating or your four-year-old will be giggling until well past midnight. You may want to capture some of the best homegrown tales for posterity. Record them using a digital audio recorder or a tape recorder so that your preschooler can listen to them again … and again … and again.

- **Melting into a puddle of ice cream:** Who says progressive muscle relaxation (tightening and releasing the tension in successive muscle groups) is just for grownups? It's a fabulously effective technique for people of all ages, including little kids. Teach your preschooler how to do it while she's lying in bed in a darkened room and she'll soon learn to love that wonderfully relaxed feeling—like she's so relaxed that she's melting into a puddle of ice cream or floating in a mug of hot chocolate topped with tiny pillows made of fluffy marshmallows. (This technique isn't for every preschooler. Some kids simply can't even stay still long enough to master the basics.)

- **Emptying my brain:** This technique works well with older preschoolers. Not only do they have a solid grasp of concepts like empty and full, they're capable of the more abstract thinking that this exercise requires. Place two large plastic juice jugs beside your child's bed. (It would be ideal if you could find a dark-colored jug for the nighttime jug and a light-colored jug for the morning jug.) The first should contain a collection of plastic objects that could each represent an idea in your child's brain, e.g., a collection of child-safe blocks, etc. If your child tends to have trouble carrying around a lot of ideas in his head—worries that make it hard for him to wind down to sleep—suggest that he empty his brain before he goes to bed by moving all his ideas from the bedtime brain to the morning brain container.

MOM'S THE WORD

"As adults, we often have trouble sleeping because we are stressed, worried, or frustrated. Preschoolers are at a very challenging stage: They are changing rapidly, and society's way of treating them is also changing. No more cute pats on the head from strangers, no more coddling at day care, more rules to follow, younger siblings to take parents' attention. Preschoolers feel this and react to it, but unlike adults, have no way of processing these emotions or handling the stress. In fact, most adults don't do this very well. So, to tackle preschool sleep problems simply from a routine or behavioral point of view is ineffective. Ways to help preschoolers and their parents wind down and handle stress would seem to be the most effective means of everyone getting good sleep."

—Jennifer, 37, mother of three

- **Variation:** If he has a lot of worries in his head, he can draw pictures of those worries on a piece of paper and then crunch up the piece of paper and throw it away. On a symbolic level at least, he can say, "Bye, bye, worries!"

- **Pictures in my head:** This one is a natural for the preschooler with an active imagination and the ability to use that imagination to think happy thoughts at bedtime, not scary thoughts! Use guided imagery to show your preschooler how this technique works so that she can use it herself when she's trying to get to sleep at bedtime or if she wakes up feeling scared or lonely in the night. Tell her to imagine a day when she felt really warm and happy. Maybe she was at the beach, walking on the toasty-warm sand; or sitting on the back porch at Grandma's, enjoying the warm, summer breeze. Ask her to remember how her arms felt and how her legs felt, what the air smelled like, what she saw, what sounds she heard, and so on. Then encourage her to turn all those wonderful sights, sounds, smells, and feelings into a movie that she can play in her head anytime she wants to relax. If she gives it a name, you can help her to remember those feelings by reminding her to treat herself to a special screening of the movie about making sandcastles or the movie about roasting marshmallows the next time she's having a hard time falling asleep.

MOTHER WISDOM

While you sometimes don't have a choice about having siblings share a room—space may be the deciding factor—if you have a choice about which siblings do or don't bunk with whom, aim for a match that bears these points in mind.

- *Age:* The youngest sibling should be at least 18 months of age before being moved in with an older sibling.

- *Compatibility:* Given what you know about their two temperaments, interests, and activity levels, are these two children likely to be able to share a room relatively peacefully or should you expect fireworks?

- *Sleep Skills:* Are they both basically good sleepers or is one sibling going to keep the other sibling up all night?

- **Dream castles:** You've told your preschooler that it's tuck-in time and she can't actually take all of her favorite toys to bed (you want her to get some sleep tonight, after all), but that doesn't mean that she can't build castles in her head. Encourage her to lie in bed drawing pictures in her head of all the things she'd love to see in real life: a castle made entirely of sugar cones, icing, and gumdrops, a library where they let you keep the books forever, etc.

- **The sound of silence:** If you cover your ears, you can hear this muted roaring sound, which, to a preschooler with an active imagination, can sound like water tumbling over a waterfall or something else equally exciting. Tell your child that if she's having difficulty zonking out any other way, she can cover her ears and listen to this cool sound, a sound that hardly makes any noise at all. Of course, it's also a great technique for drowning out any noises that happen to be driving your preschooler crazy as she's trying to drift off to Dreamland, like annoying older brothers and crying baby sisters.

- **Music:** Some parents find that music can be very soothing to their preschooler. Just make sure that you choose your bedtime tunes with care. You want something that will soothe, not inspire your child to hop out of bed and try some new dance moves. You'll also want music that's relatively consistent from start to finish. Music that changes tempo, tone, volume, or style dramatically mid-song or mid-album is likely to rouse your child from the almost-asleep stage and help her to catch her second wind.

"My three- year-old and five-year-old recently started sharing a room. The problem is that they end up playing until I go to bed. How can I let them know that it's okay to play for a while, but not for hours and hours"? Since your kids aren't settling down to sleep after a reasonable amount of playtime, you'll have to help them learn to do that. You may want to help them reorganize their room and use that as an excuse to do a bit of a toy shuffle. All the really active play toys (e.g., noisy remote-control cars) should find a home somewhere else in the house, while some of the more sleep-inducing toys (e.g., audiobooks) could simultaneously migrate to their bedroom. Establish some rules about how long the new roomies are allowed to play at night, and don't be afraid to play toy cop if you have to. "I tell them they have had all day to play and now it is quiet time," says Keri, 39, mother of seven. "If they continue to play, I remove the toy that's causing the problem."

Here's something else to consider: Not all sibling roommate matches are necessarily made in heaven. Some siblings bring out the worst in one another, especially at bedtime. You may want to rethink this particular sleeping arrangement if, after a couple of weeks, your two children are still getting consistently less sleep than they were getting before they became roomies.

Bedtime Fears

"My four-year-old starts clinging to my leg and shaking his head the moment I even mention the dreaded b-word (bedtime). Any tips on helping kids to manage their bedtime fears?" Be aware of which types of news stories and entertainment programs your child may be tuning into, even when you're positive he isn't listening. Preschoolers are like information sponges, and all it takes for them to get seriously spooked is to walk through the family room when an older sibling is watching a seemingly innocuous

PILLOW TALK

Wondering when you should be concerned about your preschooler's bedtime fears? If those fears continue unabated despite all your efforts to reassure him, if they begin to spill over into the daytime (e.g., your child won't go upstairs anymore because the monster might get him), if your child is exhibiting other worrying behaviors (e.g., excessive clinging and crying, recessive behaviors, etc.), raise the issue of his fears with his doctor. Sometimes deep-rooted fears are an indication of a more serious problem.

"family movie" that features something that's still too scary for a preschooler or when a promo for the latest horror flick comes on at the wrong moment. *Voila!* You've got one petrified four-year-old on your hands.

Help your child to feel more secure. Try giving your child a flashlight, tucking him in with his favorite stuffed animal, and playing some quiet music in his room so that he's less likely to be awakened and scared by every creak and bang. And do what else you can think of to reassure him that he's safe: "Andrew knows we have an alarm system and that we put it on every night," notes Carolyn, 40, mother of two. Remember that you get extra marks for creativity when it comes to troubleshooting your child's bedtime fears. If your child is afraid of "the monster under the bed," use that space for storage so that the monster will have to take up residence under someone else's bed. And if your child is scared of the monster in the closet, install a closet light so that the light turns on whenever the closet door is opened.

"A friend told me that I should chase the 'monsters' away by using 'magic spray.' This doesn't seem right to me." Some parents like this solution. Others prefer to avoid it because it's not telling your child the truth. At some point, your child will discover that there's no such thing as monster spray and he may understandably wonder what else you may not have been completely honest with him about.

Nightmares vs. Night Terrors

"Should we let our three-year-old come and sleep with us after she's had a bad dream?" Some children require only a few minutes of comfort after they've had a bad dream. Once they've been reassured that they are safe and their bad dream wasn't real, they're ready to be tucked back to sleep. Other children become quite upset and can take much longer to settle down. You'll have to decide whether bringing your child back to your bed is the right solution or whether it is likely to create additional problems (e.g., encourage more night waking so that your child can be rewarded with the opportunity to sleep with you).

"Should I talk to my child about his bad dream the following morning, whether or not he actually raises the subject when he gets up? Or should I let sleeping monsters lie?" Child development experts suggest that you let your child take the lead in initiating such a discussion. It's possible that your child will have forgotten all about the monster who stole his Thomas the Tank engine trains (especially when he wakes up and sees that his treasured tank engines are still on the shelf in his bedroom). But if he *does* start talking about the nightmare again, you might encourage him to make up an ending in which he chases the evil toy-stealing monster away forever and gets his prized Thomas collection back safely. It's an approach that has worked well for Jennifer, 37. "Both my husband and I remember having nightmares as children, and how terrifyingly real these fears can be," the mother of three children, ages eight months through six years, explains. "We talk them out. Luke as a preschooler told us of a monster in his closet. We asked him to describe it. He told us it was green and purple and he spit at people. He became the Spitty Monster. We then made up a story where the Spitty Monster hid in the closet because he didn't like the light. Turning on the light made him hide. Leaving his closet light on got us through a couple of nights. Then we added to the story: The Spitty Monster also didn't like being laughed at. So, if the Spitty Monster felt close, saying, 'Ha Ha' would keep him away. This worked for another few nights. Then my son wanted to add to the story, saying that the Spitty Monster really wanted to be friends, so he made friends with his imaginary monster. There have been other fears, from him and Clare, but usually a story and leaving the light on helps ease them."

"Can you explain the difference between nightmares and night terrors?" Once you've witnessed a night terror, you won't need an explanation. It's like your child has been transporting to Land of the Preschooler Zombies, except that she's still in the room with you. "Faire starts crying in her bedroom and when we go to her, it's as if she doesn't even know we're there and she's not really awake," explains Bonnie, 30, mother of two. "It's so hard because we can't stop the crying until she wakes up and can be calmed down." The only good news about night terrors (a.k.a. sleep terrors) is that, as scary as they are for parents, they aren't scary for kids. Kids aren't aware of what they're experiencing when they're having a night terror, and they don't have any memory of night terrors afterwards. Table 8.1 spells out the major differences between nightmares and night terrors, and Chapter 9 provides some additional information about night terrors.

Thunderstorms

"If there's a thunderstorm, my four-year-old tries to crawl in bed with us because she's scared. Is this normal for a preschooler?" Thunderstorms are scary to a lot of preschoolers. There's that sudden flash and then the accompanying boom. It can be really scary. Encourage your child to come and get you—or to call for you—if she's afraid. And then plan to bunk together until the storm passes over. Come daybreak, you might want to hit the library to borrow a variety of non-fiction and fiction books about thunderstorms. You might even think about purchasing a nature sounds CD that features thunderstorm sounds. (Wait! If you have a white noise machine tucked away in a drawer somewhere, maybe your make and model features thunderstorm sounds in its repertoire of soothing sounds.) But realize that it's one thing to understand what causes thunderstorms, and it's quite another to not find them scary in the night.

Sibling Sleep Deprivation

"My preschooler has been sleeping through the night since she was six months old. All that changed when we brought her baby brother home a few weeks ago. Now she's getting up in the night almost as often as he is. I'm so frustrated I could scream." Sleep deprivation times two can be almost too much to bear. In fact, for some parents, it *is* too much to bear, particularly if postpartum depression starts to factor into the equation. (See the material in Chapters 1 and 2 for some must-read information on taking care of you.) But as for your preschooler's disrupted nights, hopefully that will be a limited time offer. There can definitely be a period of adjustment for siblings when a new baby arrives, but most kids adjust relatively quickly. "After the first few weeks, my three-and-a-half-year-old no longer seemed to hear the baby at night," says Brandy, 30, mother of two. And, surprisingly, a fair number of children continue to slumber on undisturbed, seemingly oblivious to the new kid on the block who has decided to take his "town crier" responsibilities very seriously.

Help Me Make It through the Night

"I find myself losing patience with my child's night waking now that he's over three. I hadn't counted on it lasting this long. And my partner's even less patient than I am. He wants to 'Ferberize' her, starting tonight." In many ways, it's easier to be the parent of a night-waking preschooler than it is to be the parent of a night-waking baby or toddler. "Clare can tell us what she wants (a blanket, a toy, etc.) and once we give her that, she goes back to sleep quickly," notes Jennifer, 37, the mother of three. "In this way, her vocabulary has been a blessing, and takes the guess-work out of trying to help a cranky, half-asleep child." In other ways, it's more difficult. After all, when you signed up for this nighttime parenting gig, you hadn't counted on it lasting for quite this long. Some parents, like Christine, 32, mother of two, feels quite strongly that there shouldn't be a statute of limitations on nighttime cuddles or middle-of-the-night reassurance just because

Table 8.1

The Stuff of Which Nightmares and Night Terrors Are Made: A Comparison

	Nightmares	Night Terrors (a.k.a. Sleep Terrors)
Is your child awake or asleep?	Your child has a scary dream and then wakes up, frightened and upset, looking for comfort.	Your child is still asleep while the night terror is occurring, even though he may appear to be awake. His eyes may be wide open and his heart may be racing while he screams, cries, or shouts at something unseen. If he's aware of you at all, he takes only passing notice of you, and will typically go back to sleep at the end of the night terror without ever fully awakening.
Frequency	Between 10 percent and 50 percent of preschoolers have nightmares. And one in every four children has nightmares more than once a week.	Approximately 6 percent of preschoolers have night terrors.
Age at which they typically occur	Nightmares typically start when children are three to six years of age, but they occur in people of all ages.	They are most common in four- to eight-year-olds.
What triggers them	They are triggered by inadequate sleep, stress the child has experienced during the day, or a traumatic event that your child may have heard about in the news (an earthquake, a flood, or a terrorist attack). Children who have been through frightening or traumatic experiences often experience nightmares. In fact, nightmares are a symptom of post-traumatic stress disorder.	Inadequate sleep and stress trigger night terrors

Gender in which they are most likely to occur	They are equally common in boys and girls.	Night terrors are most common in boys.
Time of the night when they are most likely to occur	They typically occur between 4 a.m. and 6 a.m.	They typically occur between 1 a.m. and 3 a.m.
Sleep cycle in which they occur	They occur in REM sleep (active sleep).	They occur in NREM sleep (quiet sleep).
What you can do	Offer comfort and reassurance if your child wakes up feeling frightened by a dream. Explain to your child that the dream was not real (even though it seemed very real) and that she is safe. If your child talks about his dream in the morning, give him the opportunity to rewrite the ending of his dream so that the dream is less upsetting to him. If your child has frequent nightmares, raise this issue with your child's doctor.	Hold on to your child so that he won't hurt himself while he's thrashing around, and provide gentle reassurance, even if you're not sure he can hear you. Don't try to wake your child because this will only upset your child more. If your child continues to experience night terrors, raise this issue with your child's doctor.
Is your child likely to remember the episode in the morning?	Your child may or may not remember the dream in the morning; and even if he does remember it, he may not necessarily want to talk about it. The best advice? Let sleeping dreams lie until he brings up the subject.	Your child is unlikely to have any memory of screaming in terror in the night, but you won't forget the episode anytime soon.

a child has achieved the status of preschooler. "Preschoolers may still need cuddling, or a middle of the night drink and I don't think those things should be refused just on principle."

If we can resist the pressure to let other people tell us how we should be handling nighttime parenting situations with our kids, we're less likely to lose sight of our parenting instincts at 3:00 a.m. Consider these wise words from Todaysparent.com fatherhood columnist John Hoffman, himself the father of some long-term night wakers: "For many of us, the problem is not just disturbed nights, but the conflict we feel about it," he writes in an article entitled "Sleep Like a Baby." "So we get up to comfort our baby, but we think we aren't supposed to. Or, in desperation, we let him cry, but that doesn't feel right either." We can quickly find ourselves caught up in a rather nasty sleep snafu: the energy that we waste second-guessing our night-time parenting decisions ends up being far more exhausting and energy-zapping than our child's night-waking per se.

Little Miss Sleepyhead

"When my child was younger, she used to get up at the crack of dawn. Now that she's a little older, it's a real battle to get her up in time to go to preschool. Is there no middle ground with this child?" Perhaps not, but what you're describing isn't that unusual for children her age: 19 percent of preschoolers have difficulty getting up at least a few mornings each week (invariably the mornings when you most need her to get up on time). It could be that your preschooler is totally tuned into her world and that she may be having a difficult time winding down at bedtime and hence dragging herself out of bed the following morning. And even if your preschooler has banked a solid amount of sleep the night before, she still may crave more shut-eye time long after sun up. "In the morning, Aislin's almost acting more and more like a teenager," says Gillian, 33, who is expecting her third child. "She usually needs to be woken at 8 a.m. and is not pleased about it—this despite bedtime being about 12 hours earlier!"

Preschooler Naps: The Endangered Species List

"My daughter just turned three. How long can I expect her to keep taking afternoon naps?" Because no one has invented a nap crystal ball that will allow me to tell you how long naps will continue to be part of your daughter's reality, all I can offer you is the next best thing: a snapshot of the Law of Nap Averages. According to the National Sleep Foundation's *Sleep in America Poll* (2004), 57 percent of three-year-olds were still napping during the day, but only 26 percent of four-year-olds were still napping during the day. (See Table 3.3 in Chapter 3.) So, the odds are that your daughter will give up that nap this year.

Some parents find that their preschoolers tend to nap better when they are at day care than when they are at home. "If only I had the 15 other kids in Hayley's class over for naptime, she would go down, no problem!" says Tanys, 36, mother of two. When the moment of truth arrives and it's finally time to bid that final day-time nap goodbye, you may find that it works well to ease your preschooler into a quiet time routine so that she has a bit of a break during the day—even if it's not a full-blown nap—and you have a bit of a break, too. See Chapter 7 for more tips on helping your child to adjust when a nap disappears, and assessing your child's readiness to give up a nap.

Solutions Central—The Last Word

SLEEP PROBLEMS COME and go. Sometimes you play an active role in making them disappear as a result of carefully kept sleep logs or barely readable sleep notes. When your child starts waking up in the night again, your instinctive reaction may be to sigh deeply and think "I can't do this anymore." You're only human, after all. But then you're hit by a jolt of mother or father optimism—that morning-after fuel that keeps us going—and you realize that this might not be the same old sleep problem rearing its ugly head again: this might be a temporary visitor—a one-time visitor, even.

Your hard sleep work of the past three-and-a-half years hasn't necessarily been all for naught. Your (newly) all-star sleeper may still be in the ranks of the all-star sleepers. She may simply be an all-star sleeper with a raging ear infection. But if you *do* find yourself dealing with something more complex and less temporary in nature—say bed-wetting, sleepwalking, or night terrors—at least you have clocked enough time in the sleep-deprived parent trenches to know that you will get through this, even if it doesn't feel that way.

And having acquired all the hard-won wisdom (see "The Top 12 Sleep Solutions"), you'll be in the fortunate position of being able to make a serious difference in the life of some other desperate, sleep-deprived parent. You'll be able to pass along some of the lessons you learned—sleep solutions that really *can* make parenting a whole lot easier when a good night's sleep sometimes seems like nothing other than a cruelly deceptive mirage. After all those months of begging favors and asking random strangers for sleep advice, you finally have the chance to give something back—to pay it forward, so to speak, and in a kind, supportive, and non-bossy way. Won't that feel great?

THE TOP 12 SLEEP SOLUTIONS FOR PARENTS OF BABIES, TODDLERS, AND PRESCHOOLERS: A NO-WORRY APPROACH FOR EACH AGE AND STAGE

1. **Make sure that your child is getting adequate sleep.** According to the National Sleep Foundation, babies need 14–15 hours of sleep, toddlers need 12–14 hours of sleep, and preschoolers need 11–13 hours in each 24-hour period to function at their best. And the more sleep deprived a child is, the more likely he is to be sleepy and overtired during the day, to change sleeping locations at night, and to have more sleep problems overall. Sleep begets sleep—it can't be said often enough.

2. **Begin your child's bedtime routine when your child is sleepy but not overtired.** Ideally your baby's bedtime routine should last 30–60 minutes and your toddler or preschooler's bedtime routine should last 20–30 minutes and it should include elements that he finds genuinely enjoyable.

3. **Use the power of daylight to reset your child's sleep-wake clock.** Daylight plays a powerful role in resetting our circadian rhythms, so by exposing your child to daylight as soon as she wakes up in the morning, you'll be giving her body a powerful cue that morning has arrived.

4. **Provide your child with a sleep environment that is sleep enhancing.** That means a sleep environment that is cool (but not cold), dark, and quiet. And don't forget to check for comfort, too. Make sure that your child is sleeping on a comfortable mattress in non-itchy pajamas so that nothing can disrupt your child's trip to Dreamland.

5. **Make sure your child's sleep environment is safe, too.** (See Chapter 6 for guidelines on childproofing your child's bedroom, keeping the hall clutter-free at night, and other important nighttime parenting safety tips.)

6. **Teach your child how to soothe himself back to sleep, and be aware of how sleep associations affect your child's sleep habits.** Continue to reinforce relaxing bedtime routines and to encourage your child to soothe himself back to sleep if he wakes up in the night. About one-third of preschoolers still need some hands-on help from Mom and Dad in soothing themselves back to sleep.

7. **Keep your child on a regular sleep and nap schedule.** Your older infant, toddler, or preschooler's wake-up time and bedtime should stay within a one-hour window most of the time (a 6:30 p.m. to 7:30 p.m. bedtime works best for most toddlers and preschoolers). Obviously, you can make exceptions on special occasions, but you don't want those special occasions to be too frequent or your child's circadian rhythm (sleep-wake cycle) will start to get seriously out of whack.

8. **Don't be in any rush to eliminate naps.** And when your child does eliminate his nap, try to encourage him to replace naptime with quiet time instead. That way, he can have a bit of a break in the midst of his busy day and, on days when the two of you are home together, you can benefit from that break, too.

9. **Serve your child foods that are sleep enhancing, not sleep inhibiting.** If you serve complex carbohydrates with protein, you're giving your child a snack with plenty of lasting power. He won't wake up hungry anytime soon. On the other hand,

foods high in protein or sugar tend to give you an energy blast that can make it hard for you to get to sleep. And carbs straight up can make you very dozy. Other things to think about on the dietary front: Be particularly careful of the timing of big meals (not too close to bedtime) and watch how much caffeine your child is consuming.

10. **Use physical activity to promote sleep.** Provide your toddler or preschooler with opportunities to be physically active during the day so that he will sleep more soundly at night. And give your baby some opportunity for some "floor time," too.

11. **Avoid TV/computer and other highly stimulating forms of play right before bedtime.** Vigorous exercise can be quite stimulating, so enjoy being active as a family earlier in the day. Remember that preschoolers have particularly vivid imaginations. Monitor your preschooler's media consumption carefully to reduce fears of "the monster in the closet." And if your preschooler does develop some bedtime or middle-of-the-night fears, treat those fears seriously. Then help him to come up with a concrete game plan for dealing with the monster in his nightmare or the monster in his closet.

12. **Don't forget to practise good sleep hygiene yourself.** Not only will you have more patience and stamina to deal with whatever parenting challenges await you in the night, you'll also be modeling healthy sleep habits for your child.

CHAPTER 9

Sleep Disorders: What Every Parent Needs to Know

Sleep is the golden chain that ties health and our bodies together.
—THOMAS DEKKER

UP UNTIL NOW, this book has focused on garden-variety sleep problems—the types of issues that cause the majority of Moms and Dads to accumulate rather hefty sleep debts during the early years of their children's lives. In this final chapter of the book, we move into slightly more exotic turf by zeroing in on anything and everything that falls under the "sleep disorders" umbrella. I'll be talking about fairly common sleep disorders, like bedwetting, sleep walking, and sleep talking, as well as some sleep disorders that you may not have ever heard of—like hypnagogic hallucinations and restless legs syndrome.

The Worried Parent's Rest-Easy Guide to Sleep Disorders

SLIGHTLY PANICKED OUT about this entire subject? You're not alone. Most of us get kind of nervous when this subject comes up. But it's important to realize that there are only a few truly freaky sleep disorders (ones in which a child's health can be seriously compromised)—and even those ones don't have to the stuff of which parental nightmares are made if you seek treatment for your child.

Maybe you'll feel a little better if I start out by pinning down the definition of the term sleep disorder. The term sleep disorder is used to describe a variety of different sleep-related problems that can occur in both adults and children. Sleep disorders can be caused by physiological problems, difficulties that are related to sleep itself (e.g., problems moving from one sleep stage to another that can trigger strange sleep behaviors, like night terrors), and problems with the internal clock that tells us when to get up and when to go to sleep (e.g., advanced sleep phase syndrome—when a person wants to get up and go to sleep far too early). It can refer to everything from a relatively minor problem like bedwetting to something fairly serious like obstructive sleep apnea, when a person periodically stops breathing during sleep.

It's important to be aware of the warning signs of sleep disorders in young children. You should discuss your child's sleep patterns with his doctor if he exhibits some of the following sleep behaviors:

- difficulty falling asleep
- nighttime awakenings
- snoring
- stalling and not wanting to go to bed
- having trouble breathing
- loud or heavy breathing while sleeping
- daytime behavior like overtiredness, sleepiness, and crankiness

The good news is that most sleep problems are easily treated. Treatments options may include medication, behavior therapy, or both. It's a good idea to keep track of the frequency of any sleep disturbances that your child is experiencing (e.g., are they happening once a week, once a month, or every night?). Immediate medical attention should be sought if:

- your child's sleep is significantly disrupted
- your child is significantly disrupting the sleep of other family members

- your child is at risk of injuring himself in the night.

Sleep problems are more likely to occur when a child has a fever, or when a child is taking certain types of medications. They are also more likely to occur when a child is overtired or under stress, so you will want to:

- ensure that your child is getting adequate sleep
- establish a regular sleep-wake schedule for your child
- minimize stress
- encourage your child to go to the bathroom before he goes to bed; having a full bladder is believed to be a contributing factor to certain types of sleep disturbances in children.

For the past few years, the American Academy of Pediatrics and other leading health authorities have been recommending that doctors screen all children for snoring. What doctors are looking for are signs of obstructive sleep apnea (OSA), a sleep disorder in which a collapse of soft tissue in the throat causes a person to stop breathing for 10 seconds or longer at a time. The condition causes sleep deprivation, interferes with growth and development (by leading to sleep-deprivation-linked changes to your child's metabolic rate), and can lead to behavior and academic problems in children. OSA tends to be a particular problem in children aged two through five because this is the age at which the tonsils and adenoids are the largest in proportion to the airway size.

It's easy to start panicking about OSA—to start thinking the worst every time you hear a snuffle or snort coming out of your child's mouth. Ian Maclusky, the Director of the Sleep Disorders Laboratory at the Hospital for Sick Children (and one of the technical reviewers for this book), notes that there's a difference between run-of-the-mill snoring and "the child who snores heroically—louder than Dad." Other things to watch for are extreme restlessness (your child's bedclothes are always bunched up in the morning); pauses in your child's breathing while he's sleeping; and overtiredness during the day. See Table 9.1 for more about obstructive sleep apnea.

Table 9.1

The Most Common Types of Sleep Disorders in Young Children

Type of Disorder	Who it Affects and When	Description of a Typical Episode	What You Can Do to Help Your Child
Confusion arousals (similar to night terrors that occur in older children; in fact, some sleep experts argue that the term "confusion arousals" should be replaced with the term "night terrors" when applied to infants and toddlers)	Most likely to occur in infants and toddlers, but can also occur in adults.	Confusion arousals typically occur during the first one-third of the night. Your baby or toddler starts crying and thrashing around in her sleep. She appears to be awake, but is clearly confused and upset, and won't let you comfort her. At some point, your child will awaken briefly and decide that she wants to go back to sleep. The entire episode typically lasts under 30 minutes.	Provide comfort when your child is willing to accept it and tuck your child back in bed at the end of the episode. Make sure that your child can't injure herself while she's thrashing around in her sleep. You don't want her to bang her head on a night table beside her bed, for example.
Rhythmic-movement disorder	Occurs in 5 percent of children, but is most common in babies and toddlers; head-banging is the most common type of behavior exhibited among children with this disorder.	Your child soothes himself to sleep by engaging in head-banging, head-rolling, and/or body-rocking during the transition from sleep to wake or wake to sleep. Some children also moan or hum.	Most children outgrow this stage on their own. The treatments that are sometimes prescribed for this condition don't tend to be particularly effective.

Bed-wetting (enuresis)

Bed-wetting is so common in preschoolers (an estimated 50 percent of three-year-olds and 40 percent of four-year-olds wet the bed a couple of times each week) that doctors won't even diagnose enuresis (the medical term for bed-wetting) in children until they are at least five years of age. In general, you can expect your child to start staying dry at night approximately six months after he is staying dry during the day.

By the time children reach this age, approximately 15–25 percent of children are still wetting their bed at least some of the time, and bed-wetting is considered to be a problem if there are still at least two wet nights per month at age five to six or one wet night per month at age seven.

Your child wets the bed during the night. Children who wet the bed tend to be very deep sleepers. They may have bladders that aren't big enough to hold all the urine that is produced in the night. Their bladder muscles may not be functioning as a team (the muscles that squeeze urine out may be squeezing harder than the muscles that hold urine in). And they have a tendency not to wake up when their bladders need to be emptied. The net result? A wet bed.

In most children, the problem will resolve itself. To minimize bed-wetting, children should avoid drinking a lot of fluids before bedtime, particularly caffeinated beverages, which can act as a diuretic. It's also important for children who wet the bed to get the sleep they need. Increasing sleep by as little as 30 minutes per night may be all that it takes to help a child who was wetting the bed to start staying dry.

Don't shame or blame your child for wetting his bed. It's not something he can control.

A child has to be a willing participant in any treatment program for bedwetting. Bed alarms are the most effective treatment method for children age five and up (75 percent effective and only a 41 percent relapse rate once treatment is stopped), but this form of treatment has a 10–30 percent

continued on p. 246

Type of Disorder	Who it Affects and When	Description of a Typical Episode	What You Can Do to Help Your Child
	Bed-wetting tends to run in families. It is more common in boys because the urinary sphincter is slower to mature in boys than in girls.		dropout rate because some parents and children find that they do not like this particular treatment method. Bed alarms are generally the best bet for older children who want to stay dry for sleepovers. Other treatment methods include a nose spray (DDAVP) that decreases urine volume at night (most effective in children age nine and up), and the use of medication (controversial, due to high relapse rates and side effects). Note: Any method that rewards a child for staying dry (e.g., stickers and star charts) is generally discouraged because it overlooks the fact that bedwetting is largely out of the child's contro.
Sleepwalking	Can occur at any age, but is particularly common in children ages three through seven years. Most children outgrow sleepwalking	Your child starts sleepwalking one to two hours after falling asleep. Your child may do something odd or irrational, like trying to go to the	Keep your child safe. You may want to tie a bell to your child's bedroom door (or your own bedroom door, if you're room sharing) so that you'll

know when he's up and about. If you're bed sharing, position yourself between your child and the door so that you'll be alerted if he gets up in the night. And make sure that windows are fully secured and that floors are free of clutter so that no one will trip in the night.

If you're losing sleep because you're worried about your child wandering out of the house in the middle of the night, purchase a door alarm or turn on the door chime function on your home security system if you have one. (The door chime function makes that chirping bird sound each time someone opens an exterior door.) That should help you to rest a little easier.

Gently lead your child back to bed. You don't need to wake your child up to do this. You may end up scaring your child if you try to wake him.

Sleepwalking can be triggered by sleep deprivation, so make sure your

continued on p. 248

by the time they reach adolescence. The children of parents who were once themselves sleepwalkers are 10 times as likely to be sleepwalkers than children of parents who were not sleepwalkers.

bathroom in a closet. The sleepwalking episode may last from 5 to 20 minutes.

Type of Disorder	Who it Affects and When	Description of a Typical Episode	What You Can Do to Help Your Child
			child is getting enough sleep. Be sure to mention your child's sleepwalking to his doctor because sleepwalking is sometimes associated with sleep apnea. If your child sleepwalks on a nightly basis, your child's doctor may suggest a treatment called scheduled awakening, in which you fully awaken your child 30–45 minutes before the sleepwalking episode typically occurs. This will often interrupt your child's sleep cycles enough to prevent the sleepwalking episode.
Sleep talking	Can occur at any age; one in 10 preschoolers or school-age children talks in his or her sleep at least a few nights each week.	Your child talks, laughs, or cries out in her sleep, but is unaware of what she is doing. Consequently, she doesn't remember the episode the next day. Episodes typically last for 15 to 20 minutes.	Sleep talking is rarely cause for concern. Just let your child carry on her middle-of-the-night monologue and know that she'll soon be back to sleep. (And soon you will be, too.)

Sleep bruxism (teeth grinding or clenching during sleep)	Occurs in 14 percent of children; the frequency decreases with age (only 8 percent of teenagers grind their teeth). More common in children with cerebral palsy or severe mental retardation.	Your child grinds his teeth in his sleep. Each time your child grinds his teeth, he does so for eight to nine seconds at a time. The grinding is noisy enough for you to hear it in another room because your child is applying 88 pounds of force when he is grinding his teeth. If your child clenches his teeth in his sleep, he may wake up with sore jaw muscles and/or a headache.	Teeth grinding can damage the protective enamel on the teeth. It can also result in problems with speaking, chewing, and swallowing. Teeth grinding is more likely to occur when children are under stress or getting insufficient sleep. Anything you can do to reduce your child's stress level or help him to get more sleep should help to reduce the amount of teeth grinding. If you suspect that your child is grinding his teeth, have your child evaluated by a dentist to see if treatment is advisable or if your child is likely to outgrow his problem. Depending on your child's age and the severity of the problem, your child's dentist may suggest a hard acrylic or soft rubber oral device to prevent tooth damage.

continued on p. 250

Type of Disorder	Who it Affects and When	Description of a Typical Episode	What You Can Do to Help Your Child
Night terrors (a.k.a., sleep terrors, *pavor nocturnus*)	Occur in 1–6 percent of children; more common in boys. Runs in families. Most common in preschoolers and school-age children (four- to eight-year-olds). They can occur during naptime as well as during nighttime sleep.	Night terrors typically occur during the first one-third of the night. Your child sits bolt upright in bed and lets out a bloodcurdling scream. She may be sweating and breathing fast. Her pupils (the black dots in the centers of her eyes) may be dilated. She's totally inconsolable for the next 30 minutes, at which point she relaxes and falls back to sleep. The key thing to know about night terrors is that while they can be terrifying and upsetting to you, they are not scary for your child. Your child is oblivious to what is going on, so you can take comfort in that the next time the screaming begins in the night.	Try to eliminate any obvious source of stress in your child's life and ensure that your child is getting adequate rest. Your child's doctor may suggest a treatment called scheduled awakening, in which you fully awaken your child 30–45 minutes before the episode typically occurs. This will often interrupt your child's sleep cycles enough to prevent the night terrors from occurring that night. Not all sleep experts agree with approach, however, so you may want to do some reading on this issue so you can discuss the pros and cons of going this route in case your child's doctor suggests it. Let anyone else who takes care of your child at naptime or during the

		night know that your child sometimes experiences night terrors. That way the person taking care of your child won't panic if an episode occurs and will know how to respond (e.g., keep the child safe).
Restless legs syndrome	Restless legs syndrome (RLS) occurs in 6 percent of children. It is most likely to occur in children who are iron deficient, who exhibit symptoms of inattentiveness, and/or whose parents have RLS. Researchers are starting to believe that some nighttime complaints of leg pain in children that have been diagnosed as "growing pains" may in fact be cases of RLS.	Your child wakes up in the night because his legs are so uncomfortable—crawly, tingly, or itchy—that he can't sleep because he has an overwhelming urge to move his legs. Children interviewed in a Mayo Clinic study described the sensations as "having bugs crawling on your legs" or "like walking through snow." These feelings can make it difficult for children to fall asleep and to stay asleep.	Restless legs syndrome can often be treated by altering a child's bedtime routine. If that doesn't work, your child's doctor may prescribe iron or medications to help treat the problem.

continued on p. 252

Type of Disorder	Who it Affects and When	Description of a Typical Episode	What You Can Do to Help Your Child
Hypnagogic hallucinations and and sleep paralysis	Hypnagogic hallucinations and sleep paralysis can occur in both children and adults. They are two separate sleep disorders, but they often occur together. They are often seen in people with narcolepsy (a condition in which people fall asleep involuntarily), but can be found in others, particularly people who are sleep deprived.	A hypnagogic hallucination is a brief period of dreaming that occurs while a person is moving between sleep and consciousness. These type of of dreams tend to be frightening and can cause a child to wake with a start just before the onset of sleep. Sleep paralysis is the sensation of being fully paralyzed when you first wake up. Your mind is awake and alert, but your body feels frozen in position. It can take a few minutes until your body allows you to move consciously. If your child experiences one or both of these sleep disorders, she may be frightened and cry out for comfort. These sleep disorders can interfere with your child's ability to get a good night's sleep.	Ironically, the best way to prevent them is to prevent your child from getting sleep deprived in the first place. Talk about a Catch 22!

Obstructive sleep apnea syndrome (OSA)

Affects 1–3 percent of all children, but is most common in preschoolers because this is the age at which the tonsil and adenoids are the largest in proportion to the underlying airway size; it is most common in children who are obese, who have head and neck abnormalities, and who have large tonsils or adenoids.

There is also an association between OSA and learning or behavioral difficulties which mimic attention-deficit/hyperactivity disorder. The constant sleep disruption is believed to be responsible for the behavioral symptoms.

Your child snores loudly, has difficulty breathing during sleep (e.g., gasps, snorts, and actually stops breathing), is a restless sleeper, breathes through his mouth when he is sleeping, or sleeps in unusual positions when sleeping. Infants with OSA may have difficulty feeding. Allergies, asthma, and gastroenterological reflux disorder are all contributing factors to OSA in young children.

Children with OSA are also likely to have problems with bed-wetting.

In 2002, the American Academy of Pediatrics recommended that all children be screened for snoring, in an attempt to raise awareness of OSA. You should flag your child's breathing problems for your child's doctor (as opposed to waiting for your child's doctor to screen him for potential breathing problems) if:

- he snores loudly most nights
- he snores and gasps so loudly in his sleep that he sometimes wakes himself up
- he pauses, gasps, snorts, and actually stops breathing at times
- he is a restless sleeper
- he sleeps in unusual positions
- he sweats heavily at night
- he exhibits behavioral problems during the daytime (the symptoms of OSA can mimic the symptoms of attention-deficit hyperactivity

continued on p. 254

Type of Disorder	Who it Affects and When	Description of a Typical Episode	What You Can Do to Help Your Child
			disorder (ADHD), namely concentration problems, impulsiveness, and fidgetiness)
			• he is difficult to wake up in the morning
			• he has headaches (particularly morning headache)
			• he is irritable, aggressive, and/or cranky
			• he is sleepy and/or dreamy
			• he has a nasal tone to his voice and breathes through his mouth during the day.
			Some children with OSA will benefit from having their tonsils and adenoids removed. Others will benefit from nasal continuous positive airway pressure (CPAP), although getting children to sleep with a CPAP mask on at night can be extremely difficult. It involves sleeping with a noisy mask on your face.

| Nocturnal seizures | Most likely to occur in children with epilepsy. Nocturnal seizures tend to become worse—not better—with age. | You may not realize that your child has had a seizure until the following morning, at which point your child may have a headache, which you may be able to detect when he starts pulling at his ears in the absence of an ear infection; muscle aches, be extremely groggy or want to sleep in for hours past his usual time, be uncommunicative, unable to concentrate, extra clingy, lose urinary control throughout the day, and other symptoms. If you happen to witness the episode, you may notice a repetitive one-sided rhythmic motion which eventually becomes a more generalized rhythmic movement. The movements will tend to be quite similar from one episode to the next. | Have your child assessed by a pediatrician to confirm that he is experiencing nocturnal seizures. *Tip:* If you're unsure whether your child is experiencing a nocturnal seizure or something else (a nightmare or a night terror), videotape the episode so that your doctor can view the episode and, if necessary, send it on to a specialist. Offer comfort and support to your child. |

Solutions Central—The Last Word

THE MAJORITY OF sleep disorders are highly treatable. Some don't even require formal treatment. Your child will outgrow them as his body matures. Talk to your doctor about your child's sleep problems so that you can obtain an accurate diagnosis and learn the best ways of managing your child's sleep disorder until the recommended treatment—or time—begins to resolve the problem.

Sleep Tools

Sleep Tool 1

Sleep Problem Solver—A Six-Step Action Plan for Solving Your Child's Sleep Problems

What This Step Involves	What to Do
Step One	
Review the basic facts about babies, toddlers, preschoolers, and sleep (whichever stage is most relevant to your child). If your baby was born prematurely, don't forget to adjust the sleep information to reflect your child's developmental stage rather than her chronological age.	• Read (or re-read) Chapters 6, 7, and 8. • Consult the appendices for leads on other suggested resources if you want to do some more in-depth research on this subject (optional).
Step Two	
Gather information about your child's sleep patterns and start thinking about whether or not your child actually has a sleep "problem." If you think your child has a sleep problem, how would you	• Make some notes about your child's current sleep patterns (e.g., naptimes, bedtimes, total amount of sleep in a 24-hour period, who put the child to bed, basic bedtime/soothing routines, sleeping location, level of tiredness, sleep cues, foods eaten before bedtime, any other information that you think would be

continued on p. 258

What This Step Involves	What to Do
Step Two: (Continued)	
define the problem? What are your short-term and long-term sleep goals for your child? What steps need to be accomplished in order for your child to achieve these goals? (Remember, it's your definition of the word "problem" that counts.)	helpful/relevant. Use the sample sleep log provided (Tool 5). You may also wish to follow the links to some of the online sleep logs and sleep worksheets that I've provided at www.sleepsolutionsbook.com. Or, if you prefer to design your own sleep log, simply start keeping notes in a calendar or a notebook (you may want to find one with graph paper) or on your computer—whatever works best for you.
	• Write out your sleep goals for your child. Be sure to break down "big" sleep goals like "sleeping through the night in her own bed" into a series of little steps, e.g., "going to bed without being rocked to sleep by a parent, sleeping in her own bed all night, not waking up in the night, etc." Then think about any individual sleep problems that you will need to work on in order to address each of these smaller problems, and the order in which you would like to tackle them. Once again, you can use the template provided (see Sleep Tool 5), design your own sleep tools, or use some of the ones that I've linked to online.
Step Three (May not apply to everyone)	
Have your child evaluated by your family physician if you have any questions or concerns about any underlying health issues, or if you just want to discuss his sleep issues with someone you trust.	Set up an appointment with your child's health care provider. Bring copies of any notes you've made about your child's sleep patterns and a list of any sleep-related questions you may have, as well as any other questions or concerns you may have about your child's health. Be sure to read through the list of why children wake up in

the night (See Sleep Tool 4) to see if that list raises any red flags for you that you will want to raise with your child's health care provider. Also, if you're unsure about the pros and cons of the various sleep-training philosophies (see Sleep Tool 2), you may also want to ask your health care provider to weigh in with his opinion. (Just remember that in the end, you're the one who has to decide what will ultimately work best for your child.)

Step Four

Consider the various sleep-training approaches and decide on an option—or a series of options—that seem to be well-suited for your family. Remember that it's possible to borrow the best elements of a number of different sleep approaches to come up with your own customized sleep solution. (See Sleep Tool 2 for a summary of what parents like and dislike about each of the major sleep training approaches.)

- What matters most to you in a sleep-training method?

  ( ) solving the problem quickly
  ( ) not allowing any crying
  ( ) minimizing crying
  ( ) finding a method that is in synch with your other parenting philosophies
  ( ) finding a method that emphasizes opportunities for learning for the child
  ( ) finding a method that respects your child or family's history/needs (child who was adopted; parents' history of infertility/loss; child/parents' history of trauma; other issues)

- What matters most to your partner?
- Are you basically in synch when it comes to this issue? If not, can you find some common ground?

Step Five

Decide if this is a good time for you to focus on helping your child to improve her sleep habits.

Issues to consider:
- What else is going on in your life?
- What else is going on in your child's life?
- Can you minimize the other stresses in your life while you're helping your child to master some new sleep skills?

continued on p. 260

What This Step Involves	What to Do
Step Six Keep track of your child's progress so that you can see where you are, where you've been, and where you'd like to be. The key is to keep records that are just detailed enough to be useful, but not so detailed that the record-keeping becomes an arduous chore after just a few days.	Use the sample sleep log (see Sleep Tool 5) as a template, or develop your own custom sleep log. Think about the following issues on an ongoing basis so that you will remember to celebrate your mini-victories and to set new goals at the same time: • your action plan for the next week • how you will measure success over the short term • how you will measure success over the long term • how you will know when your baby's problem has been solved for good (What is your current definition of "sleep success" for your child? Has it evolved over time?)

Sleep Tool 2

A Comparison of the Major Sleep-Training Methods for Babies, Toddlers, and Preschoolers

	The no-cry method (a.k.a. gentle sleep solutions)
How it Works	You temporarily shift your child's bedtime a little later so that you'll be putting him to bed at a time when he is likely to feel sleepy. Then you help your child make the connection between a series of pleasurable bedtime routines (each of which is, in turn, reinforced with lots of encouragement and praise from you) and the experience of falling asleep. Then, you gradually shift your child's bedtime to an earlier time. (You move it in 15-minute increments at a time.)
What Some Parents Like About It	You are teaching your child about sleep and helping him to develop some positive bedtime routines and self-soothing skills. Studies have indicated that this method is relatively quick to implement (you can expect results in less than a week) and that pre-bedtime tantrums can be replaced with sleep-friendly bedtime routines with minimal fuss or unhappiness for you or your child. This method is a lot easier to implement than some of the other methods, which can either require a lot of patience on your part or leave you feeling anxious and stressed because of the need for prolonged periods of crying.
What Some Parents Don't Like About It	You need to be committed to establishing a predictable bedtime routine for your child and sticking with that routine over the long term. (You can't abandon the more pleasurable bedtime routine once your child is going to bed more easily or he'll be likely to start resisting bedtime again.) Disruptions such as illness or family travel during the initial days or weeks of this program could make it difficult to achieve the desired results. Not all parents are open to the idea of temporarily shifting their child's bedtime to a later time, which is what the initial stage of this technique requires.

continued on p. 262

Bedtime Fading	
How it Works	You focus on teaching your child to learn how to sleep independently. You might initially be providing comfort by picking your baby up, but eventually you'll progress to the point where you're be providing verbal comfort from across the room, down the hall, etc. This method also focuses on preventing or minimizing sleep associations that may work against your child's ability to learn to self-soothe (e.g., the nurse-to-sleep association). Another common solution offered in gentle sleep books involves having the parent move into the child's bedroom for a period of time ("parent's continuous presence"). The parent sleeps in the child's bedroom, but doesn't take the child out of his crib/bed at night. There is no verbal contact or eye contact. The parent pretends to be asleep no matter what. The parent does this for an entire week in order to reassure the child that the parent is nearby. Then, after a week, the parent tries moving out into the hall or to his or her own bedroom while monitoring the child's reaction. Most books offering no-cry solutions offer a "gentle" cry-it-out method as a last resort for parents who have found themselves at their wits' end and who feel like they absolutely have to do something about their child's sleep problems now. (And some of the newer variations on the traditional "cry-it-out" theme now feature some "gentler" parenting solutions.) The techniques for gently encouraging a child to go to sleep can be particularly helpful to parents with young babies. If you decide to use this method, you'll likely find that some of these techniques become a permanent part of your parenting toolkit, for both daytime and nighttime use.
What Some Parents Like About It	The idea of avoiding or minimizing crying, or being present to offer comfort while crying occurs, is appealing to many parents. Most gentle sleep solution methods offer helpful strategies for gradually reducing nighttime nursing and making the transition from co-sleeping to solo sleeping as stress-free as possible for young children. This is a child-friendly and parent-friendly approach to sleep-training. It is respectful of infant development and acknowledges that young children need their parents around the clock, not just during those hours of the day when it's convenient for parents to be "on call."

This method involves taking a step-by-step approach to teaching your baby to self-soothe and learning how to sleep independently, e.g., providing comfort while picking your baby up, without picking your baby up but while offering soothing pats, providing verbal comfort from across the room, from out in the hall where baby can't see you, etc.

What Some Parents Don't Like About It	Some gentle sleep solutions books fail to alert you to the downside of going on and off your sleep training plan. (Some encourage you to abandon your sleep plan anytime you or your baby find it too difficult to stick with the sleep program and to simply try to get back on track tomorrow.) While this is a wonderfully nurturing idea in theory, it sets up an intermittent reinforcement schedule that can undermine some of your efforts to solve your child's sleep problems. By following your sleep plan inconsistently, you could end up encouraging your child to cry every time you attempt to reintroduce the sleep plan again, in the hope of getting you to put the sleep plan on hold again. (See information on intermittent reinforcement schedules below.)

Many gentle sleep solution books don't fully explain how to make the "parent's continuous presence" method work in the real world, so parents are left with a lot of unanswered questions.

Gentle sleep solutions take longer than other sleep solutions. That's not necessarily a bad thing. (Sometimes slow is better.) But you should be aware of this going out of the gate.

Extinction with parental presence (parent's continuous presence); one variation of this method is known as the chair method

How it Works	This method seeks to provide children with the comfort and reassurance that comes from having the parent physically present in the room while simultaneously giving that child the very clear message that night-time is for sleeping.

Variation one: You move into your child's bedroom for a period of time in order to reassure your child that you are nearby. There is no verbal contact or eye contact between you and your child. You pretend to be asleep. You do this for an entire week and then move back to your own bedroom.

Variation two, The chair method: You sit in a chair in your child's room, providing verbal reassurance, but not physically touching your child. Gradually you move the chair farther and farther away from your child's crib. Eventually the chair is out of your child's room entirely.

continued on p. 264

Extinction with parental presence *(parent's continuous presence); one variation of this method is known as the chair method* **(Continued)**	
	Note: Some of the gentle sleep methods rely on these methods as well.
What Some Parents Like About It	Parents who don't feel comfortable with full-blown extinction methods but who want a quick (or quicker) fix may be inclined to try this method.
What Some Parents Don't Like About It	For full-blown extinction to occur, you have to ignore your child's cries while you're in the same room as your child, which can be hard on you and your child. If you decide to provide intermittent comfort in order to make the process easier on your child and yourself, you slow down the process and could end up training your child to cry longer and harder to get your attention the next time around (see note about intermittent reinforcement schedule below). Some children find it extremely upsetting to have you in the room, but not picking them up (particularly in the variation of this method that has a parent sitting in a chair next to the crib). This method fails to explain how your child is supposed to adapt when you move back to your own bedroom or the chair disappears entirely—a major knowledge gap.
Pick up, put down *(positive routine-stimulus control techniques)*	
How it Works	The parent establishes a positive and calming bedtime routine for the child. The pleasurable routine is halted each time the child cries or throws a tantrum (e.g., putting the child down in bed and then picking the child up when the child stops crying, or having the parent leave the room until the child stops crying). When the child stops crying or throwing a tantrum, the positive bedtime routine resumes. The "pick up, put down" method as described above works best in situations when older babies and toddlers are sleeping in a crib.
What Some Parents Like About It	The child has the choice to stop crying and to have his/her positive behavior reinforced with a reward—a continuation of the positive bedtime routine.

What Some Parents Don't Like About It	This routine requires a lot of patience. You may have to stop and start the bedtime routine countless times until your child begins to make the connection between the stopping and starting of the bedtime routine and what it takes to elicit the desired behavior from you. You may find it hard not to pick up your child when he is crying. (You have to wait until your child stops crying to give your child attention because you want to reinforce the positive behavior.)
Modified cry-it-out **(a.k.a. graduated extinction, controlled crying)**	
How it Works	The parent puts the child to bed, and if the child starts to cry, the parent provides comfort to the child at predetermined intervals. One method has the intervals between parental checks on the child increasing; another has the length of the time spent with the child decreasing in length. With each of these methods, the goal is the same: to gradually wean the child off needing parental help in getting to sleep or getting back to sleep so that the child can master this important skill on his own. This method should not be used on newborns or young babies. Young babies require feeding in the night as well as the reassurance that comes from knowing that someone will respond to their cries.
What Some Parents Like About It	Studies have indicated that most parents using this method get results within one week. Because this method allows parents to check on their child frequently, parents are more likely to stick with this particular program and to follow the rules of the program (as compared to the full-blown cry-it-out method, which has a high rate of parents either abandoning the sleep program altogether or modifying the program to such a degree that it can actually make their child's sleep problems worse).
What Some Parents Don't Like About It	In some cases, a child can be trained to cry for longer and longer periods in order to obtain the reward of having Mom and Dad come in and offer comfort—not exactly what most parents are hoping for when they sign up for this particular sleep program. The problem occurs when parents inadvertently set up an intermittent reinforcement schedule. (See explanation below.)

continued on p. 266

	Cry-it-out method (a.k.a. extinction technique)
How it Works	The parent puts the child to sleep at a designated time and ignores the child's cries until a certain time the next morning. Some variations on this method will allow the parents to intervene under certain circumstances (e.g., if the child has thrown up, in which case the parent is instructed to change the sheets in a matter-of-fact manner and get the child back to bed as quickly as possible). With this sleep-training method, you respond to your child if you think your child could be hungry, but you ignore the crying at other times of the night. You can expect a temporary increase in crying (an "extinction burst") when you first start with this method. This method should not be used on newborns or young babies. Young babies require feeding in the night as well as the reassurance that comes from knowing that someone will respond to their cries.
What Some Parents Like About It	This method tends to deliver the speediest results. It is also easy to understand and follow in the middle of the night. You don't have to keep track of complex reinforcement schedules.
What Some Parents Don't Like About It	Some parents find this particular sleep training method completely unacceptable. Others find that they can't stick with this method long enough to make it work for them (even though studies have shown that this method usually works within three nights). Those who do attempt it often find it difficult to follow the method 100 percent: They may comfort their child intermittently, which can actually set up an intermittent reinforcement schedule in which the child learns that her cries in the night are reinforced some of the time, which can make nighttime crying louder and more persistent! (Do some research on Skinner and his pigeons and you'll find out what's happening here. Intermittent reinforcement is powerful stuff! Skinner discovered that behavior that is reinforced intermittently is much more difficult to extinguish or get rid of than behavior that is reinforced on a consistent basis.)

Some children become resistant to extinction methods. Others will engage in gagging, vomiting, or self-injurious behaviors, which can be very upsetting to parents. Relapses can occur, so you may have to go through this less-than-fun process more than once.

Scheduled awakenings (the parent wakes up the child)	
How it Works	You wake your child up approximately 15 to 30 minutes prior to the time when he typically wakes you up in the night, in the hope of reprogramming his sleep cycles so that his usual night-time awakenings eventually stop. Once your child is awake, you soothe him back to sleep in the way you normally would if he had awakened on his own (e.g., giving him a cuddle, offering reassurance, tucking him back into bed). The interval between awakenings is gradually increased until your child is eventually sleeping through the night.
What Some Parents Like About It	This method has proven to be successful in increasing the length of children's nighttime sleep periods.
What Some Parents Don't Like About It	You're still missing out on much-needed sleep. You may have to set your alarm to wake yourself up repeatedly in the night so that you can wake your child. And you can expect to do this for seven weeks before your child's sleep problems are resolved. Not all sleep experts recommend the use of this technique, and those who do are more likely to recommend it for tackling a sleep disorder (e.g., night terrors) as opposed to a run-of-the-mill sleep problem (night waking). Some parents are reluctant to mess with their child's natural sleep patterns, too. This method doesn't teach children how to fall asleep on their own, nor does it provide parents or children with any tools for dealing with bedtime struggles. In fact, some sleep experts have suggested that this method should not be used with children who have both night-waking problems and bedtime-resistance problems.

continued on p. 268

	Scheduling to improve the quality of your baby's sleep
How it Works	Most of these programs—which are targeted at parents with young babies—promise to have your baby sleeping through the night in a matter of weeks if you follow a prescribed schedule. Some schedules consist of some basic guidelines that you apply to your baby's situation; others are so detailed and prescriptive that you will want to keep your Palm Pilot handy to ensure that your baby is staying on track.
What Some Parents Like About It	The idea of solving your baby's sleep problems by getting your baby on to a strictly enforced eating and sleeping routine can be very appealing to some parents, particularly since many of these programs promise results in a matter of weeks.
What Some Parents Don't Like About It	Other parents reject this whole school of thought, feeling that scheduling—or overscheduling—our kids lives' tends to happen soon enough. Enough with the "baby boot camp" hyper-scheduling! Besides, rigid scheduling taken to the extreme has been proven to be detrimental to the health of young babies. One program which advised feeding newborns at three to three-and-a-half hour intervals beginning at birth and eliminating night feedings by age eight weeks was associated with failure to thrive, poor weight gain, dehydration, breast milk supply failure, and involuntary early weaning.

Sleep Tool 3

Bedtime-Resistance Checklist: Common Reasons for Bedtime Resistance in Toddlers and Preschoolers

Common Reasons for Bedtime Resistance	What You Can Do About the Problem
Your child isn't tired yet	Pay attention to your child's sleep cues. Note the approximate time each evening when your child starts to become genuinely sleepy. Begin to adjust your child's bedtime accordingly, bearing in mind what time he has to get up in the morning (if your family has a fixed morning schedule) and how many hours of sleep are appropriate for a child his age (don't forget to tally up all of his daytime and nighttime sleep).
	Get biology on your side at bedtime. When your child is put to bed when he is sleepy, his body produces melatonin, a calming hormone. If he becomes overtired, his body starts producing cortisol, a stress-related hormone that leaves him feeling wired. He'll have a harder time getting to sleep and staying asleep. Cortisol can even affect the quality of his sleep the next day, which can, in turn, make it difficult for him to settle down at bedtime the following night. Talk about a dastardly domino effect.
Your child is making a declaration of independence	Understand that you're dealing with normal toddler development. Your child is asserting her ability to do the exact opposite of what you want her to do at any given time, so if you want her to go to bed, well, you know what side of *that* argument she's likely to end up on.
Your toddler's mantra these days is "You snooze, you lose."	Introduce a relaxing pre-bedtime wind-down routine (so the transition from "fun-time" to "bedtime" isn't quite so abrupt) and remind your child that there will be fun things to do tomorrow, after she's had a good night's sleep.

continued on p. 270

Common Reasons for Bedtime Resistance	What You Can Do About the Problem
Your child hasn't had enough physical activity during the day, so her body may still have some get-up-and-go left by the time bedtime rolls around	Your child needs at least 30 minutes of moderate physical activity each day, and at least 30–60 minutes of more vigorous physical activity each day. Not only is this good for your child's heart and lungs, it will help to improve the quality of his sleep by relaxing him and making it easier for him to fall asleep, to move between sleep cycles, and to sleep more soundly. Just make sure you schedule the Backyard Olympics for sometime well before dinner otherwise your tot will be in workout mode rather than wind-down mode when you're ready to start his nightly bedtime routine.
Your toddler just had a big meal or she recently ate some foods that are making it difficult for her to fall asleep	It's hard for anyone to sleep well on a full stomach, kids included, and what's in their tummies can also have an impact on the quality of sleep. Caffeine (or, worse, caffeine plus sugar) can leave children as well as adults feeling fully wired. (See Chapter 2 for some tips on foods that help promote rather than interfere with sleep.)
Your toddler's sleeping environment isn't as sleep-friendly as it could be	Your child's sleep environment may go overboard in attractions (could you fall asleep in the middle of Toyland if you were a kid?) or be too uncomfortable (too cold, too noisy, too bright, too anything!). See Chapter 2 for tips on creating a sleep-friendly environment.
Your toddler is too scared to fall asleep in the same room as the monster in the closet	Your toddler or preschooler may be willing to go head-to-head with his siblings, but as for taking his chances with the monster in the closet, surely you must be joking? You'll find that the monster won't stick around for long if you take your child's fears seriously and reassure him that there really aren't any monsters in the closets or anywhere else. Provide your child with a toddler-safe flashlight so that he can get rid of any creepy shapes and shadows instantly, if he's feeling scared. And make sure that the bedtime stories that you're reading to your child are of the distinctly non-spooky variety. The last thing your child wants or needs is more scary fodder for his already active imagination.

Common Reasons for Bedtime Resistance	What You Can Do About the Problem
The bedtime routine at your place is just that—*routine*—and in kid parlance, "routine" is another word for "boring"	There's nothing wrong with coming up with a predictable bedtime routine, as long as it isn't such a bore that your child refuses to buy into the bedtime routine at all, choosing instead to entertain herself by doing circuit training up and down the hall until she's caught her second, third, and fourth winds. So if you suspect that your child has outgrown or grown bored with certain elements of her existing bedtime routine (or she hides in a closet at the first sign that bedtime may be on the agenda), perhaps it's time to come up with something new. Remember, if she's fighting you every inch of the way, your supposedly soothing bedtime routine is more of an exercise in kid wrangling— great fun for her, but highly ineffective if your goal is to encourage her to settle down to sleep anytime soon.
Your toddler's overall sleep habits aren't anything to write home about	The longer it takes your child to fall asleep, the more likely it is that bedtime is going to be an ordeal for your child and for you. So if you can work on improving your child's sleep habits overall (see Chapter 4 for the low-down on what separates the good sleepers from the not-so-great sleepers and what you can do to tip the sleep roulette wheel in your child's favor), you'll reap huge dividends on the bedtime front.

Sleep Tool 4

Reasons Why Babies, Toddlers, and Preschoolers Wake in the Night

Reasons for Nightwaking	How to Help Your Baby (Newborns and Older Babies)	How to Help Your Toddler or Preschooler
She's hungry	If your baby is a newborn, being hungry in the night is perfectly normal. Simply feed your baby and know that the day will come when your baby will dine by day and sleep by night. Once your baby gets to be about six months old, her sleep patterns will be less tied to the time of her last feeding and more tied to her circadian (day/night) rhythms. However, even after she starts sleeping through the night on a regular basis (which means being able to sleep for at least a five-hour stretch at night), she may wake up looking for a middle-of-the-night feeding for a couple of nights whenever she's going through a growth spurt. You can minimize the nighttime waking by ensuring that she's getting enough to eat during the day.	Your child may have gotten in the habit of eating in the night, even though most children her age have learned to eat during the day rather than at night. It's also possible that she's nursing more for comfort than for nutrition, or she's simply learned to associate falling asleep with being at the breast. (See Chapter 6 for some tips on gradually weakening the powerful nurse-to-sleep association.) With older toddlers, you can introduce new elements to the bedtime routine after you finish nursing (e.g., story time or cuddle time after you finish nursing) and you can gradually teach your child that we sleep at night (when it's dark) and eat during the day (when it's bright outside).
She's overtired	It's difficult for children to get a good night's sleep when they are overtired. If your child missed her nap and/or went to bed late, she's likely to find it difficult to get to sleep at bedtime and more likely to wake up during the night. Help her wind down by using whatever techniques she finds most soothing and focus on ensuring that she gets her naps tomorrow.	

Reasons for Nightwaking	How to Help Your Baby (Newborns and Older Babies)	How to Help Your Toddler or Preschooler
She's over-stimulated	If your child was engaged in highly stimulating activities right before naptime or bedtime, she may have a hard time winding down to go to sleep. Try to structure your child's day so that there's a bit of transition time between play periods and sleep periods	
She has a wet or dirty diaper or she needs to go to the bathroom	If your baby has a tendency to wet through her diapers in the middle of the night, experiment with different types and brands of diapers. Some parents find that cloth diapers keep their babies dryer while other parents swear by dispos-ables. There's also considerable variation when it comes to the fit of each particular brand of diaper. You may have to experiment a bit before you hit upon the brand that fits your baby just right and is suitably absorbent for overnight wear. Studies have shown that the new "gel"-style disposable diapers tend to keep babies driest because they are capable of wicking both urine and moisture from bowel movements away from baby's tender skin. Note: Some parents find that their babies dirty their diapers shortly after they tuck them into bed and that the babies end up waking	Your child may be waking up because she needs to go to the bathroom in the night or because the sensation of being in a wet or dirty diaper is waking her up. (She may be newly sensitive to this now that she's reached the toilet-training stage.) Children with full bladders sometimes have difficulty falling back to sleep after a brief sleep awakening. Children who sleepwalk, sleep talk, or who have difficulty with night terrors are most likely to experience this problem. (See Chapter 9 for more on sleep disorders.) If it's a wet bed that's waking her up, don't get upset with her. She's not wetting the bed on purpose. Think about encouraging her to use the bathroom before she goes to bed (if she's started the process of toilet-training) and putting her to bed in a more absorbent night-time diaper or pull-up and make her bed up in layers (plastic sheet, regular

continued on p. 274

Reasons for Nightwaking	How to Help Your Baby (Newborns and Older Babies)	How to Help Your Toddler or Preschooler
	up crying a short time later because they want their diapers changed. One way to avoid this problem is to move the pre-bedtime feeding ahead a little in the hope that your baby will have that bowel movement before she goes to bed. Of course, the downside is that you end up decreasing the interval of time before her next feeding since the feeding clock is ticking away while you're waiting for that bowel movement to occur. It's a tough call.	sheet, plastic sheet, regular sheet) so that you can all get back to sleep more quickly.
She has a painful diaper rash	Some babies and toddlers are more prone to diaper rashes than others. If your child has extra-sensitive skin, you can minimize the chances of her experiencing a flare-up by:	

- changing her wet diapers frequently (at least every two hours during the daytime when she's a newborn and whatever you can manage at night; less often as she begins to urinate less frequently), changing soiled diapers right away, and wiping baby well to remove all traces of urine and stool

- using unscented wipes or wet washcloths, adding a protective barrier of rash cream (either petroleum ointment or white zinc oxide) to protect your baby's bottom if she's particularly prone to rashes, and experimenting with different brands of disposable diapers if you're using disposables (since every brand fits slightly differently and therefore some will cause less friction and less leakage for your baby)

- rinsing cloth diapers well (adding a half-cup of vinegar to the rinse cycle helps to remove the alkaline that can be so irritating to baby's skin)

Reasons for Nightwaking	How to Help Your Baby (Newborns and Older Babies)	How to Help Your Toddler or Preschooler
	It's also possible that your baby could be reacting to something in the disposable diapers or—if you're using cloth diapers—the laundry detergent or the bleach you are using to wash her diapers.	
She's ill or in pain or she has a medical condition that is making it difficult for her to sleep	• If your child sleeps only for a short time (just long enough to take the edge off her fatigue) or she is comfortable only when she's sleeping in a particular position (e.g., sitting up), it could be that she's in pain because of an illness or teething. Medical conditions that can interfere with sleep include gastroesophageal reflux (GER), ear infections, itchiness (dermatitis), eczema, pinworms, epilepsy, asthma, allergies, food intolerances, stomachaches, headaches, and sleep disorders. (Note: Check the index to find the relevant sections of this book dealing with specific health complaints.) • Your parental intuition can be a powerful tool in trying to diagnose the problem, so take some time to observe your child to try to see if you can figure out what's going on. Watch how she's acting (e.g., falling asleep, only to wake up crying?) and when she seems to be most comfortable (when she's lying down?) • Babies with ear infections often find it very uncomfortable, or even painful, to sleep in a fully reclined position. This is because ear infections can lead to an accumulation of fluid in the ear that can cause severe pain when the baby is lying down, making it difficult for baby to sleep. If your child's doctor suggests that you elevate your toddler's crib mattress to help your child to deal with the pain associated with an ear infection (most children are more comfortable in such a position), make sure that the incline is gradual so that your child won't roll around and end up with his feet elevated rather than his head; elevate the crib mattress (as opposed to the whole crib); and make sure that the sleeping surface is smooth and firm. You need to be conscious of providing a safe sleeping environment, even into the toddler and preschooler years.	

continued on p. 276

Reasons for Nightwaking	How to Help Your Baby (Newborns and Older Babies)	How to Help Your Toddler or Preschooler
She's teething	While the experts continue to debate whether teething pain results in disrupted sleep or pain to babies and toddlers (the naysayers point out that teething tends to coincide with a period in which night waking tends to recur anyway), if your baby is up in the night pulling on her teeth and gums, you don't care what any double-blind study says. It's obvious to you that your child is in pain! For tips on managing teething pain, see Chapter 6.	
Something about her sleeping environment is making it difficult for her to get a good night's sleep	• It will be difficult for your child to get a good night's sleep if her sleeping environment is the incorrect temperature, if she's over- or underdressed for that environment (add or subtract layers accordingly), if the pajamas someone gave her for her birthday are trimmed with super-itchy lace, or if there are car doors slamming outside on the street all night long. Find ways of dealing with the problem that's at the root of the problem so that her sleep won't be disturbed. • To check your baby's temperature, feel the back of her neck to see if she's sweating, and her tummy to see if she feels cold. *Note:* Your baby's hands and feet don't provide a very reliable indication of her overall temperature. • Don't forget to check your baby over thoroughly, particularly if she's inconsolable: A clothing tag could be poking your baby's skin. A thread or a piece of hair could be wrapped around one of her fingers or toes or, in the case of a little boy, his penis. (These types of tangles occur more often than you might think.) If you can't remove the hair or thread on your own, take your baby to the health care provider's office. There are hair-dissolving creams that will do the trick.	
She hasn't learned how to fall back to sleep on her own	Babies with poorer self-soothing skills and more challenging temperaments may tend to wake up when they enter periods of light sleep. These transitions occur about once every 60 minutes. That's a lot of	Toddlers and preschoolers who have less developed self-soothing skills and more challenging tempera-ments may tend to wake up when they enter periods of light sleep. You may want to take a two-tiered

Reasons for Nightwaking	How to Help Your Baby (Newborns and Older Babies)	How to Help Your Toddler or Preschooler
	opportunities for a baby to wake up each night. If there's anything else that disturbs them as they make this transition—hunger, noise, cold, wetness—it's game over in terms of baby's sleep and yours	approach to dealing with this issue: simultaneously providing comfort to your child and helping her to develop the self-soothing skills she needs to get back to sleep on her own. (See Chapter 6 for more on this important issue.)
She wants some extra comfort or reassurance, perhaps due to some recent changes to her routine or because she's reacting to something that's going on in the family	Change is tough enough for grownups, and we've got a full repertoire of self-soothing skills to fall back upon, so why are we so surprised that young children, who have yet to develop a full repertoire of self-soothing skills, react so powerfully when they are faced with a perceived threat to their own safety and security? If your baby is feeling a little unsettled as a result of some recent upheaval in her life, her sleep patterns might bear the brunt of it. Focus on providing her with the comfort and reassurance she needs.	If your toddler is dealing with a major change in her life—the arrival of a new baby brother or sister or a move to a new house, for example, provide her with the reassurance she's seeking by keeping as much of her day-to-day routine as consistent as possible. (If a new baby has just arrived on the scene, try not to move to a new house, change daycares, and start toilet training all at the same time.) Even one major change can be a lot for a toddler to deal with. And while your child is waking in the night, find that common-sense middle ground where you provide just enough reassurance to get your child back to sleep, but not so much middle-of-the-night cuddling that you end up reinforcing a new night-waking habit that can be hard to break down the road.

continued on p. 278

Reasons for Nightwaking	How to Help Your Baby (Newborns and Older Babies)	How to Help Your Toddler or Preschooler
She's experiencing separation anxiety	Separation anxiety (not wanting to be separated from the people they love most in the world—even in the middle of the night!) is a common cause of sleep interruptions during the second half of the first year of life. Your baby will need some extra reassurance from you. Introducing a lovey may help.	While separation anxiety tends to reach its peak when babies are around nine months of age, toddlers can experience a second wave of separation anxiety between ages two and three years. And, as we all know, these developmental time lines tend to vary from toddler to toddler, so if you notice separation anxiety-like behavior from your toddler at any point, chances are it's the real thing. Introducing a lovey may help.
She's recently achieved a developmental milestone (e.g., sitting, standing) or she's in the process of mastering a new skill and she wants to work on it night and day	Who has time to sleep when there are sitting up and standing up skills to be mastered? Give her the chance to practice her new skills during the day, and show her how to get back down from the position she is "stuck" in at night. And be patient. She'll soon be on to the next developmental stage.	Just as your baby wanted to work on her sitting-up and standing-up skills at 3 a.m., your toddler may be determined to work on putting on her own shoes or practising a song that she learned at day care in the wee hours of the morning. You may want to listen to her moonlight serenade for a few minutes (to see if she'll go back to sleep on her own), but if it seems like she's going to keep going until daybreak, you'll probably want to go in and remind your toddler that it's sleepy time, not singing time. Then tuck her back in bed with a cuddle and a kiss.

Reasons for Nightwaking	How to Help Your Baby (Newborns and Older Babies)	How to Help Your Toddler or Preschooler
She's gotten into the habit of waking up in the night	Sometimes children simply get into the habit of waking up in the night. This is particularly common after a child who previously slept through the night starts waking in the night due to illness or teething. Even once the underlying problem has been resolved, the child may still tend to wake up in the night out of sheer habit. Some children will eventually start sleeping through the night again on their own. Others may need some gentle encouragement from their parents. See Sleep Tool 2 for an overview of the basic sleep training techniques and Sleep Tool 1 for some guidance on developing a sleep plan that feels right for your family.	
She's dealing with some special challenges	If your child has special needs that affect her ability to sleep or spent a lot of time in hospital when she was younger and now has to readjust to the sleep routine at home, sleep may be an extra challenge for her. Depending on your child's medical condition, she may have some sleep disorders (see Table 9.1) or she may simply be lagging behind other children her age when it comes to achieving various sleep-related milestones. Talking to your child's doctor and other parents who have children with special needs may help you set realistic sleep goals for your child and get the support you need to cope with what could be an extended period of nighttime parenting.	
She recently joined your family after being adopted	If your child was recently adopted, she may still be adjusting to the new routines in your family. That may require some extra time and patience on your part. Anything you can find out about her pre-adoption sleep routines and what types of techniques she finds soothing will be extremely helpful as you ease her into your family's routines and help her to develop some self-soothing skills over time.	

Sleep Tool 5: 7-Day Sleep Log

KEEPING A SLEEP log can give you a visual snapshot of your child's sleep-wake cycles. Here's how to use this sleep log to learn more about your child's sleep patterns and behaviors.

- Note the start and end of your child's sleep period (nap or nighttime sleep) by shading in the blocks of time in the sleep log. (See example in first row of sleep log below.)

- Tally up your child's total number of hours of daytime and nighttime sleep.

- Start keeping track of your child's sleep associations. In other words, note what conditions have to be present for your child to be able to fall asleep. Does your child need to be nursed to sleep, rocked to sleep, tucked in bed with his favorite stuffed animal, etc.? Note this information in the Notes field. (Because this field is relatively compact, you'll probably want to use acronyms or symbols, or cross-reference your entries in a separate logbook so you can keep track of different sleep associations and sleep-related behaviors at once.)

- Make some basic notes about your child's sleep routine. Be sure to note whenever you make significant changes to your child's sleep routine as these changes may affect your child's sleep patterns during the days ahead. Also make note of anything else that could be affecting your child's health: illness, over-tiredness, a change to his usual routine, and so on.

- Make some basic notes about your child's mood, energy level, attentiveness, etc., so that you can assess if your child is receiving adequate sleep. Realize that there are many factors that can throw your child's sleep patterns out of whack, either for the short or long term. Even those much-anticipated early childhood mile-stones can lead to temporary disruptions on the sleep front.

Day/Date	12 am	1	2	3	4	5	6	7	8	9	10	11	12 pm	1	2	3	4	5	6	7	8	9	10	11	Total Hrs. sleep	Notes
Example Sat. Feb. 2																									13	Nursed to sleep each feeding

Directory of Organizations

The following organizations are excellent sources of information if you want to delve a little deeper into the world of sleep.

Sleep Associations: General

AMERICAN

Academy of Dental Sleep Medicine
BDSM National Office: American
Board of Dental Sleep Medicine,
One Westbrook Corporate Center,
Suite 920 Westchester, IL 60154
Phone: 708-273-9335
Website: www.dentalsleepmed.org

American Academy of Sleep Medicine
1 Westbrook Corporate Center
Suite 920, Westchester, IL 60154
Phone: 708-492-0930
Fax: 708-492-0943
Website: www.aasmnet.org

National Institutes of Health
National Center on Sleep Disorders
Research
6705 Rockledge Drive, Suite 6022
Bethesda, MD 20892-7993
Phone: 301-435-0199
Fax: 301-480-3451
E-mail: ncsdr@nih.gov
Website: www.nhlbi.nih.gov/about/
ncsdr/index.htm

National Sleep Foundation
1522 K Street NW, Suite 500,
Washington, DC 20005
Phone: 202-347-3471
Fax: 202-347-3472
E-mail: nsf@sleepfoundation.org
Website: www.sleepfoundation.org

**National Sleep Medicine Education
and Research Foundation**
1 Westbrook Corporate Center
Suite 920, Westchester, IL 60154
Phone: 708-492-0930
Fax: 708-492-0943
Website: www.aasmnet.org

Sleep Research Society
1 Westbrook Corporate Center
Suite 920, Westchester, IL 60154
Phone: 708-492-1093
Fax: 708-492-0943
Website:
www.sleepresearchsociety.org

CANADIAN

Canadian Sleep Society
School of Psychology
(École de psychologie)
Laval University (Université Laval)
Ste-Foy, QB G1K 7P4
Phone: 418-656-3275
Website: www.css.to

Sleep Organizations: Sleep Disorders

American

American Sleep Apnea Association
1424 K Street NW, Suite 302
Washington, DC 20005-2410
Phone: 202-293-3650
Fax: 202-293-3656
E-mail: asaa@sleepapnea.org
Website: www.sleepapnea.org

Narcolepsy Network, Inc.
P.O. Box 294
Pleasantville, NY 10570
Phone: 401 667 2523
Fax: 401-633-6567
E-mail: narnet@narcolepsynetwork.org
Website: www.narcolepsynetwork.org

Restless Legs Syndrome Foundation, Inc.
819 Second Street SW
Rochester, MN 55902-2985
Phone: 877-INFO-RLS (877-463-6757)
507-287-6465
Fax: 507-287-6312
E-mail: rlsfoundation@rls.org
Website: www.rls.org

Canadian

Sleep/Wake Disorders Canada
3080 Yonge Street, Suite 5055
Toronto, ON M4N 3N1
Phone: 416-483-9654
Fax: 416-483-7081
E-mail: swdc@globalserve.net

Sleep Safety and Juvenile Safety Standards Organizations

American

First Candle/SIDS Alliance
1314 Bedford Avenue, Suite 210
Baltimore, MD 21208
Phone: 800-221-7437
E-mail: info@firstcandle.org
Website: www.firstcandle.org

National SIDS/Infant Death Resource Center
8280 Greensboro Drive, Suite 300
McLean, VA 22102
Phone: 866-866-CRIB (866-866-7437)
703-821-8955
Fax: 703-821-2098
E-mail: sids@circlesolutions.com
Website: www.sidscenter.org

U.S. Consumer Product Safety Commission
Washington, DC 20207-0001
General information: 301-504-7923
CPSC's toll-free hotline:
1-800-638-CPSC (1-800-638-2772)
TTY: 1-800-638-8270
E-mail contacts for reporting unsafe products: www.cpsc.gov/talk.html
Website sign-up form for safety alerts:
www.cpsc.gov/cpsclist.asp
Website: www.cpsc.gov

Canadian

Canadian Foundation for the Study of Infant Deaths
586 Eglinton Avenue E, Suite 308
Toronto, ON M4P 1P2
Phone: 800-END-SIDS(Canada)
(800-363-7437) 416-488-3260
Fax: 416-488-3260
E-mail: sidsinfo@sidscanada.org
Website: www.sidscanada.org

Health Canada Consumer Product Safety Office
Product Safety Programme
MacDonald Building
123 Slater Street, 4th Floor A.L. 3504D
Ottawa, ON K1A 0K9
Phone: 613-952-1014
E-mail: CPS-SPC@hc-sc.gc.ca
Website: www.hc-sc.gc.ca/
cps-spc/index_e.html

Infant and Toddler Safety Association
385 Fairway Road S, Suite 4A-230
Kitchener, ON N2C 2N9
Phone: 519-570-0181
Fax: 519-570-1078

Juvenile Product and Sleep Product Manufacturers Associations

AMERICAN

Better Sleep Council
501 Wythe Street
Alexandria, VA 22314
Phone: 703-683-8371
Website: www.bettersleep.org

Juvenile Products Manufacturers Association
15000 Commerce Parkway, Suite C
Mt. Laurel, NJ 08054
Phone: 856-638-0420
Fax: 856-439-0525
E-mail: jpma@ahint.com
Website: www.jpma.org

CANADIAN

Better Sleep Council Canada
P.O. Box 170
Streetsville, ON L5M 2B8
Website: www.bettersleep.ca

Major Pediatric Health Associations

AMERICAN

The American Academy of Pediatrics
National Headquarters
141 Northwest Point Boulevard
Elk Grove Village, IL 60007-1098
Phone: 847-434-4000
Fax: 847-434-8000
E-mail: (list of key contacts)
www.aap.org/visit/contact.htm
Website: www.aap.org

CANADIAN

Canadian Paediatric Society
2305 St. Laurent Boulevard
Ottawa, ON K1G 4J8
Phone: 613-526-9397
Fax: 613-526-3332
E-mail: info@cps.ca
Website: www.cps.ca

Directory of On-line Resources

T he following are the best on-line sleep resources that I came across while I was researching this book. I will be providing link updates and new links, sleep news updates, and other relevant information via the official website for this book, sleepsolutionsbook.com.

Sleep: Reference Guide

American Academy of Sleep Medicine: www.aasmnet.org

Ask Dr. Sears: *Sleep Issues*
www.askdrsears.com/html/7/T070100.asp

BabyCenter.com: *Baby Sleep Questions:*
www.babycenter.com/expert/faq-babysleep.html

BabyCenter.com: *Toddler Sleep Questions:*
www.babycenter.com/expert/faq-toddlersleep.html

Berkeley Parents Network: *Advice About Sleep:*
www.parents.berkeley.edu/advice/sleep/

Canadian Sleep Society: www.css.to

Centre of Excellence for Early Childhood Development: *Sleeping Behaviour:*
www.excellence-earlychildhood.ca/theme.asp?id=12&lang=EN

Dr Greene.com: *Sleep* www.drgreene.com/54_23.html

eMedicine Consumer Health: *Sleep—Understanding the Basics:*
www.emedicinehealth.com/articles/42421-1.asp

KidZZZSleep.org: *Patient Handouts:*
www.kidzzzsleep.org/phandouts.htm

National Institutes of Health: *Star Sleeper:*
www.nhlbi.nih.gov/health/public/sleep/starslp/index.htm

National Sleep Foundation: www.sleepfoundation.org

National Sleep Foundation: *Cycles of Sleeping and Waking with the Doze Family:* www.sleepfoundation.org/doze

SleepEducation.com: www.sleepeducation.com

Sleepnet.com: www.sleepnet.com

Sleepsolutionsbook.com: www.sleepsolutionsbook.com

Todaysparent.com: *Sleep:*
www.todaysparent.com/baby/sleep/archive.jsp

University of Michigan Health System: *Your Child: Sleep Problems:*
www.med.umich.edu/1libr/yourchild/sleep.htm

World Federation of Sleep Research & Sleep Medicine Societies:
www.wfsrs.org

Zero to Three: *The Sleep of Infants and Why Parents Matter:*
www.zerotothree.org/coping/index.html

Sleep Research and Sleep

Journal of Sleep Research: www.blackwell-synergy.com/loi/jsr

Journal Sleep: www.journalsleep.org

Kellymom.com: *Studies on Normal Infant Sleep:*
www.kellymom.com/parenting/sleep/sleepstudies.html

**Mother-Baby Behavioral Sleep Laboratory, Department of Anthropology,
University of Notre Dame:** www.nd.edu/~jmckenn1/lab/

The New York Times: *Sleep:*
www.topics.nytimes.com/top/news/health/
diseasesconditionsandhealthtopics/sleep/index.html

ParentingLibrary.com: *Parenting News:*
www.parentinglibrary.com/parentingnews.html

Sleep Problems and Disorders

American Sleep Apnea Association: www.sleepapnea.org

Canadian Sleep Society: *Sleep disorders brochures:*
www.css.to/sleep/brochures.htm

Narcolepsy Network Inc.: www.narcolepsynetwork.org

Restless Legs Syndrome Foundation, Inc.: www.rls.org

Zero to Three: *Coping When Your Baby Has Reflux or GERD: You Are Not Alone:*
www.zerotothree.org/coping/index.html

Sleep Health and Safety

American Academy of Pediatrics: *A Parents' Guide to Safe Sleep:*
www.healthychildcare.org/pdf/SIDSparentsafesleep.pdf

American Academy of Pediatrics Policy Statement: *The Changing Concept of Sudden Infant Death Syndrome: Diagnostic Coding Shifts, Controversies Regarding the Sleeping Environment, and New Variables to Consider in Reducing Risk Task Force on Sudden Infant Death Syndrome Published on-line October 10, 2005:*
http://pediatrics.aappublications.org/cgi/content/full/peds.2005-1499v1

American Dental Association: *Statement on Early Childhood Caries (Baby Bottle Tooth Decay):*
www.ada.org/prof/resources/positions/statements/caries.asp

American Massage Therapy Association: www.amtamassage.org

Canadian Foundation for the Study of Infant Deaths: www.sidscanada.org

Canadian Massage Therapy Alliance www.cmta.ca

Canadian Paediatric Society: *Recommendations for Safe Sleeping Environments Paediatrics & Child Health 2004; 9(9), 659–663; Reference No. CP04-02:* www.cps.ca/english/statements/CP/cp04-02.htm

Canadian Paediatric Society: *Recommendations for the Use of Pacifiers:*
www.cps.ca/english/statements/CP/cp03-01.htm

Caring for Kids: *Product Recalls and Health Warnings Affecting Children:*
www.caringforkids.cps.ca/productrecalls.htm

First Candle/SIDS Alliance: www.firstcandle.org

Health Canada: Early Childhood Tooth Decay:
www.hc-sc.gc.ca/hl-vs/oral-bucco/care-soin/child-enfant_e.html

Health Canada: *Juvenile Product Advisories:*
www.hc-sc.gc.ca/cps-spc/advisories-avis/child-enfant/index_e.html

Health Canada: *Juvenile Product Recalls:*
www.hc-sc.gc.ca/cps-spc/index_e.html

Juvenile Products Manufacturers Association: *Safe and Sound for Baby: A Guide to Baby Product Safety, Use, and Selection:*
jpma.org/consumer/SafeSoundBabyBrochure/SafeSoundBaby1Up.pdf

MedPage Today: *Back Sleeping and Pacifiers at Bedtime Reduce SIDS Risk:*
www.medpagetoday.com/Pediatrics/2005AAPMeeting/tb/1902

Minnesota Department of Health: *Safety Tips for Bedsharing with Your Baby:*
www.health.state.mn.us/divs/fh/mch/mortality/safetytips.html

Mothering Magazine: *Sleep Environment Safety Checklist:*
www.mothering.com/articles/new_baby/sleep/safety-checklist.html

National Association for Holistic Aromatherapy: www.naha.org

National Safety Council: *Crib Safety Tips:*
www.nsc.org/library/facts/cribtips.htm

National SIDS/Infant Death Resource Center: www.sidscenter.org

Sleep Products Safety Council: *SafeSleep.org for Grown-ups*:
www.safesleep.org/grownups/grownups.html

Sudden Unexpected Death in Childhood: www.sudc.org

U.S. Consumer Product Safety Commission: www.cpsc.gov

Moms' Sleep

**Mother-Baby Behavioral Sleep Laboratory, Department of Anthropology,
University of Notre Dame:** www.nd.edu/~jmckenn1/lab/

Womenshealthmatters.ca:
www.womenshealthmatters.ca/news/news_show.cfm?number=248

Postpartum Support and Sleep Solutions

British Columbia Reproductive Mental Health Program
www.bcrmh.com/disorders/postpartum.htm

Childbirth and Postpartum Professional Association: www.cappa.net

DONA International: www.dona.org

Mamazine.com: *Postpartum Depression, Reflux, and the Sex Life of Ms. Frizzle:*
www.mamazine.com/Pages/feature37.html

National Association of Postpartum Care Services: www.napcs.org

Our Sisters' Place: www.oursistersplace.ca

Pacific Post Partum Support Society: www.postpartum.org

The Postpartum Resource Centre of New York, Inc.:
www.postpartumny.org/whatisPPD.htm

Postpartum Support International: www.postpartum.net

Mother Fuel

Brain, Child: *The Magazine for Thinking Mothers:* www.brainchild.mag

LiteraryMama.com: www.literarymama.com

Mamazine.com: www.mamazine.com

Mother of All Blogs: www.motherofallblogs.com

WeeWelcome.ca: www.weewelcome.ca

General Pediatric Health and Development Information

American Academy of Pediatrics: www.aap.org

Canadian Paediatric Society: www.cps.ca

Invest in Kids: www.investinkids.ca

Johnson and Johnson Pediatric Institute: www.jjpi.com

U.S. Department of Agriculture Food and Nutrition Center: www.nal.usda.gov/fnic/

U.S. Department of Health and Human Services: Breastfeeding: www.4woman.gov/breastfeeding/

Zero to Three: www.zerotothree.org

Useful Sleep-Related Product Information

Avalon Music: www.avalonmusic.com

Halo Sleep Sack: www.halosleep.com

Obus Forme: *Sound Therapy Relaxation System:* www.obusforme.com/product_nav.asp?ID=75

Solitudes Nature's Spa: www.solitudes.com

Recommended Reading

I found the following books helpful while researching this book. In some cases, the entire book was invaluable. In other cases, one section of the book—or the author's take on one particular subject—was more helpful than other parts of the book. If you'd like to access the mini-reviews that I've written of many of these books, please visit the sleep page at ParentingLibrary.com. You will also find downloadable book lists, parenting book club reading list suggestions, and other useful information on a variety of parenting topics in that section of the site.

Cohen, George J. *American Academy of Pediatrics Guide to Your Child's Sleep: Birth Through Adolescence.* New York: Villard, 1999.

Dement, William C., and Christopher Vaughan. *The Promise of Sleep: A Pioneer in Sleep Medicine Explores the Vital Connection between Health, Happiness, and a Good Night's Sleep.* New York: Dell, 1999.

Ferber, Richard. *Solve Your Child's Sleep Problems,* Completely Revised and Updated Ed. New York: Fireside Books, March 2006. (New edition was forthcoming as my book went to press.)

Garabedian, Helen. *Itsy Bitsy Yoga: Poses to Help Your Baby Sleep Longer, Digest Better, and Grow Stronger.* New York: Fireside Books, 2004.

Gordon, Jay, and Maria Goodavage. *Good Nights: The Happy Parents' Guide to the Family Bed (and a Peaceful Night's Sleep!).* New York: St. Martin's Griffin, 2002.

Hogg, Tracy, and Melinda Blau. *The Baby Whisperer Solves All Your Problems (by Teaching You How to Ask the Right Questions): Sleeping, Feeding, and Behavior—Beyond the Basics from Infancy through Toddlerhood.* New York: Atria Books, 2005.

Idzikowski, Chris. *Learn to Sleep Well: A Practical Guide to Getting a Good Night's Rest.* San Francisco: Chronicle Books, 2000.

Jackson, Deborah. *When Your Baby Cries: 10 Rules for Soothing Fretful Babies and Their Parents.* London: Hodder Mobius, 2004.

Karp, Harvey. *The Happiest Baby on the Block: The New Way to Calm Crying and Help Your Newborn Baby Sleep Longer.* New York: Bantam Books, 2003.

Kryer, Meir. *A Woman's Guide to Sleep Disorders.* New York: McGraw-Hill, 2004.

Kurcinka, Mary Sheedy. *Sleepless in America: Practical Strategies to Help Your Family Get the Sleep It Deserves.* New York: Harper Collins, 2006. (Forthcoming as my book went to press.)

Martin, Paul. *Counting Sheep: The Science and Pleasures of Sleep and Dreams.* New York: St. Martin's Press, 2004.

Mindell, Jodi A. *Sleeping through the Night: How Infants, Toddlers, and Their Parents Can Get a Good Night's Sleep*, Rev. Ed. New York: HarperCollins, 2005.

Pantley, Elizabeth. *The No-Cry Sleep Solution for Toddlers and Preschoolers.* New York: McGraw-Hill, 2002.

_____. *The No-Cry Sleep Solution: Gentle Ways to Help Your Baby Sleep through the Night.* New York: McGraw-Hill, 2005.

Reichert, Bonny. *In Search of Sleep: Straight Talk about Babies, Toddlers, and Night Waking.* Toronto: Sarasota Press, 2001.

Sadeh, Avi. *Sleeping Like a Baby: A Sensitive and Sensible Approach to Solving Your Child's Sleep Problems.* New Haven: Yale University Press, 2001.

Sears, William. *Nighttime Parenting: How to Get Your Baby and Child to Sleep (La Leche League International Book).* New York: Plume Books, 1999.

Sears, William, Martha Sears, Robert Sears, and James Sears. *The Baby Sleep Book: The Complete Guide to a Good Night's Rest for the Whole Family (Sears Parenting Library).* New York: Little Brown, 2005.

Walsleben, Joyce, and Rita Baron-Faust. *A Woman's Guide to Sleep: Guaranteed Solutions for a Good Night's Rest.* New York: Three Rivers Press, 2001.

Weissbluth, Marc. *Healthy Sleep Habits, Happy Child: A Step-by-Step Program for a Good Night's Sleep,* 3rd Ed. New York: Random House, 2003.

West, Kim, with Joanne Kenen. *Good Night, Sleep Tight: The Sleep Lady's Gentle Guide to Helping Your Child Go to Sleep, Stay Asleep, and Wake Up Happy.* New York: CDS Books, 2004.

Wolfson, Amy. *The Woman's Book of Sleep: A Complete Resource Guide.* Oakland: New Harbinger Press, 2001.

Note: Because the leading pediatric health authorities in Canada and the U.S. changed their health recommendations regarding safe sleep in November 2004 (in the case of Canada) and in October 2005 (in the case of the U.S.), some of the information in pre-2006 editions of these books may not necessarily be fully compliant with those recommendations. Use the information in Chapter 6 as well as the links to the American Academy of Pediatrics and Canadian Paediatric Society websites (provided in Appendix B) to familiarize yourself with current safe sleep practices so that you can avoid putting your baby at risk as a result of any outdated information on safe sleep practices that may be contained in the books listed above or any websites or other sources cited in this book.

Index

noises
differentiating, 107–108
waking early and, 209
non-REM (rapid-eye movement)
sleep, 73, 75
nose sprays, 246
nursing. *See* feedings
nurture, 111
nutrition
caffeine, 225
sleep-enhancing, 239–240
sleep strategies (mom's), 57–58,
63–65
snacks, 211, 224
turkey, 59

O
obesity, 253
obsession with sleep, 10–11
obstructive sleep apnea (OSA),
243, 248, 253–254
Ohye, Bonnie, 21
overheating
hot water bottles and, 167
sleep sacks and, 151
swaddling and, 147, 151, 162
in tummy-sleeping position, 146
overparenting, 108
overstimulation
colicky babies, 170
effect of, 89, 273
intense child and, 116
and motion, 165
overtired children
effect on, 272
highly active child, 115
naps and, 109, 212
recognizing, 89, 91–92, 199
waking early, 177–178, 207–208

P
pacifiers
finding, 178
for GER, 188
recommendations for using,
151–152
SIDS and, 103
sleep association and, 102, 104
as soothing technique, 168
weaning from, 214–215
pajamas
choices, 196, 222
favorite, 120
irritation from, 117, 201, 239,
276
safety, 153
Pantley, Elizabeth, 142
parenting team
agreeing on plan, 128
division of duties, 36–37
effects on relationships, 37–40
issues in developing plan,
128–133
mom-only sleep association
and, 175–176
nighttime feeding associations
and, 180
strengths of partners, 32–33
weaning nighttime feedings,
205
parent's continuous presence, 262,
263–264
partners. *See* fathers; parenting
team
patience
effect of sleep deprivation, 25
in sleep plan change, 132
pavor nocturnus, 232, 234–235, 244,
250–251, 273